James Allen
On F1 - 2011
Vettel Steals The Show

James Allen
On F1 − 2011
Vettel Steals The Show

Photography by Darren Heath

Speed Merchants Limited

First published in 2011
by Speed Merchants Ltd

Cataloguing in Publication Data is available from the
British Library

ISBN: 978-0-9564187-2-2

www.jamesallenonf1.com

*Printed and bound in England by CPI Antony Rowe Limited,
Chippenham, Wiltshire*

Contents

Foreword
By Christian Horner
Team Principal, Red Bull Racing

This year was clearly a remarkable one for Red Bull Racing. The car, RB7, was competitive from the first test and we managed to pick up where we left off at the end of 2010. We turned up at the first race, won it and didn't look back from there. This was a great satisfaction to the whole team and testimony to the tremendous team effort.

We have improved in every area: operationally, strategically, from a performance and reliability point of view. And, of course, Sebastian was in a class of his own this year. He put together a pretty impressive campaign, which meant that he won the drivers' title with four races to go and the team clinched the constructors' crown with three races remaining.

It was a combination of things with Sebastian: he had confidence from winning his first title, he had more experience and he was also quicker than most drivers to adapt to the new Pirelli tyres. He seemed to understand what the tyres needed and what was the best way to get the most out of them. He was also fantastic under pressure, if you think back to races like Barcelona and Monaco, for example.

To have retained the double world title places us in a fairly elite group now. Our target for next year will be to try to retain both of the championship titles. Our opposition will never get easier: Ferrari, McLaren and Mercedes Benz are all quality teams with great resource and infrastructure behind them. But Red Bull Racing has demonstrated that 2010 was no flash in the pan.

On a personal level it's been very satisfying. When I came into the team, which had been bought from Jaguar, it was a team that seemed confused in terms of its identity, what it was trying to be. It was obvious that there were some very skilled people there but in Jaguar, with the rotating door of management, it looked like a supermarket trying to run a corner shop. F1 is a niche business you need to be fast responding and self-critical as you are judged every two weeks as you compete through the year. The team lacked technical leadership and that's where the first focus was placed and who better to do that than Adrian Newey?

His arrival was the first milestone for the team, Sebastian's was the second and the 2009 regulations were the third and biggest because we were able to test the group we'd built against the other teams with a clean sheet of paper. It's a people sport and it's about making sure the right people are in place and then empowering them.

It's great to see that this year we've been able to apply the lessons we learned last year, and the team has taken another step forward. It's a great privilege to lead this team. We keep it simple. You have to do the basics well and that's been my philosophy in every category in which I've competed. This year we've done the basics very well; we had a quick car and we maximised our opportunities.

It's great that this season the focus has been on the racetrack. There has been some great racing this year and I think that the introduction of the Pirelli tyres in particular, as well as the DRS wing have added another dimension – there were well over 600 passes on track this year!

I hope you enjoy looking back through this collection of stories and insights into a great year for Formula 1.

Introduction

After several seasons of thrilling title battles with close fought finishes, I suppose it was inevitable that sooner or later we'd get a championship where one driver dominated, as Michael Schumacher did between 2000 and 2004. We've subtitled this book "Vettel Steals the Show" because there really was only one man in it. Sebastian Vettel clinched his second world title and dominated both qualifying and the races. He has achieved more at the age of 24 than any driver in F1 history, and he is still getting better.

This is hard for some fans to accept; they see him as a driver whose success is entirely due to the performance of the car. It's rather like Nigel Mansell in 1992, when the active ride Williams was way out of reach of Ayrton Senna's McLaren and Michael Schumacher's Benetton. But Vettel's success this year was more hard fought than it looked. Yes, he took pole most of the time, but his teammate Mark Webber was rarely alongside him, so it can't have been just the car. Then, at various times through the year, he was under huge pressure in races but managed to hold on to take the win, breaking the record for most laps led in a season, previously held by Mansell, and taking it to another level.

McLaren were the best of the rest, but it wasn't Lewis Hamilton leading the charge, it was his older and wiser teammate Jenson Button who was the second best driver of 2011. Button found a way of managing the new Pirelli tyres and although he wasn't the fastest in qualifying, his race performances were fast and consistent. Meanwhile, Hamilton got lost in a world of distractions with off-track relationships taking their toll, and within the paddock he became an angry young man. In many ways it looked like he was doing his growing up in public as Button's success seemed to rattle him, as did the formidable combination of Vettel and Red Bull. Suddenly the golden boy found he wasn't so golden after all as a younger man came along and picked up a second world championship, something Hamilton has not come close to achieving since his triumph in 2008.

Martin Whitmarsh had rather disparagingly described Vettel as the "Crash Kid" in 2010, but a year later it was his own driver Hamilton who deserved that nickname after a series of race collisions with Felipe Massa.

Ferrari underperformed again and replaced their technical director with less than a third of the season gone. Mercedes disappointed too, the second year of Michael Schumacher's comeback did not yield the results expected from the three-pointed star. However, we did see Schumacher himself back on form, particularly in the second half of the season where he outraced his teammate Nico Rosberg.

This was a year when the midfield battles were particularly interesting with Force India, Sauber and Toro Rosso all having their moments in a very tight scrap for points. Renault suffered greatly from the absence of Robert Kubica, sidelined by a horrific arm injury before the season started.

If the outcome of the championship and many of the races was never in doubt, there was some good racing this year thanks to two new innovations: the DRS wing and the introduction of Pirelli tyres. Both contributed to there being almost 700 on-track overtaking moves during the year. It also contributed to some frantic pit lane action as well, with tyres that were designed not to last.

This made race strategy once again a very significant factor in the sport and at *JA on F1* we were onto that, producing the Strategy Briefing and Report in association with Swiss bank and F1 global partner UBS. These reports proved very popular with fans around the world: in addition to running on the *JA on F1* website, they appeared in eight different languages on some of the leading sites in territories around the world, reaching in excess of eight million fans.

It was a great year for *JA on F1*. We continued to find innovative ways to bring the fans closer to the sport, giving 14 fans a chance to go to the British Grand Prix, something they would not otherwise have done. We were centrally involved in the staging of three FOTA Fans' Forum events, in Montreal, Woking and Milan, where fans had the chance to interact with the teams and their racing heroes face-to-face. We also sent a Fan Ambassador to Abu Dhabi in November in collaboration with our partner Shell.

We were particularly proud to stage an amazing event in May – one of the first screenings in London of the award-winning film *Senna*, for an audience of 200 fans and special guests from Senna's life, including mechanics and engineers as well as Sir Jackie Stewart, Martin Brundle, Professor Sid Watkins and Terry Fullerton, whom Senna credits with being the best driver he ever raced against. I did a Q&A session on the stage with the film's director Asif Kapadia and writer Manish Pandey and brought the special guests in one by one. It was an unforgettable night.

Off-track it was a relatively benign year in F1 politics, although there was some to-ing ad fro-ing over the Bahrain Grand Prix as the sport misread the signals on the significance of the Arab Spring, and there was a struggle over the new engine regulations for 2014, which will see a move to small capacity turbo charged hybrid engines.

It felt like the calm before the storm, which is likely to break in 2012, as a new Concorde Agreement is negotiated between teams, the FIA and the commercial rights holders Bernie Ecclestone and CVC. There were some intriguing side stories though, like the fraud trial of Gerhard Gribkowsky, a former chairman of the F1 holding company and an executive of BayernLB, which sold the commercial rights in the sport to CVC in 2006. As the season wound to a close there were signs that the FIA and the teams were finding shared objectives; an alliance between those two stakeholders would pose a substantial threat to Ecclestone and CVC.

The confusion over the Lotus name in F1 was resolved after two court cases and a year of battling, with Tony Fernandes rebranding his team Caterham F1 Team and giving the Team Lotus name to Group Lotus. It appears that for the moment at least the team will continue to be known as Lotus Renault GP, but the chassis name will be Lotus.

F1 is like life on fast forward. It's a sport that never stays the same for long, never rests, as new partnerships are formed, new cars released, new drivers hired. It is a sport that is on permanent auto-refresh and that is one of the main reasons for its popularity. But on a human level the strain is immense. There is an insecurity that comes from standing on shifting sands, and in F1 the sands shift constantly whether it be in politics, sporting fortunes or technical innovation.

Telling these stories is the lifeblood of *JA on F1*, as are the many thousands of comments we get from readers each month, to which F1 insiders and fans around the world pay attention. With the stunning images of F1's leading photographer, Darren Heath, this book tells the stories behind the stories in 2011.

For help in producing this book and throughout the year on *JA on F1* I'd like to thank Pip Calvert. Thanks also go to Bill Allen, Phill Appleton and Andrew Hirsch at John Brown Group, Geoff Fisher at CPI, Julian Flanders, Sara Linney and Jon Lloyd at Grand Prix Legends, Mandy Scott-Johnson, Darren Heath, Alex Salter, Neil Campbell, Darren Odam, Pete Young, Simon Ryley, Christian Horner for the Foreword, Sebastian Morrison, Mark Newman, Matt Meadows and Sue Varley.

Thanks to our sponsors: Jean Christophe Babin, Rob Diver and Francoise Bezzola at TAG Heuer; Bjorn Waspe, Jonas Karpf, Tanja Cvetko and Preethi Nair at UBS; Richard Bracewell, Stuart Humm at Shell and Ansar Ali at Caterham.

Thanks finally to the readers of *JA on F1* for making 2011 so enjoyable.

James Allen
London, November 2011

This book is dedicated to Mary Allen (1933-2011)

Chapter One
January 2011

It was quite a quiet winter by F1 standards. Unlike the year before there were no earthquakes – like Michael Schumacher coming back to race for Mercedes or Jenson Button moving to McLaren.

Ferrari was very much the team in focus after the trauma of losing the world championship at the final race of 2010. They avoided any knee-jerk reaction, but in early January there were signs coming out of Maranello that heads would roll for the shocking error in strategy that cost Fernando Alonso the world championship. As predicted by the Italian media in the days after the Abu Dhabi fiasco, it was the most senior operations engineer Chris Dyer who took the bullet. There had been hints from the management of "changes". The concept of a team winning together and losing together is fine, but with the pressure which clearly had been bearing down on Ferrari, especially with Ferrari president Luca di Montezemolo's political rivals carping at him, someone had to be singled out to get the chop, not least "pour encourager les autres".

Dyer falls on sword; Martin becomes Head of Strategy
4 January 2011

Ferrari have finally announced the major changes that team boss has Stefano Domenicali has hinted at. According to the team's website, "Neil Martin takes on the role of heading up the new operations research department. A 38-year-old Englishman, Martin previously worked for Red Bull and prior to that McLaren, and he will now report directly to technical director, Aldo Costa.

"At the same time, Costa's deputy, Pat Fry will, in addition to his current role, take on the job of head of race track engineering. Up until yesterday, this position was held by Chris Dyer whose role within the company will be redefined in the next few days."

So, as predicted, Dyer falls on the sword for the strategy mistake in Abu Dhabi.

Meanwhile, Neil Martin is an interesting appointment. He comes from the financial services field and wrote a paper on risk assessment that he realised had uses for F1 strategy. He showed it to McLaren boss Martin Whitmarsh who hired him on the strength of it.

Martin was originally headhunted by Red Bull and headed up their strategy unit until last year when he promptly left the team. Last summer there were suggestions he would be joining Ferrari, but I got a categorical denial from Ferrari when I asked if that was true. On the face of it, it seems that the events of Abu Dhabi have prompted a rethink. Ferrari say this is not the case and that Martin was hired before Abu Dhabi.

Although Ferrari say that Martin's role is not specifically to run race strategies, it is more of a strategic overview role looking at ways of improving operations across the board, his appointment will also have been at the behest of Fry with whom he worked at McLaren. It takes up part of the role Fry was due to have and has been done because Fry has now put his head in the lion's mouth, making the big calls as head of track operations, an area where Ferrari have struggled a few times in recent years.

A few days after this announcement, I was honoured to be invited to the Wroom media event in Madonna di Campiglio, where the Ferrari drivers and management hang out with the media over several pleasant days of skiing and eating nice meals.

Against the backdrop of the snow-covered Dolomite Mountains, 45-year-old Stefano Domenicali looked relaxed and positive after a very difficult end to the 2010 season. He said that after a lot of soul searching after the Abu Dhabi strategy disaster, he and the team had picked themselves up and were now 100 per cent focused on 2011.

He made a great deal of the idea that the team needs "to be perfect, right from the start" of the year, with the car and drivers being competitive. Alonso, he said had been "extraordinary" in the second half of 2010 and he expected him to start at that level, "Certainly Fernando starts from an extraordinary baseline after a second half of the season which was almost perfect."

There was a lot of discussion about the other driver, Felipe Massa, who will have extra pressure on him this year. Domenicali said that he expects Massa to be able to pull himself together and put in a competitive season. I asked him how that would be measured – by Massa getting 60–70 per cent of Alonso's points, for example? But if he has such a figure in mind, which would be the normal way to measure performance, Domenicali didn't share it publicly,

"I'm expecting, because Felipe is very strong, for him to be closer to Fernando, or even better," he said. "I'm sure that the technical problems Felipe suffered last year will be solved. I saw him already in the first day of the Pirelli test with a different face. He knows that he has the full support of the team."

It was not to be. Massa seemed once again adrift at times in the 2011 season, discounted by rivals when planning strategy and unable to get close to his teammate's level for most of the season, with a few exceptions.

Domenicali said over and again that a perfect start to the season is essential, not just from the drivers but also from the car. This is a logical way to approach the season after what happened last year and it gets everyone focused on maximising those early races, but it also put pressure on and begged the question, what happens if they have a less than perfect first few races?

As it turned out, compared to Red Bull Racing they never really got started.

In the background Montezemolo added to the pressure still further by saying "We have to win" at the launch of the new F1 car. The Ferrari president was busy building up his political powerbase within Italy, getting his Italia Futura movement into position ready for him to be asked to replace the discredited Berlusconi government, should the call come. He named the 2011 Ferrari F1 car the F150 – in honour of Italy's 150th anniversary as a nation – but when Ford complained that this was the same name as its best-selling pick-up truck the name was hastily changed to 150 Italia. Despite its lofty ambitions, sadly for Ferrari and Italy it was not a well-born car.

Then, out of the blue a story broke which was to hang over F1 and create uncertainty in the F1 world for the whole season.

3

Former chairman of F1 holding company arrested
5 January 2011

Formula 1 finds itself on the financial pages again tonight, but not for the right reasons. Gerhard Gribkowsky, the 52-year-old former chairman of SLEC, the holding company of F1's commercial rights which have been sold to CVC, has been arrested in a probe on bribery, breach of trust and tax evasion.

According to German prosecutors in Munich, the BayernLB bank, of which Gribkowsky was a senior executive, sold its stake without it being properly evaluated and that he personally received $50 million in payments disguised as two consultancy agreements via companies in the British Virgin Islands and Mauritius into a foundation he set up in Austria called Sonnenschein (Sunshine). They claim that because Gribkowsky didn't declare the money as income in Germany, he may also have evaded taxes.

However Gribkowsky's Austrian lawyer told the Austrian Press Agency tonight that the foundation was investigated in 2006 and nothing came of it and that the money was "fully taxed".

CVC, which still owns the majority stake in the F1 commercial rights holder, issued a statement tonight saying, "CVC confirms that it has no knowledge of, nor any involvement in, any payment to Mr Gribkowsky or anyone connected with him in relation to CVC's acquisition of Formula One."

BayernLB got involved in F1 when the Kirch Group, to whom Bernie Ecclestone had sold a stake in the F1 commercial rights holder, went under in 2002, leaving three banks, including Gribkowsky's, holding the F1 assets.

He became a regular figure in the paddock and even co-hosted a dinner for a small group of British media at Magny-Cours, with Ecclestone. During this time BayernLB became the main bank in the consortium and Gribkowsky therefore became chairman of SLEC in 2005. This was at the height of the threat from the manufacturers to break away and start their own series.

Williams strikes oil with Venezuelan sponsor deal
15 January 2011

The Williams team is in Venezuela at the moment and today the team announced the long-awaited tie up with PDVSA, the state-owned oil company. It is a massive boost to the team, which said goodbye to important sponsors RBS and Philips at the end of last season.

Venezuela has the world's sixth largest oil reserves and is in the top ten oil exporters. It has by far the largest oil business of any Central or South American country.

"They are a substantial partner and can make a meaningful difference to our fighting ability," said the team's figurehead, Frank Williams. This is true. Like every other team Williams' ability to attract talented engineers and to be able to develop cars is dependent on resources. This deal will make a difference to their ability to fight Renault at the fringes of the top four teams, rather than in the midfield with Force India and Sauber.

The deal is very much the work of the new Williams chairman Adam Parr who has been aggressively pursuing investment in both Venezuela and Qatar in the last six months. The arrival of Pastor Maldonado has changed the tone at Williams, which is now a very South American focussed team. Maldonado's teammate this season is Brazilian Rubens Barrichello, starting his 19th season in F1.

Maldonado is very much flying the flag for a country in which having a sportsman on a world stage is a major deal. PDVSA has supported Maldonado's career through the feeder series and the substantial long-term backing undoubtedly swung the drive his way in competition with Nico Hulkenberg.

The Williams team is F1's great survivor. So many have gone by the wayside over the years, but Williams has always proven Darwin's theory that you have to adapt to survive in a competitive and hostile world. They have always been adaptable when it comes to selling the team to sponsors and have gone through many phases of sponsorship: Saudi money in the early 1980s, Japanese money in the Honda years and an ingenious BMW total buyout of the livery in the early 2000s. There were a couple of tobacco phases, with Camel and then Rothmans, which coincided with the team's most successful period between 1991 and 1997, but on the whole the team was always far less reliant on tobacco money than McLaren or Ferrari.

Yesterday Maldonado did a demonstration drive of the Williams car on a special road course in Caracas in the presence of the Venezuelan president Hugo Chavez and a crowd of thousands. He will start testing in earnest at the start of February in Valencia.

Williams was in focus at the start of the year, not just for this deal but also for its plans to float the F1 team on the stock market. Their objective was to "secure the long-term ownership of Williams" in a way that remains true to the ideals with which Frank Williams and Patrick Head started the team in 1977. This involves remaining independent beyond the time when Williams and Head are no longer around.

Head wanted to exit and take his money out of the business and it was felt that the safest way to do this was a flotation, rather than a sale of equity to a third party.

The Williams F1 team floated on the Frankfurt Stock Exchange on 2 March. The listing, of 2.4 million shares, was fully subscribed at €25 per share, which valued the team at €250 million. The sale means that €60 million has been raised, principally for Head, whose stake in the team was reduced to just 5 per cent.

Chapter Two
February 2011

Of all the dramas to hit F1 during 2011, to me the most startling was the accident which sidelined Robert Kubica while taking part in a rally in Italy. The images were horrific – a piece of steel barrier piercing the floor of his car. The reality for Kubica was that it partially severed his right hand and caused serious damage to the right side of his body.

It was a huge blow for the Pole, whose career star was in the ascendant and who was on the verge of getting a call-up from Ferrari. It was also a disaster for the Renault GP team, which lost its lead driver and reference point. As the season went on they slid backwards in competiveness.

Kubica may miss start of F1 season after rally crash
6 February 2011

Renault F1 driver Robert Kubica has been injured in a high-speed accident while competing for fun in a rally in Italy. The Polish driver, who set the fastest time in last week's F1 test in Valencia, has suffered a very serious hand injury, according to *La Stampa* in Italy, his right hand was crushed and surgeons are working to restore functionality. He also has fractures to his right arm and leg. According to the BBC he is unlikely to be ready to start the F1 season, which starts just over a month from now.

Kubica has always enjoyed honing his skills in rally cars, but this accident, so close to the start of what was set to be a crucial season for him and the Renault team, will inevitably call into question the wisdom of F1 drivers taking part in extra-curricular activities such as this. Kubica is not the first such victim. A shoulder injury while motocross riding (although he claimed it was a tennis injury) wrecked Juan Pablo Montoya's introduction to the McLaren team and one always had the impression that Ron Dennis lost faith in him at that point.

Kubica's career has already been overshadowed by injury. He broke his left arm in an accident during his F3 days, which threatened to slow his progress through the junior ranks. He also suffered a huge accident in the Canadian Grand Prix in 2007, and was lucky to escape without serious injury. It seems likely that this recent accident will have a long-term effect on his participation in F1, though one hopes this will not be the case.

With a radical new car and a confident technical department, Renault looked set to challenge the front-runners more regularly this season. The loss of their lead driver at this stage will upset plans greatly. Bruno Senna is at the top of the list to replace him, an amazing opportunity and a real turnaround in the fortunes of the Brazilian. The sight of the Senna yellow helmet in a black and gold Lotus sponsored car will be too much to resist for the marketing people. Senna and Romain Grosjean are the reserves, but along with the other race driver Vitaly Petrov, are they a potent enough force to start the season scoring the kind of points Renault need to challenge for a top four place? Renault spoke to Kimi Raikkonen last summer but the dialogue ended in bitterness. Renault's engineers will miss the technical ability Kubica would have brought to the testing programme. Nick Heidfeld is also an available and experienced option.

The Italian surgeons – hand reconstruction specialists – worked on Kubica for seven hours. After the operation, Dr Igor Rossello said that although amputation was still a possibility, "the hand is alive". He added that, "we will have to wait a week before we know if it will survive." More surgery might well be needed. He also said that a recovery period of a year was to be expected.

Although it is only speculation, as we do not know all the facts about the accident, the doctor's announcement that the recovery period might be as much as a year indicates that Kubica's injury is extremely severe. The footage shows that the energy in the accident was very great. This is backed up by the fact that Kubica also broke his leg and his arm. His hand seems to have been crushed by some Armco that came up through the floor.

Tonight I called a friend in London, Richard Young, who is a plastic surgeon specialising in hand reconstruction at Chelsea and Westminster Hospital, for some insight into hand crush injury, of which he has extensive experience. I wanted to know what the risks are and the likely recovery times in a situation such as this.

He explained that an injured hand is at risk of amputation when the blood supply has been severed. The surgeon's first job is to restore this; then comes a wait to see if the blood vessels will function properly. After that it's a question of whether the doctors can repair the nerves and tendons to restore full functionality, in Kubica's case to the level required by an F1 driver.

The hand has many small muscles, tendons and nerves, which if crushed are likely to reduce the ability to roll the fingers in and to make fine movements, such as picking up a pin or in the case of an F1 driver operating the buttons and dials on the steering wheel. Damage to the nerves will impair feeling and this can take at least three months to return.

In terms of rehabilitation, sometimes when athletes break a bone they can speed up the repair by sitting in a chamber to boost oxygen or blood flow, but that will not apply in this case. Here we are dealing with tendons and these must be protected for up to three months before any effort can be put through them, otherwise the tendons rupture again. Also, if there is severe damage to nerves in the hand or forearm, the ability to make fine movements can be lost forever.

We had a lot of comments from readers in response to the story of Kubica's crash; many were mystified why the driver took such risks in his spare time and how Renault could have allowed it. As the son of a racing driver, I'm well aware of the mentality of racers and I tried to articulate this in a follow-up piece.

Why racers take risks and why we love them for it
7 February 2011

"Did you never think of stopping Robert [Kubica] from taking part in rallies?" asked *L'Equipe* newspaper to Renault team boss Eric Boullier today.

"Not for one second," replied Boullier, "He could just as easily have been knocked over by a bus. Robert is a racer, he loves cars and he lives for nothing but racing. Competing is his essence. At 14 he slept in a kart factory because he loved racing. From the outset it was agreed among us that

Robert would do rallies as well as F1. It was vital for him. His strength comes from that passion. I never thought about the risk. Motor sport is dangerous, but he loves it."

I have found the reaction to Robert Kubica's accident fascinating and enlightening. First we have the team principle, as explained by Boullier above, which expresses understanding and justifies Renault's decision to let him compete in a sport away from F1. Then we have the reaction of rival team bosses who are both appalled by the injury and surprised at Renault's relaxed attitude to their lead driver's potentially dangerous hobby. The fans and the media are similarly split: some castigate him for taking unnecessary risks so close to the start of the season, while others simply feel terribly sorry for him and his plight.

Latest bulletins from the doctors suggest a horrendous injury to his right arm, which caused him to lose a lot of blood. Despite some heroics by his surgeons, experts in the field to whom I've spoken suggest he may never regain fine motor function in that hand. If so, his F1 career is unlikely to continue. Of course, there are always miracle comebacks, and it looks increasingly like that is what will be required for him to race an F1 car again. Renault disagree with this prognosis, claiming that the doctors are exaggerating and that he will recover within a year.

Whatever your opinion, the question remains why did Kubica take part in the rally? Why did he take the risk of losing everything just to satisfy some urge to drive fast? And will this put an end to drivers doing anything but the safest hobbies in future?

I grew up with a father who was a racing driver. He was a Lotus works driver in the 1960s. If you've not lived with it, it's hard to explain the 'daredevil gene' racers have, which forces them to race. It's a restlessness; a need to challenge oneself. At the margins it's almost a kind of rage.

I don't have it, I recognised that early on, but in 22 years working in F1 I've seen it countless times in the eyes of the racers I've encountered. Why else did Valentino Rossi and Kimi Raikkonen do rallies while holding down major roles with leading teams? Why did Jim Clark or Stirling Moss drive every kind of car they could get their hands on?

Juan Manuel Fangio once said, "There are those who keep out of mischief, and there are the adventurers. We racing drivers are adventurers; the more difficult something is, the greater the attraction that comes from it." This is the best quote I've ever come across to explain why racers race and why we love them for it. Nowadays F1 cars are still challenging to drive on the limit, but they are so safe that drivers have become quite matter-of-fact about the risks in their job.

In the 1970s F1 driver Patrick Depailler used to enjoy hang gliding in his spare time. He had a bad accident and was still recovering from it when he was killed in F1 testing in 1980. Today no one would allow an F1 driver to go hang gliding, but the question is, in this age of ultra professionalism, should drivers be forced to avoid all dangerous sports in their spare time? I think they might after this… and a little bit more of that racer spirit will be lost.

Renault team owner Gerard Lopez must now be mulling over the wisdom of his policy to allow Kubica to race rally cars. Other team principals I've spoken to today say that their drivers would not be able to take part in such activities. Of course, insurance is a major factor. Though its relatively cheap to insure an F1 driver for F1 driving because the cars are so safe, a team will pay much more to insure against the drivers being unavailable to them. If a driver is unavailable, the insurance company will pay out for his replacement and possibly for the original driver's salary as well.

The driver will in turn typically insure himself against injury and loss of earnings. Premiums rise significantly for more dangerous sports… such as rallying. Kubica's manager Daniel Morrelli is a very precise, careful individual and he will no doubt have taken care to ensure that his client was correctly insured.

But, whatever the whys and wherefores, one thing's for sure – Renault will have to look for someone else to drive for them this year.

They turned, as predicted, to Nick Heidfeld, who had been Kubica's teammate at BMW Sauber. It was not a harmonious relationship and despite a promising start with a podium in Malaysia, Heidfeld was dropped from Spa onwards in favour of Bruno Senna. Heidfeld maintained that this was because Senna brought budget to the team, but the fact is he also failed to lead the team as Kubica would have done and failed to outpace teammate Vitaly Petrov, whom Kubica had destroyed the year before.

But outside of F1 the world was changing, particularly the Middle East as the "Arab Spring" took hold. It was amazing to see the events unfolding in Egypt, Yemen, Syria and Libya as people took to the streets demanding to be heard. Some wanted a change of regime and achieved it through bloody struggle. Others just wanted some changes, but still had to go through a degree of bloody struggle to make their voices heard. One such country was Bahrain, host of a Grand Prix since 2004.

The event had become a popular stop on the F1 calendar, with the ruling family integrating itself into F1 life, buying a stake in McLaren and inviting many of the sport's leading figures to break bread with them during Grand Prix weekend. So it was uncomfortable in the extreme for many of F1's leading figures to witness the bloody scenes at Pearl Roundabout as the regime sent in the troops to crush the uprising.

F1 did not cover itself in glory over the episode, its administrators failing or refusing to appreciate the seriousness of the situation. In February the race was called off, but later in the year a clumsy attempt to reinstate it made the sport look bad.

Although as the season came to an end there were still many problems in Bahrain, it was given a place on the 2012 calendar in the first part of the season.

Bahrain GP is off – organisers say it's official
21 February 2011

The Bahrain Grand Prix due to take place on 13 March has been called off according to race organisers. The Crown Prince of Bahrain telephoned F1 promoter Bernie Ecclestone this morning to tell him of the decision. The reason given was that the country needs to focus on its own internal issues at this time.

"At the present time the country's entire attention is focused on building a new national dialogue for Bahrain," said the Crown Prince. "After the events of the past week, our nation's priority is on overcoming tragedy, healing divisions and rediscovering the fabric that draws this country together;

reminding the world of the very best that Bahrain is capable of as a nation once again united."

It is not yet clear whether attempts will be made to reschedule the race for later this season, although the wording of the statement from Bahrain suggests that they expect it to be rescheduled, rather than cancelled. Fitting it into an already packed schedule that runs to the end of November will be difficult without having three back-to-back races or extending the season into December.

Today's decision follows a volley of intense media coverage of the situation with mounting criticism of the sport for not calling the event off. But for legal, insurance and commercial reasons the teams wanted to push the decision onto FOM and FOM needed to push it onto the Bahrainis. This has now happened. It is the first time in modern F1 that a race has had to be cancelled.

Williams chairman Adam Parr said, "It is obviously disappointing for everyone involved in the organisation of the event, but it is clear that to race in Bahrain at this time would be inappropriate given the current circumstances. It is always Williams' intention to contribute positively to the countries we compete in and so we fully support the Crown Prince's decision to cancel the test and forthcoming Bahrain Grand Prix. We now look forward to a season debut in Melbourne and returning to Bahrain when it is right to do so."

FOTA met to discuss what to do about the fourth test session, originally scheduled to take place in Bahrain. It was decided that the teams would now reconvene in Barcelona on 8 March for four more days of testing. This is not what Pirelli were hoping for. They badly wanted some hot weather running to evaluate their tyres, which have come in for criticism for the way they behave in cold conditions.

It is not yet clear whether the teams will attempt to run again before the first race in Melbourne on 27 March. But pushing the test back to 8 March indicates that they will probably not hold an extra test in place of the Bahrain GP. One sticking point is tyre supply, with Pirelli committed to a certain test supply and the ones destined for the Bahrain test are already in transit.

Some teams are likely to want extra running. The dropping of the Bahrain race certainly will help McLaren and buy them some more time to fix the initial problems they have encountered with their new car.

Chapter Three
March 2011

Vettel commits to Red Bull until 2014
14 March 2011

World champion Sebastian Vettel today committed himself to the Red Bull team until the end of 2014 at least. Vettel is just 23 years old now and will only be 27 – traditionally seen as the age when a driver enters the peak period of his career – at the end of this contract extension. Fernando Alonso is in that period now; he turns 30 this year and will be 33 when Vettel's contract runs out. By that time Alonso will have been in F1 for 14 years.

The move will certainly put an end to stories about Vettel and Ferrari for a while, which will be a relief, but they are bound to come back when the contract gets close to its expiry date. He looks like a natural successor to Alonso: it's hard to imagine them working together in the team – the cost would be a major issue too – so it's really a question of whether Alonso is still cutting it at 33, how much longer he wants to race and what Red Bull's plans are at that stage. Vettel will have been driving in F1 for them (and Toro Rosso) for eight years when this latest deal ends he will surely want to think about his future.

For now though, Vettel is showing great loyalty to Red Bull. I don't know the details of his extension package, but I imagine that he has moved from a small retainer plus large bonus deal to something more akin to what Alonso and Lewis Hamilton have where they earn in the region of €15 million a year, with the retainer being the larger of the two portions. Even more important, Vettel's prospects of getting results look pretty rosy this year; the RB7 looks like the car to beat going into the first race next week.

The novelty and great unknown of the 2011 season was the adjustable rear wing, known as DRS (Drag Reduction System), which was brought in to improve overtaking. For some fans this was a degree too much of artificiality. The Pirelli tyres were designed to degrade much more quickly than the Bridgestone, which was going to contribute to the "show", but the DRS wing looked like it might turn F1 into the racing equivalent of WWE Wrestling. On the eve of the new season, the FIA issued a statement with thoughts from race director Charlie Whiting about how the DRS would work.

The statement explained that the rear wing could be used at any time in practice and qualifying. But Whiting spelled out how the system would work in the race to allow a following car to use his rear wing to attempt a pass: "Proximity to the car in front will be detected before the straight on which the wing may be activated," he wrote. "If the car behind is less than one second behind (as judged by the installed timing loops in the track) the driver will be told that his system is "armed", however, he may only use it when he reaches the designated point on the following straight. This point is likely to be 600 metres before the braking point for the following corner, though this may be adjusted according to data gathered during testing and practice.

"There will be marks (lines) on the track to show the area where proximity is being detected and a line across the track at the point where the driver whose system is armed may deploy it.

"Furthermore, the television broadcasters will be sent a signal each time a system is armed and this will be displayed to the viewers."

Race Control was keen not to be seen as "interfering" too much in the outcome of a battle or a race. This is sensitive ground and interestingly Whiting said that the idea was "a proposal the teams made to the FIA" – spelling out whose bright idea this was in the first place, perhaps in case it didn't work so well.

From the simulation work done so far it appeared that the difference between a car using the wing and one not using it was likely to be in the region of 6–8 mph at the end of the straight. And that's pretty much how it worked out.

But with well over 200 comments left on the post I wrote about the FIA's statement, the majority surprisingly negative, in the interests of giving fans a chance to make their voices heard, I posted two responses.

Fans react to adjustable rear wing reality
16 March 2011

We've had a strong reaction from readers to the story I posted yesterday about the DRS. Until now the adjustable rear wing has been a concept and more recently an item on the cars during test sessions. As the racing season comes into view Charlie Whiting's comments on the way the system will work have drawn many fans to feel negative about the idea. But there are also some who feel that the system should be given a chance. Here are two posts from readers, which I feel articulate the debate and deserve a wider audience.

Tom Mitchell speaks for many when he says: "If most other fans were in favour of DRS, then fine. But reading here, it seems that practically nobody is. Whitmarsh et al will say that they are listening, like when he said that if it doesn't work then they would remove it. But what he doesn't get is that we don't want it to work – because that would mean they've successfully made the racing artificial.

"Now there is a clear distinction between real fans and those they're aiming to please with DRS. The former are people like those on this website who have been watching F1 through the good and bad. The latter are people who know nothing about F1 (aka 'new markets'), and I suspect are 'the only good bits are the crashes' type people. Now I have nothing against new people becoming fans, but not at the very clear expense and anger of the loyal fans, who the F1 insiders clearly do not give a damn about and take for granted."

However, Sebee argues that, as with many innovations in F1, it needs to be given time: "I applaud the FIA for at least trying something for 2011. Over the years all the driver aids have resulted in cruise control racing and the fans have complained that lack of passing is an issue, now we have the DRS, KERS and fragile tyres. I'm all for well-thought-out variables being brought into the mix. We accept automatic paddle shifting gearboxes now, weren't they a gimmick at some point? Will anyone here seriously argue that their introduction took away from the spectacle, the driver skill, and most importantly passing opportunities? Since manual gearboxes aren't a realistic option in F1 today – DRS and KERS it is.

"Also, James is right when he says he's reserving judgment, but perhaps he's viewing it with questions and wishes to be proved wrong.

"Let's let a few races take place and see what they come up with. I recall some major UK newspaper declaring that you should put down a layer of paint next to your TV in 2010 because it's more interesting to watch it dry than F1 will be after Bahrain. We could discuss if it was pure or due to peripherals (as per Fan's View a few months ago), but whatever your conclusion – you can hardly say 2010 was a boring show.

"Rome wasn't built in a day. Give the 2011 spec a chance. If it doesn't work, will it really be that hard to remove DRS and KERS from the cars? I think not.

"Now, will someone please show me photos of F1 hardware arriving in Australia. I'm developing an anxiety twitch."

The new season was upon us. Pre-season testing had revealed some anxiety about the durability of the Pirelli tyres, with some predicting we could have as many as four pit stops per race at some venues. Pirelli remained calm and said that the cold conditions in Spain during testing had contributed to this prediction and that in warmer conditions, most races would be a choice between two or three stops.

There was also anxiety surrounding McLaren. The new car had been painfully slow in testing and looked un-driveable when I saw it in Barcelona. McLaren boss Martin Whitmarsh took a bold gamble weeks before the first race and ordered his technical team to rework the car, removing some extreme solutions particularly around the exhausts and the rear end aerodynamics. The gamble paid off. Although the McLaren wasn't capable of challenging for the win straight away, it was there or thereabouts and, over the course of the season, they evolved their car in such a way that they could optimise it around the original design.

It was clear to me that Sebastian Vettel and Red Bull Racing would be hard to stop, as they would go into the new season on a wave of confidence after winning the world title the year before. And so it proved. Ferrari had looked quite competitive in pre-season testing, but once again couldn't carry it through once the racing started.

Thoughts as I board the plane to Melbourne
23 March 2011

It's a grey, chilly morning in London. The traffic has been intense, the news programmes are full of the Libya intervention, the Japanese earthquake, problems in Yemen and the prospect of the British chancellor bringing in a tax on private jets. And Karun Chandhok has just been given the reserve driver role at Lotus this morning.

Formula 1 seems trivial in comparison to the seismic events going on in the world, However, sport and politics have already overlapped this season with the cancellation of the Bahrain Grand Prix and I'm sure they will overlap again as F1 forges paths into new markets in an unsettled world.

The new season is here and I'm getting onto a Malaysian Airlines flight to Melbourne via Kuala Lumpur. I'll arrive on Wednesday night in time for a shower, dinner and hopefully a good sleep before the business starts on Thursday. I'm interviewing Hamilton, Vettel, Webber, Heidfeld among others for Australian TV that day. The everyday interactions of F1 life will quickly get back into step; the lunge and parry of the drivers and media, the mischievous politicking of those higher up the food chain, the bustle in the paddock.

It's a great feeling, the start of a new season and this is the 22nd time I've felt it.

Every year we travel hopefully, wanting it to be a good season low on politics and high on good racing. Lately it's been pretty good, with seasons going down to the wire more often than not. This season I reckon we'll have loads of fun with the Pirelli tyres. It's going to make the strategic side of the racing so much more important.

I've started a content strand, kindly supported by F1 sponsor UBS, where I will do a deep dive into the race strategy and how the decisions get taken, with inputs from insiders. I hope you like it; it should help fans to understand in more depth why things happened as they did in the races. I'm also doing pre-race strategy planning content which will sit on the UBS F1 website.

I predict a good battle for the title between Vettel and Alonso, which might get a bit fractious at times. Webber will give it everything to be part of the battle, Hamilton too. I worry a little bit about his decision to take on Simon Fuller as manager. Hamilton came into F1 with a single-minded focus on racing, his dad's strict discipline saw to that. Then he split with his dad, got more into the LA lifestyle with his pop star girlfriend and now Fuller is going to make him into a brand.

Rumblings of unhappiness with the team that brought him into the sport have emerged since that management contract was signed. The relationship between the man and his team is changing. McLaren tried to be clever with this year's car and it caught them out. Now it's another uphill fight to catch the front-runners.

In terms of other predictions I also think we'll see a stronger Schumacher this year, mixing it with the younger front-runners at times. I also expect quite a split in the middle of the grid with the stronger drivers in slower cars getting ahead of the weaker drivers in faster cars. There is a lot for the drivers to deal with this year with new tyres, KERS and the adjustable rear wing. I think it's a tough time to be a rookie.

Vettel in total control in season opener in Melbourne
28 March 2011

Sebastian Vettel won the Australian Grand Prix in Melbourne from pole position, leading home Lewis Hamilton and Vitaly Petrov, who became the first Russian to stand on the podium in only his 20th Grand Prix start. It was an eventful, if not spectacular race. There was plenty of overtaking, not much of it due to the new adjustable rear wing, but rather to good driving and different levels of grip from the tyres from car to car.

The weather was the best of the weekend, sunny with track temperatures of 27°C.

At the start Vettel held his position, Hamilton battled with Webber and held his second place. Behind them Vitaly Petrov went from sixth to fourth in the Renault, while Felipe Massa had a great start, moving from eighth to fifth and ahead of Alonso in the process. Alonso dropped down to eighth but started moving back through the field, passing Rosberg, and by lap 6 was up to seventh place.

Button was all over Felipe Massa in the early stages and tried to pass him on the pit straight using the adjustable rear wing. Massa was told that his brakes were getting too hot. As Massa held Button up, Alonso joined them. Button then used an escape road to pass Massa but was unable to give the place back as Alonso had passed Massa straight after. This meant Button had to serve a drive-through penalty for the illegal overtake, which added an extra 23 seconds to his race time.

Meanwhile, on lap 10 Hamilton was closing down on Vettel, and had the tactical advantage of being able to pit first. Webber's tyres started going off on lap 11, his pace dropping by 2 seconds a lap. He pitted first on lap 12, switching to hard tyres and rejoining in traffic behind Kobayashi. Alonso pitted on lap 13, with Massa in a lap later. Both Ferraris went for soft tyres, as did Vettel on lap 15.

Vettel had doubled his lead through the first round of stops; Alonso was up to fifth place behind his old friend Vitaly Petrov. Several drivers tried the adjustable rear wing on the pit straight, but without it leading to an over-take. Button finally managed it on Kobayashi on lap 26.

Rubens Barrichello scythed past Kobayashi for P9, then tried a very ambi-tious pass on Rosberg, leading to a collision. Rosberg's car was damaged in the radiator area. Barrichello was given a drive-through penalty for the incident. Schumacher had also retired from the race, making it a miserable start to the season for Mercedes.

Webber had no pace on the hard tyres; he was a second a lap slower than the leaders and fell to 20 seconds behind by the time of his second stop on lap 27. He took soft tyres as did Alonso a lap later, both drivers clearly choosing a three-stop strategy, where their rivals went for two. Alonso was much faster than Webber and started catching him at over a second a lap.

On lap 37 Vettel, Hamilton and Petrov all pitted for hard tyres that they would take to the end of the race. Petrov had a slow release. On lap 40 Sergio Perez set the fastest lap to that time having only pitted once. Webber and Alonso were ahead of Petrov at this stage. Webber pitted on lap 41. He made a mistake on his out lap and when Alonso pitted a lap later, the Spaniard took the place. Petrov meanwhile moved back into third place.

Button passed Massa for P6 on lap 48. Perez was lapping faster than the leader on lap 50 as he closed in on the back of Massa, despite the fact that the Mexican had only stopped once, a remarkable achievement. Massa had to pit with nine laps to go.

"The sun came out today and the car was perfect," said Vettel after his winning start. "It was crucial to get past Jenson at the first stop, I was on new tyres, he was on old ones. I was able to control the gap to Lewis. I'm very happy. Compliments to Pirelli. I was giving them a hard time over the winter, but we did less stops [than expected]."

Vettel was coy on the use of the rumoured "start only" KERS. "I was pressing some buttons, yes," he said. There were no TV graphics of his start, but a replay of Webber's start showed that he did not use KERS, although the system was armed. Later Vettel said that the team had suffered some problems with KERS reliability through the weekend and that he wants them to get a reliable system as soon as possible. It seems that many teams have had problems with cooling the KERS batteries and were not able to use it during the weekend.

Hamilton was delighted with second place. "Everyone says I have an aggressive driving style and today I was able to prove that's not the case, I looked after the tyres better than the guy next to me," said Hamilton in reference to Vettel.

Sauber's perfect Sunday was spoiled when scrutineers found that their rear wing was not in conformity with the rules and they were excluded. They are appealing the decision. It meant that Paul di Resta got a point on his F1 debut.

Australian Grand Prix
Melbourne 58 laps

1.	Vettel	Red Bull-Renault	1h29:30.259
2.	Hamilton	McLaren-Mercedes	+22.297
3.	Petrov	Reault	+30.560
4.	Alonso	Ferrari	+31.772
5.	Webber	Red Bull-Renault	+38.171
6.	Button	McLaren-Mercedes	+54.300
(7.	Perez	Sauber-Ferrari	+1:05.800) *
(8.	Kobayashi	Sauber-Ferrari	+1:16.800) *
9.	Massa	Ferrari	+1:25.100
10.	Buemi	Toro Rosso-Ferrari	+1 lap
11.	Sutil	Force India-Mercedes	+1 lap
12.	Di Resta	Force India-Mercedes	+1 lap

13. Alguersuari	Toro Rosso-Ferrari	+1 lap
14. Heidfeld	Renault	+1 lap
15. Trulli	Lotus-Renault	+2 laps
16. D'Ambrosio	Virgin-Cosworth	+3 laps

excluded for rear wing infringements

Drivers' Championship Standings
1. Vettel   25 pts
2. Hamilton 18
3. Petrov   15
4. Alonso   12
5. Webber   10
6. Button   8

Constructors' Championship Standings
1. Red Bull-Renault   35 pts
2. McLaren-Mercedes   26
3. Ferrari   18
4. Renault   15
5. Toro Rosso-Ferrari   4
6. Force India-Mercedes 3

What is Hispania's place in Formula 1?
31 March 2011

At last weekend's Australian Grand Prix, Hispania Racing's Narain Kartikeyan and Tonio Liuzzi became the first drivers not to qualify for a Formula 1 Grand Prix for almost a decade. There's no shame in that – Niki Lauda and Nelson Piquet once failed to qualify for a race, in the days when there were far more teams than places on the grid.

Having failed in its attempt to buy the Toyota cars, the team decided to build its own car very late. It failed to turn a wheel in pre-season testing and was still being built when practice began on Friday. Despite turning 11 laps each in qualifying, both drivers failed to make the cut under the new 107 per cent rule and the stewards rightly denied them a place on the grid.

They travel to Malaysia for next weekend's race, with hopes of making it through to Sunday. But what should we make of this team – which echoes the weekend warriors of the early 1990s, like Andrea Moda and Forti – at a time of unprecedented competence on the rest of the grid? And what of the claims from some, inside and outside the team, that once they fit the correct front wing the car will be faster than Virgin?

I spoke to Hispania's Geoff Willis on Sunday morning at length. He has been around: was part of Adrian Newey's team at Williams in the glory days, was in charge at BAR in their heyday and played a role in building Red Bull up to where they are now. He knows what he's doing, in other words.

Clearly he now finds himself in less than ideal circumstances and is putting a brave face on it. But listening to him talk, you realise that he believes in what he's doing and that he's looking forward to shocking a few in the paddock who think Hispania shouldn't be there.

The construction of the car was outsourced to Italian composites firms in which Willis has confidence. However, the front wing failed a crash test and so the car ran in Melbourne with last year's front wing for which the aero package was not designed. All being well the revised wing will pass its test in the coming days and Hispania will be able to do some set-up work in the four hours of practice at Sepang.

When it does, Willis believes that it will push Virgin to the back of the grid. Already Virgin's Timo Glock – who looked a haunted man on the Sunday night plane to Kuala Lumpur – has expressed concern that the car is miles off and that a fast Red Bull lap in Q1 could push them out of the race. But to be beaten by a car which has had hardly any running would be very painful indeed for Nick Wirth's engineers.

The problem at Hispania, clearly, is money. The owner, Jose Carabante, is still learning how F1 works, especially its cash demands. I worked for someone like that at Brabham in the early 1990s, who had underestimated how much an F1 team cost to run. Back then it was £1 million a month. Now it's a minimum of four times that.

Carabante said on Spanish radio that the team would have a €45 million budget this season and promised a "new aerodynamic package" for the Spanish Grand Prix. "It will be enough to be ahead of Lotus and Virgin," he said. "Last year we were in a worse condition than now and we ended up ahead of Virgin with twice our budget, and behind Lotus due only to one accident."

Lotus has taken a big step forward on performance and is now closer to Force India on pace, but Virgin is vulnerable and the whole digital design philosophy is coming under question.

Within months both Hispania and Virgin had new owners as the turbulent life at the back of the grid took its toll. With the Russian billionaire Andrei Cheglakov taking a greater degree of control at Marrussia Virgin Racing, the team's poor start to the year put paid to Nick Wirth's digital car revolution as his Wirth Research group was dropped and former Renault engineering director Pat Symonds brought in to create a technical department in a new building in Banbury.

Meanwhile, Spanish investment firm Thesan Capital acquired Hispania and adopted the name HRT. Geoff Willis left the team, to reappear later in the season at Mercedes GP.

Chapter Four
April 2011

The start of April saw a visit to the Paris headquarters of FIA president Jean Todt for an exclusive interview, which I wrote up for the Financial Times *and* JA on F1. *Over the course of two hours Todt said some interesting things. He spoke a little of the increasing spat between him and Bernie Ecclestone, which was one of the themes of the year and is sure to be a feature of 2012.*

Ecclestone had called the FIA a "joke" a few weeks before our meeting. Todt also took the opportunity to lay down a marker for future negotiations on the 2013 Concorde Agreement by saying that he would be looking for a better deal financially for the FIA, even though the FIA had sold the F1 commercial rights to Ecclestone for 100 years.

What was very clear was that he plans to fight for the best interests of the FIA in the same way as he fought – often controversially – for Ferrari's interests during his 16 years at the helm of the Scuderia. He wears a different hat now, but his modus operandi is the same.

In 2001, following a demand from the EU that the FIA separate the regulatory and commercial side of F1, a deal was signed by then FIA president Max Mosley whereby the commercial rights were assigned to Ecclestone's company for 100 years for a fee of US$360 million, which was paid upfront. This money sits in the FIA Foundation in London, which is a separate institution and which runs the FIA Institute and programmes like the young driver academy and global road safety programmes. Todt is not able to get the FIA's hands on any of this money.

Although the fee looks very light now in comparison to the value of TV rights and circuit licence deals being done, Todt said that at the time it was "a good initiative, a wise decision in 2001 to sell the rights", but that he has done a thorough study of the agreement, which came into force at the start of 2011, and "it cannot be changed. It is what we have."

Interestingly, he also spelled out that he would take the opportunity of the next Concorde Agreement negotiations to robustly pursue a deal for the FIA which reflects current values. "Now it is my responsibility to make the best out of it and to secure the best future for F1," he added. "And you know that it is a commercial agreement, called the Concorde Agreement, which is on much shorter periods and the term of the current one is the end of 2012. So, together with the commercial rights holder and the teams, we will have to discuss the next Concorde Agreement.

"I will make sure everybody realises that times have changed since the [100 year] agreement was signed. Fifteen years ago you didn't have all the sophisticated electronics you can enjoy today when you watch the TV. All that has a cost. Definitely we need to take that into consideration because I must make sure that the funding for the FIA is correct. Our costs are greater than they were ten years ago. Evolution has a price.

"When the agreement was made I wasn't president of the FIA. They [CVC] are very smart people. They have left Bernie total freedom to run the business and he has done an outstanding job as its promoter. But he is not alone: it's like a movie, you have the director but you must also have the actors, and the actors [in F1] have been strongly participating in the show and in the success of the show.

"What is important now is to consider what everyone has contributed in the evolution of what was F1, what is F1 and what F1 has to be in the future. And to have a healthy discussion about how to share the revenues and the costs."

Appropriately, around this time Ecclestone's company reported turnover figures for the sport, showing just how robust its financial health is.

F1 turnover tops $1 billion again as teams' share rises
6 April 2011

Turnover for F1's commercial activities exceeded $1 billion last year according to annual figures released by Formula One Administration. This represents a $19 million increase on the previous year. The teams' share increased by $114 million to $658 million.

Although this equates to an average of $54 million for each of the 12 teams in F1 last season, it doesn't work out that way as the money is not split evenly. It is paid out according to several columns laid out in the Concorde Agreement whereby prize money share goes with success: the champion team receives more than lower placed teams, while there is also a column rewarding teams with a long history of success, like Ferrari, McLaren and Williams.

The interesting thing about the FOA accounts is that the sport has been able to marginally increase revenues at a time when the world has been going through a severe economic downturn. The addition of new races obviously contributes to the rise, as do new Global Partner deals like the ones with UBS, DHL and LG as well as new TV rights deals and renewals.

Despite this increase, revenue doesn't match up to what was expected when the debt was taken out on the business shortly after CVC took a stake in 2005. According to a document produced by RBS and Lehman Brothers in 2006, when the F1 debt package was offered to the markets, the projected turnover for 2010 was $1.28 billion. In contrast, payments to teams for 2010 were projected at $622 million, less than they actually received.

We heard from Jean Todt at the weekend that he would like to review the FIA's share of the commercial revenues of the sport and the teams will also be looking to increase their share when the parties sit down to discuss the new agreement. There is a lot of positioning and messaging going on at the moment from the various parties, but the hard talk has yet to start.

Every season there is a "must have" technical gizmo which one team perfects and the others all rush to copy. This year's was the exhaust blown diffuser, which started last season when Red Bull really got to grips with it. As the teams perfected the technology it became clear how much downforce the device was generating, far more than Pirelli had projected when designing the tyres, for example. One thing that definitely caught my eye after Australia was the statement from Renault that they used 10 per cent more fuel during the race in order to maximise the exhaust gas pressure on the overrun in the corners.

Here's what they said: "To power a blown floor effectively and generate additional downforce, an engine must produce significant amounts of exhaust gas. Simply put, the more fuel burned, the more exhaust and potentially more downforce is produced. Since the RS27's fuel consumption rate is extremely good, the Renault-equipped teams were able to burn 10 per cent more fuel than normal during the Australian Grand Prix without running out, therefore giving more exhaust flow to its partners using the blown diffuser."

That is something like 15kg of extra fuel needed, which around Albert Park equates to about 0.6 seconds compared to not carrying that fuel. Renault's boast here is that their engine is so much more efficient than the other engines that they can have the gain of the diffuser without carrying more fuel than their rivals. That's quite a benefit. I'd like to drill down into that a bit more over the coming weeks.

Renault and Red Bull were the pioneers of the return of the exhaust blown diffuser last season and they seemed to have an advantage here. Meanwhile, their rivals Ferrari and McLaren enjoyed a bit of an advantage on KERS, having optimised their second versions this year. Red Bull used a different kind of KERS from the Renault and it proved unreliable in the early part of the season. I was given a strong heads up that they were using a start-only system in Australia but that appears not to have been entirely correct. It's only a matter of time before someone uncovers the truth behind what they are actually doing with it.

Vettel keeps his cool in all-action Malaysian Grand Prix
10 April 2011

Sebastian Vettel maintained his 100 per cent success record this season with another win from pole position in the Malaysian Grand Prix. Jenson Button finished second and moves into that position in the championship, while Nick Heidfeld gave Renault a second consecutive podium, one which was again based on a sensational start.

The race gave a very vivid example of F1 2011 style with the DRS adjustable rear wing and the high wear Pirelli tyres leading to a lot of overtaking, some of it absolutely thrilling. We had three cars abreast into the final corner at one point and a very spirited battle between Lewis Hamilton and Fernando Alonso that led to contact.

Despite Vettel's smiles, it was a day when reliability issues at Red Bull raised their heads again with both drivers unable to use KERS during the course of the race, a big disadvantage. This was highlighted by its failure on Mark Webber's car at the start, which lost him positions and then made his chances of recovering more difficult. He was carrying the extra weight of the system with none of the performance. Later in the race the same was true of Vettel.

Conditions were dry, with track temperature of 31°C and humidity at an incredible 88 per cent. With rain a distinct prospect, drivers were told to look after their tyres.

At the start, Vettel got away cleanly, Hamilton was boxed in behind him and this allowed Heidfeld to sweep around the outside into second place from sixth on the grid. Behind them a frustrated Webber was swamped by other cars. Both Ferraris went through, with Massa getting past Alonso in the process.

On lap 11 Webber was forced to pit for slick tyres, his first stop of four on the day. He took a different strategy from his rivals, partly because he is heavier on his tyres, but he made a good recovery from ninth on the opening lap to finish fourth.

Hamilton pitted on lap 14, but then rain started to fall. Luckily for him Red Bull pitted Vettel a lap later for dry tyres as did Jenson Button. Alonso came in on lap 15. Kobayashi ran long on the first stint, running second around lap 17. It set him up for a two-stop strategy, one less than everyone else, and a strong finish in seventh place using the Sauber's gentle action on the tyres to good effect.

Vettel drove a measured race at the front, maintaining his margin, keeping his lap times consistent and fast while managing the tyres and the engine revs. Behind him a lot changed over the course of the race. Any one of five drivers could have joined him on the podium and for most of the race it looked like it would be Hamilton plus either Alonso or Button. But Hamilton had a series of problems, including the collision with Alonso, which knocked the front wing off the Ferrari.

Although the result wasn't what Ferrari had hoped for, they will draw encouragement from having competed with McLaren and one of the Red

Bulls after their lack of pace in Australia and in qualifying at Sepang. "Today we were fighting wheel-to-wheel with the McLarens and with Webber so that was a nice surprise," said Alonso, who added that the collision with Hamilton was due to his DRS wing not working on the straights, forcing him to race Hamilton in the corners. He was called to the stewards after the race and had 20 seconds added to his race time so he dropped to sixth. Hamilton was similarly punished, so Alonso stayed sixth, Kobayashi was classified seventh with Hamilton eighth.

No doubt a major talking point from the weekend is the amount of overtaking and the more "chaotic" style of racing. Purists will argue that a lot of the passing was artificial – caused by the new DRS wings, KERS and the on-off nature of the Pirelli tyres. I thought it was entertaining, if rather hard to follow at times. But if the Bridgestone years were like being in a sweet shop and getting only the odd goody, today felt like we'd eaten all we could see. There was a bit too much going on. But I imagine that new fans of the sport will say, "F1's pretty cool, isn't it?"

Vettel thought it was pretty cool and well he might. He now has twice as many points as his nearest challenger. "A great day," said Vettel. "It was quite different to what we saw two weeks ago with the tyres. It was difficult [to judge the stops]. Lewis had a problem and I realised Jenson was behind and I could comfortably control the gap. KERS is something we have to work on, it was crucial at the start and it gave us what we needed there, but we had a problem and had to turn it off. We cannot stop pushing, things were much closer here than in Australia."

Button finished second, having managed a 19-lap final stint on the hard tyres. It was McLaren's 200th podium in partnership with Mercedes.

Malaysian Grand Prix
Sepang 56 laps

1. Vettel	Red Bull-Renault	1h37:39.832
2. Button	McLaren-Mercedes	+3.261
3. Heidfeld	Renault	+25.075
4. Webber	Red Bull-Renault	+26.384
5. Massa	Ferrari	+36.958
6. Alonso	Ferrari	+37.248 (+ 20 sec penalty)

7. Kobayashi	Sauber-Ferrari	+1:07.239
8. Hamilton	McLaren-Mercedes	+49.957 (+ 20 sec penalty)
9. Schumacher	Mercedes	+1:24.896
10. Di Resta	Force India-Mercedes	+1:31.563
11. Sutil	Force India-Mercedes	+1:45.000
12. Rosberg	Mercedes	+1 lap
13. Buemi	Toro Rosso-Ferrari	+1 lap
14. Alguersuari	Toro Rosso-Ferrari	+1 lap
15. Kovalainen	Lotus-Renault	+1 lap
16. Glock	Virgin-Cosworth	+2 laps
17. Petrov	Renault	+4 laps

Drivers' Championship Standings
1. Vettel   50 pts
2. Button   26
3. Hamilton 22
4. Webber   22
5. Alonso   20
6. Massa   16

Constructors' Championship Standings
1. Red Bull-Renault   72 pts
2. McLaren-Mercedes   48
3. Ferrari   36
4. Renault   30
5. Sauber-Ferrari   6
6. Toro Rosso-Ferrari 4

Another poor showing by Ferrari sent alarm bells ringing at Maranello. The car was too conservative to compete with the breathtaking audacity of Adrian Newey's Red Bull design. Only a few months after firing one of their key operational engineers, Chris Dyer, for the failure in Abu Dhabi, now it was technical director Aldo Costa who found his head on the chopping block.

Ferrari managers fly home for emergency meeting
13 April 2011

Despite there being only a week's break before the Chinese Grand Prix this weekend, the three main managers of Ferrari's F1 team have made a 48-hour return trip to Italy to try to resolve some issues relating to the performance of the cars.

Team boss Stefano Domenicali, technical director Aldo Costa and his deputy Pat Fry made the journey trip to investigate why the cars are not performing the way the simulation tools say they should. Massa said on the eve of the Malaysian race that they are not getting the best from the front wing and it's clear that their rivals are also getting more from the exhaust blown diffuser. But the problem is also more basic than that.

Speaking on Ferrari's website Domenicali said, "We'll try to have something ready for China but we know that first we'll have to work out why the figures in the wind tunnel do not correspond with those we have seen on the racetrack. If we don't have a clear picture of things here, we'll have to approach the development of the car from a different angle."

They spent a lot of time on Friday in Malaysia doing aero tests instead of setting up the car – time they never made back. Wind tunnel correlation problems are nothing new in F1; Renault had them a couple of years ago as have plenty of other teams. Until they are understood and rectified, it's very hard for a team to move forward on development. And with strong rivals like Red Bull, McLaren, Renault and even Mercedes likely to make big gains in the coming weeks and months, you can see the urgency to solve the problem.

Ferrari president Luca di Montezemolo raised the bar at the launch of the car in January when he said, "This year we have to win". After Sunday's race he said, "I am definitely not satisfied with the way the season has begun, but I have complete faith in the people here who know how to react when the situation is tough."

Their main problems are in qualifying, where Alonso was 0.9 seconds off Vettel's Red Bull and 0.8 seconds off Hamilton's McLaren. Massa was 1.3 seconds off the pole. They are also worried about the Renault: Nick Heidfeld split the Ferraris in qualifying and with his car's awesome starts and straight line speed, he threatens to be in front of them on the opening lap and hard to pass, unless they can keep him behind them on the grid.

On the plus side Ferrari were much stronger in the race. Even if Vettel was cruising, the McLarens definitely weren't and Alonso was giving them a hard time. Add in the fact that Alonso's DRS rear wing wasn't working and there is some encouragement for the team. Their strategy decisions were pretty sound too, even if they had some problems with the execution of the pit stops.

Hamilton beats Vettel to win thrilling Chinese Grand Prix 17 April 2011

Lewis Hamilton won the Chinese Grand Prix, breaking Sebastian Vettel's stranglehold on F1 this season in a thrilling race, which featured the Holy Grail of a pass for the lead in closing stages. It was Hamilton's first win since September last year and the 15th of his 74-race career.

And it wasn't because of the DRS wing, the pass Hamilton pulled on Sebastian Vettel happened in Turn 7, one of the faster corners on the track, when Vettel least expected it and it came about because of differences in strategy.

Hamilton had learned from his problems in Sepang, saving a new set of soft tyres for the race, and it played its part. His strategy planning began on Saturday. Varying strategy and resulting overtakes was the story of the race and what made it such a thriller, as the new style racing really hit its stride. Drivers who went for three stops found that their tyres had life in them in the closing stages and they were able to make up places.

There were complaints after Malaysia that the DRS wing had made overtaking too easy. But here there were many passes which were not in the DRS zone, particularly from Hamilton and Webber, who recovered from 18th on the grid to finish on the podium, proving he is always at his best when chips are down. He might have beaten Vettel if he had not lost so much time in the first stint on hard tyres, where he actually lost a place to Sergio Perez. KERS also played its part in the overtakes, but this race was all about Pirelli tyres creating the spectacle.

Hamilton's race wasn't without its dramas. Before the start his engine flooded. The mechanics managed to get him onto the grid with less than a minute to spare before the pit lane closed.

At the start Vettel got away slowly allowing Button and Hamilton to pass him. Behind them Massa again outperformed Alonso off the start line and got ahead, while the Force India cars again had strong starts, picking up places – Di Resta was seventh and Sutil eighth at the end of the first lap.

The Mercedes drivers stopped earlier than their rivals, Rosberg came in on lap 14, indicating a three-stop strategy. The leaders bunched up behind Button approaching their stops, Vettel and Massa passed Hamilton and then pitted, following Button in. At this point three stops was an option for Vettel. Button made a mistake, driving into the Red Bull pit box, losing around three seconds in the process and Vettel jumped him and as they emerged, but Rosberg was first out.

Button was the first of the front-runners to make a second stop, followed by Rosberg and Hamilton. Vettel stayed out having committed to a two-stop plan, which turned out to be the wrong choice. The Ferraris had also committed to two stops, which was a shame for Massa who had good pace in this race and even passed the race winner at one point. Nevertheless he restored his reputation by finishing 14 seconds ahead of Alonso.

From then on it was all about how the differing strategies would play out. Everyone is still learning about the new Pirelli tyres and how best to use them and today showed how finely balanced the decisions are.

There were many highlights to the race and some sublime overtakes. Hamilton was faster than Button and was forced to overtake his teammate on lap 36. Button gave him room, as Hamilton was in a determined mood. Webber came through the field very rapidly, his team pitting him in order to give him some clear air to push in. Once the third stops were made it was clear that the three-stop plan was starting to come into its own. Webber passed Alonso for sixth, then took Massa, Alonso and finally Button.

Meanwhile, Hamilton closed on the leader Vettel, who made it as hard for him as he could, particularly in the DRS zone into Turn 14. But Hamilton was an irresistible force and he went past midway through the following lap, as Vettel struggled for grip on his tyres which were seven laps older than Hamilton's.

"The strategy we came up with into qualifying seemed to help," said an emotional Hamilton. "Quite a few things came together; the pit stops, the car felt great. I tried to keep my tyres. The guys at the front had to do quite a bit of overtaking. I wasn't worried [about the problem before the start], it was important to stay as calm as possible."

One final note: Heikki Kovalainen finished 16th for Lotus, ahead of Perez and Maldonado, marking the first time since the team arrived in F1 last season that one of the new teams has battled with established team cars. Trulli's fastest race lap was only 0.3 seconds slower than Maldonado's, set in similar circumstances on new tyres in the closing stages.

Chinese Grand Prix
Shanghai 56 laps

1. Hamilton	McLaren-Mercedes	1h36:58.226
2. Vettel	Red Bull-Renault	+5.198
3. Webber	Red Bull-Renault	+7.555
4. Button	McLaren-Mercedes	+10.000
5. Rosberg	Mercedes	+13.448
6. Massa	Ferrari	+15.840
7. Alonso	Ferrari	+30.622
8. Schumacher	Mercedes	+31.206
9. Petrov	Renault	+57.404
10. Kobayashi	Sauber-Ferrari	+1:03.273
11. Di Resta	Force India-Mercedes	+1:08.757
12. Heidfeld	Renault	+1:12.739
13. Barrichello	Williams-Cosworth	+1:30.189
14. Buemi	Toro Rosso-Ferrari	+1:30.671
15. Sutil	Force India-Mercedes	+1 lap
16. Kovalainen	Lotus-Renault	+1 lap
17. Perez	Sauber-Ferrari	+1 lap
18. Maldonado	Williams-Cosworth	+1 lap
19. Trulli	Lotus-Renault	+1 lap
20. D'Ambrosio	Virgin-Cosworth	+2 laps
21. Glock	Virgin-Cosworth	+2 laps
22. Liuzzi	HRT-Cosworth	+2 laps
23. Karthikeyan	HRT-Cosworth	+2 laps

Drivers' Championship Standings
1. Vettel   68 pts
3. Hamilton 47
2. Button   38
4. Webber   37
5. Alonso   26
6. Massa   24

Constructors' Championship Standings
1. Red Bull-Renault   105 pts
2. McLaren-Mercedes   85
3. Ferrari   50
4. Renault   32
5. Mercedes   16
6. Sauber-Ferrari   7

It was around this time that stories began to emerge about Rupert Murdoch's News Corp showing an interest in F1. The rumour – albeit put about by a reporter on Sky News, a channel owned by News Corp – spoke of Murdoch looking to buy out the commercial rights of F1 from CVC in a consortium with Carlos Slim. The initial rumour brought an almost instant denial by Bernie Ecclestone.

However, media coverage gave the idea some credence, though many seasoned people saw it as a smokescreen or negotiating ploy aimed at other interested parties. An official statement released later confirmed that the interested parties were, in fact, News Corp and Exor, the Agnelli's family company and the ultimate owners of Ferrari.

Then the Murdochs' world turned upside-down with the phone hacking scandal at the News of the World. *But in August they came through to buy the TV rights for the UK in a bold deal, which rewrote the terms of the Concorde Agreement on whether F1 had to be on free-to-air television.*

In a changing media world where newspapers are in decline News Corp has always been on the lookout for the right assets to grow the business. It looked at buying Manchester United a few years ago, for example, and has long had aspirations to control a global sport, which it can exploit commercially. F1 seems like a natural choice.

It is a fabulous global platform – a relatively simple structure with 12 teams, 24 drivers and a 19-race calendar and some areas that have huge potential for commercial exploitation in the future, like online and mobile. The company already has extensive business with Formula 1: it buys rights for Sky Sports Germany and across Asia with the Star Sports Network among others.

News Corp has a wide reaching global platform of its own and the ability, via a deep understanding of the market, to exploit the commercial rights of a sport. The English Premier League is an interesting example, as it has similar global appeal to F1 but significantly higher commercial returns despite asking fans to pay to watch games.

The EPL has been on Sky in the UK for almost 20 years and is a commercial powerhouse. Its UK TV package is worth £600 million a year while overseas sales are slightly higher. The 20 Premier league teams collect £40 million each with the champions earning £70 million for a season, more than F1 teams, of which there are only 12.

News Corp weren't the only ones looking at building a business around F1. Team Lotus boss Tony Fernandes had a busy 2011, with a court battle against Group Lotus over which of them had the right to be called Lotus in F1. That case was heard in April and before it ended Fernandes activated his plan B, to buy an existing small sports car manufacturer called Caterham.

Fernandes confirms Caterham acquisition
27 April 2011

The consortium behind Team Lotus today confirmed that it has acquired the Caterham road car business. Team owner Tony Fernandes explained his thinking: "we will link the Formula 1 team and the car company close together. Then we will look at building technology and marketing links."

He said that adding the road car platform to the F1 programme is where he wanted to be 12 months ago with Group Lotus, but that came unstuck due to a clash with Group Lotus CEO Dany Bahar. "Now it's our baby and we will build from a solid base into something in the same vein as Air Asia," he said.

It has emerged that Fernandes was approached by Caterham's owner and former Lotus executive Ansar Ali shortly before Christmas last year about buying the company and the deal was done quickly. Ali had previously led a management buyout of Caterham in 2005. He will stay on in his existing management role at the company.

Caterham will continue to build the iconic 7 but will also add new models to the range. There has been a lot of talk about the spirit of Colin Chapman, the Lotus founder whose widow and son aligned themselves with Group Lotus at around the time Fernandes and Ali started negotiating.

Fernandes is trading off the heritage of Team Lotus, which he bought from David Hunt last autumn, and not the heritage of Lotus cars. In turn he believes that Group Lotus, which is a sponsor of the Renault F1 team, does not have the right to trade on Team Lotus' heritage.

Ali is very careful to endorse this view saying that the Lotus heritage is not important to Caterham, "My honest belief is no, the legacy doesn't make that much difference to Caterham. But the historical relevance of the 7 is important."

He added that, "I'd be lying if I didn't say that the (Team) Lotus connection was attractive to both of us. I think the credibility is there and it reinforces the providence and the *raison d'être* of the acquisition."

Although the use of the Lotus name is the subject of a legal battle, which Fernandes launched last year against Group Lotus and which could be resolved with a judgement in the next couple of weeks, Fernandes is now moving into road car territory via Team Lotus Enterprises. "Caterham has a unique place at the heart of the motoring world," he said. "As well as being proudly and staunchly British, it has an enviable and uniquely unblemished reputation within the industry for performance, handling and engineering excellence.

"Caterham Cars has remained wholly faithful to Colin Chapman's philosophy of 'less is more', and the DNA of the original 7 can still be traced to the newest additions to Caterham's product offering.

"It is already a successful business with sales across Europe, Japan, Australia and the Middle East, and under the guidance of the existing management team, we now have all the ingredients and the launch pad to further evolve that spirit and take Caterham to new exciting horizons with innovative products and greater global brand exposure."

Chapter Five
May 2011

Ferrari wasn't the only team having a rethink in light of a poor start to the season. Three races in and Williams was still without a point, heading for its worst start to a season since before its winning years which began at the end of the 1970s. Chairman Adam Parr had suggested that changes were needed and in early May he set the course for the future, basing the technical department around Mike Coughlan, the man at the heart of the McLaren/Ferrari spy scandal of 2007.

Williams makes controversial appointment as Sam Michael resigns
3 May 2011

Williams has announced details of the long expected changes to its technical department with the controversial appointment of Mike Coughlan as chief engineer. Chairman Adam Parr said that the team needs "a fresh approach".

Sam Michael has resigned after 11 years as technical director and will leave the team at the end of the season. His short-term role will be to oversee development of the 2011 car to unlock its potential, which has not been seen to date. The team will evaluate Coughlan's suitability to become technical director during the year. Also falling on his sword after a start to the season, which Frank Williams described as "not at the level that it needs to be," is Jon Tomlinson, who was chief aerodynamicist. Meanwhile, Parr has also indicated that Patrick Head will retire at some point this year.

Michael resigned a few weeks ago and is likely to find a role elsewhere in the pit lane, where his skills are well known, but it is the appointment of Coughlan which is so controversial. His role in the scandal whereby Ferrari technical secrets were passed to McLaren ahead of the 2007 season came to light when his wife took a dossier of Ferrari technical information to a copy shop in Woking and the manager alerted Ferrari. It led to McLaren receiving a record $100 million fine while Coughlan and his co-conspirator Nigel Stepney at Ferrari were banned from F1 for two years.

Coughlan popped up again at the start of last season with the abortive Stefan GP team, which tried to get an entry along with other new teams using Toyota chassis.

There has been no official reaction to the news from Ferrari. However, in private, they were furious about his reappearance at Stefan GP and will not be overjoyed to see him reappear now. Of course, it would have been far worse for them if Stepney had reappeared.

Frank Williams says, "He [Coughlan] left Formula One in 2007 because of conduct which he acknowledges was wrong and which he profoundly regrets. His two-year ban from the sport expired some time ago and Mike is now determined to prove himself again. Williams is delighted to be able to give him the opportunity."

Coughlan himself says, "My experience in 2007 was life changing."

Parr said that the team thought hard about Coughlan's past before making the appointment but he believes that everyone has a right to move on in life once they have paid the penalty for their misdemeanours. "My view is quite simple: you do something wrong, you get a penalty, you serve your time and you acknowledge what you did was wrong. Everyone has the right to move beyond that – otherwise, what was portrayed as a two-year penalty would be a lifetime penalty, and that is not right," he said.

Speaking to reporters this morning, Parr also confirmed that Patrick Head, who has been centrally involved on the technical side at Williams for over 30 years, would also be leaving the company, "Patrick has made it clear that he will be retiring this year, so that will happen at some point," he said. "It has nothing to do with the restructuring, it's just the fact that he's turning 65 and had already signalled that it's time for him to move on to his next set of interests in life."

Williams, of course, was inextricably linked with the death of Ayrton Senna, in the eyes of many the greatest driver the sport has produced. The documentary film made about his life had premiered in Japan and Brazil in late 2010 with a good response in both countries, but when it opened in Europe and particularly the UK it soon became a smash hit, going on to become the most successful UK produced documentary film ever, even getting a shot at an Oscar.

I was delighted that JA on F1 *played its part in spreading awareness about the film last year, and this year we hosted the first UK screening of the film in front of an audience of over 200 fans, together with many figures from Senna's life, including some of his mechanics, engineers, fellow drivers and even a few special guests. The evening raised money for the Grand Prix Mechanics Charitable Trust, of which I'm a patron.*

It was a very proud night for JA on F1 *to be able to put on an event like this. And we had a few surprises up our sleeve.*

Emotional night at *Senna* screening
4 May 2011

Last night *JA on F1* hosted a screening of the award-winning documentary *Senna* at the Curzon Mayfair in London. The event, supported by TAG Heuer, was introduced by Sir Jackie Stewart, chairman of the Grand Prix Mechanics Trust.

After the screening we did a Q&A session with the film-makers Asif Kapadia and Manish Pandey. There were also contributions from Senna's rival in F3 Martin Brundle; Dave Ryan, the ex-McLaren team manager; Clive Hicks and Kenny Szmanski, who were Senna's mechanics at Lotus; Professor Sid Watkins, one of Senna's closest allies in F1, and finally Terry Fullerton, the kart racer whom Senna once said was the best driver he ever raced against. They spoke about Senna, his qualities and how well the film represented him.

Brundle explained how the film had made him reconsider much of what happened when he raced against Senna, and explained certain things that took place which he hadn't understood before. For example, how, on the podium at Monza in 1992, Senna told him that they were going to be teammates at Williams the following year.

Professor Watkins spoke about Senna's humility and what a rare quality that is in racing drivers. He told a story about a time when Senna came for an appointment at his hospital in London and waited in the waiting room with the other patients, pushing a lady ahead of him in the queue in her wheelchair.

But the appearance of Fullerton was amazing. In the light of Senna's tribute to him in the film, it was incredible to hear his thoughts on what it felt like to be described by arguably the greatest F1 driver ever as the best he'd raced against.

It was an emotional occasion, the first time that the film has been shown to the public in the UK and over 200 fans, who bought tickets through this site, were there to experience it and share in the fascinating discussion afterwards. It goes on general release in the UK on 3 June.

Vettel sticks to Plan A and wins the Turkish Grand Prix 8 May 2011

Sebastian Vettel won the Turkish Grand Prix with something to spare today, leading from pole position and staying "very much in control" as he put it. It was Vettel's 13th career victory, his third of the season and his sixth win in the last eight races. Mark Webber finished second and Fernando Alonso third.

In front of a thin, but better crowd than in recent years, it was a day on which many team strategists told their drivers to move to Plan B – meaning four pit stops rather than three, because tyre wear was significant due to the loads in Turn 8 and the higher temperatures.

It was another race full of overtaking moves, but the undercurrent from the drivers was a feeling of dissatisfaction that many of the overtakes were too easy, thanks to the adjustable DRS wing. Alonso's pass on Webber and Webber's pass on Alonso were cases in point. But there were plenty of others where, unlike China, the driver behind was able to sail past in the DRS zone, even with tyres of relatively similar ages.

Many of the overtakes had multiple phases to them, with drivers passing and re-passing each other in extended battles. The final sequence of corners at Istanbul contributed to this, with the follow-up opportunity to pass again into the first corner.

But regardless of the impact DRS had on the action, there were some fantastic battles between Hamilton and Button, Button and Massa, Kobayashi and

Schumacher, who seemed to get hit by several cars. At times it was hard to keep up with the flow of the race.

The start was electric with Rosberg passing Webber for second place behind Sebastian Vettel. Lewis Hamilton lost ground trying to go around the outside of Webber, dropping to sixth.

Webber sailed past Rosberg using the DRS wing on lap 5, while Hamilton and Button got into a fierce scrap which lasted a few laps during which positions changed several times. Button had the edge as Hamilton seemed to be suffering more from wear on the rear tyres. He was passed by Massa on lap 10 and both pitted at the end of the lap. McLaren turned their man around more quickly and Hamilton got back out ahead.

The first stops came early (laps 10 and 11), but Vettel really came into his own just before the second when he was able to pull away from Webber and Alonso at a second a lap. However, Alonso's pace in the Ferrari was the real surprise of the afternoon. Able to lap at the same pace as the Red Bulls in the second stint, he actually passed Webber for second place in the third stint on lap 30. He managed to hold onto the place despite pitting after Webber for the third stop.

Rosberg tried a different tactic from the others, choosing to run the hard tyres in the second and third stints, which cost him some places, but put him on the faster tyres for the final part of the race. Vettel used his new set of tyres in the third stint to pull away and consolidate his lead on a day when his team's tactics were as perfect as his driving.

In the closing stages, after the drivers had made their fourth stops, the real action was Webber closing on Alonso, while Hamilton – on tyres that were seven laps newer than his teammate – closed in on him. They were 30 seconds behind Alonso at this stage, showing how remarkable the turnaround by Ferrari and Alonso had been.

"Throughout the race we had a cushion and I was able to react rather than act. But this one is for the guys [mechanics] because I damaged the car on Friday. I'm obviously very happy," said Vettel. "Of course, the tyres are tricky to handle, we saw today different strategies with different people. At times the tyres go away from you and you have to deal with that. But we had the pace to react and we never had anyone close behind."

Turkish Grand Prix
Istanbul Park 58 laps

1. Vettel	Red Bull-Renault	1h30:17.558
2. Webber	Red Bull-Renault	+8.807
3. Alonso	Ferrari	+10.075
4. Hamilton	McLaren-Mercedes	+40.232
5. Rosberg	Mercedes	+47.539
6. Button	McLaren-Mercedes	+59.431
7. Heidfeld	Renault	+1:00.857
8. Petrov	Renault	+1:08.168
9. Buemi	Toro Rosso-Ferrari	+1:09.300
10. Kobayashi	Sauber-Ferrari	+1:18.000
11. Massa	Ferrari	+1:19.800
12. Schumacher	Mercedes	+1:25.400
13. Sutil	Force India-Mercedes	+1 lap
14. Perez	Sauber-Ferrari	+1 lap
15. Barrichello	Williams-Cosworth	+1 lap
16. Alguersuari	Toro Rosso-Ferrari	+1 lap
17. Maldonado	Williams-Cosworth	+1 lap
18. Trulli	Lotus-Renault	+1 lap
19. Kovalainen	Lotus-Renault	+2 laps
20. D'Ambrosio	Virgin-Cosworth	+2 laps
21. Karthikeyan	HRT-Cosworth	+3 laps
22. Liuzzi	HRT-Cosworth	+5 laps

Drivers' Championship Standings
1. Vettel   93 pts
2. Hamilton   59
3. Webber   55
4. Button   46
5. Alonso   41
6. Massa   24

Constructors' Championship Standings
1. Red Bull-Renault   148 pts
2. McLaren-Mercedes   105

3. Ferrari	65
4. Renault	42
5. Mercedes	26
6. Sauber-Ferrari	8

After all the hype about DRS wings making overtaking too easy and the Pirelli tyres requiring too many pit stops, this was really the first race in which everything was a bit too much. There were too many pit stops – 82 in all – and countless passes which were too easy in the eyes of both fans and drivers.

I picked up a distinct undercurrent from drivers after the race that they hadn't enjoyed being able to sail past each other so easily. Mark Webber said that his run in China had made him aware that the tyre situation and the DRS were making things artificial, "You come up against drivers like Fernando, Jenson and Nico, you catch them at 2.5 seconds a lap. It's nice but it's not rewarding because they've got nothing to fight back with."

The problem in Turkey was that the DRS zone was placed halfway along the straight from Turn 10 to Turn 12, where the cars were already travelling at around 180mph. Opening the DRS gives a sudden electric burst of speed, which takes the car past its rival with no real problems. The car in front was a sitting duck.

Many fans reacted badly to the race, this comment by JA on F1 reader Dmitry summed up the views of many, "I am getting more and more sure with each race, that F1 became too artificial with DRS... of course it is nice to watch when one car passes another, but when it is performed in such a fashion as today – thanks, but no thanks."

Alonso commits long-term future to Ferrari
19 May 2011

Fernando Alonso today committed his future to the Ferrari team, signing a five-year deal that will take him though to the age of 35. Alonso spoke of "no doubt ending my F1 career" at Ferrari.

Alonso, who narrowly missed out on last year's world championship in his first year with the team, was described by Ferrari president Luca di

Montezemolo as "a driver who has always demonstrated a winning mentality even in the most difficult circumstances," a reference to the disastrous final round of 2010 in Abu Dhabi where the strategy let him down, and also praised him for his attitude and efforts with a disappointing car so far this season.

Apart from an impressive rally last autumn, where the car was developed into a competitive enough package to allow him to win races and challenge for the title, so far the overall balance sheet for Ferrari with Alonso has not matched expectations. The two-time champion has had to be patient as the team overcomes calibration issues with the wind tunnel and a restructuring of the technical management team.

Alonso's commitment to Ferrari is therefore a bold statement of faith on both sides. Like Vettel's new three-year contract with Red Bull, these commitments are the cornerstone of both teams' medium to long-term plans.

The other driver of that calibre who has yet to decide his long-term plans is Lewis Hamilton. McLaren are delighted with the pairing of Hamilton and Button, as are their sponsors, and all the signs are that they intend to stick with it. However, there are some destabilising forces, such as Red Bull's management, which enjoys dropping compliments and hints about Hamilton joining their squad.

Are they serious or are they just trying to destabilise McLaren? And is Hamilton listening? The Englishman recently dismissed Red Bull as merely "a drinks manufacturer", but their continued dominance on the track does not support this view. Hamilton is in a position, in which many leading drivers have found themselves in the past, where he needs to decide whether to stick with McLaren because they are always there or thereabouts, or to try to get himself into the best car.

Hamilton's idol, Ayrton Senna, won three world titles with McLaren, but eventually moved to Williams in 1994 because they had dominated the sport for the two previous seasons with their Adrian Newey-designed car. Hamilton is eager to match Senna's three titles, but his opposition is fierce and he needs to know that he will have access to a winning car.

Red Bull don't need Hamilton in order to win because they already have Vettel (and Newey, come to that). But this is a company that has always done things differently and Hamilton's appeal is that he could re-energise the team if they could persuade him to move at the end of 2012. Should this start to look like a reality, a new one-year deal for Mark Webber would bridge the gap before Hamilton's arrival.

News of Alonso's new contract really caught everyone by surprise, not because the Spaniard would want to stay at Ferrari, but that he would tie himself to the team for five years, in all likelihood the rest of his F1 career. With the rise of Red Bull and the stability of its technical group, Ferrari have endured three uneven seasons: not being compet-itive in 2009 or 2011, and with Alonso only getting back in the game in the second half of the season to fight for the championship in 2010.

The announcement came on the eve of Alonso's home race, the Span-ish Grand Prix at Barcelona. Although the Ferrari wasn't fast enough to give Alonso a shot at the win, news of the contract produced a real feelgood factor among the Spanish crowds.

Vettel holds off Hamilton to win tense Spanish Grand Prix 22 May 2011

Sebastian Vettel won his fourth race of the season in today's Spanish Grand Prix, holding off a charging Lewis Hamilton in the closing laps and extending his championship advantage to 41 points. It was a very tense battle between two young world champions at the top of their game.

Jenson Button finished third, over half a minute behind, the only front-runner to do three stops rather than four, with pole sitter Mark Webber fourth and Alonso a distant fifth. Michael Schumacher had his best race this year in sixth, staying ahead of his teammate Rosberg having passed him with a superb start.

The Red Bulls had qualified a full second ahead of the McLarens, but in race trim there was nothing between them with the McLarens seemingly more comfortable on the hard tyres.

Vettel's 14th career win was one of his most hard fought with intense pressure from Hamilton. Vettel did not have KERS for much of the race, yet another reliability issue that he had to deal with both in qualifying and in the race. Sooner or later that is going to really start costing Red Bull, especially as McLaren are right there on race pace. But, in a great display of defensive driving, Vettel used the advantage in the faster corners to keep Hamilton at bay in the crucial DRS zone.

The start was sensational. Both Red Bulls got off the line well but struggled for pace on the long run to Turn 1. Vettel weaved a couple of times to block Alonso, but the Spaniard dived down the inside and squeezed past both Webber and Vettel to take the lead. It was a very determined move and gave him the tactical advantage of track position at the start.

Expectations that the DRS wing would encourage overtaking on this track, which has been notoriously difficult to pass on, were dashed early on and there were only a handful of DRS passes today, while the tyres did produce plenty of overtakes.

The first round of stops came early, with Vettel the first of the leaders to come in on lap 10. Alonso and Webber covered him, making their stops on the following lap. Vettel had to pass Button and Massa on his out-lap and did so decisively to keep his challenge alive. Webber wasn't so lucky, hitting traffic and losing third place to Lewis Hamilton in the undercut. This was where his strategy went wrong and he didn't recover from it.

Hamilton took the lead when Alonso pitted and had great speed on his worn tyres, setting the fastest lap of the race to that point on lap 21. He stayed out and managed to make his older tyres work for him to lap faster than Alonso, and when he pitted on lap 24 he was ahead of Alonso and Webber. On tyres that were four laps fresher he pulled away from the Ferrari and got to within 1.6 seconds of Vettel by lap 31, when Webber and Alonso stopped again.

Button made his second stop on lap 31, and rejoined in fifth place. He closed up on the battle between Alonso and Webber, who were much slower on the hard tyres. They passed and re-passed each other on lap 34, as Vettel came in for his third pit stop. Hamilton retook the lead and then pitted a lap later, coming out right behind Vettel.

Button passed Webber for fourth place on lap 36, his soft tyres making all the difference, and he passed Alonso later on the same lap. He then set about building a margin over them, which he would need in the final stint when they would be on soft tyres. He made it work perfectly and took his podium; a great result after a poor start and tenth place on the opening lap. He made his three-stop strategy work brilliantly

In the closing stages Hamilton was right with Vettel on the hard tyres, getting all the details right, but he couldn't get close enough in the middle sector to make it count along the pit straight.

"It was pretty tough," said Vettel. "I don't understand where Fernando came from at the start. We got him at the first stop. Lewis was very strong [on hard tyres]. He gave us a very hard time. But we made it. A great result."

Hamilton said, "I don't think we can be disappointed. We had some serious pace, but it was hard to get past Sebastian – they were massively quick in the high downforce. I gave it my all."

After the race four drivers, including Hamilton, Button and Webber, were investigated by the stewards, which included Mark Blundell as the driver steward, for not slowing under yellow flags. They were not given a punishment, instead being told not to do it again.

Spanish Grand Prix
Barcelona 66 laps

1. Vettel	Red Bull-Renault	1h39:03.301
2. Hamilton	McLaren-Mercedes	+0.630
3. Button	McLaren-Mercedes	+35.697
4. Webber	Red Bull-Renault	+47.966
5. Alonso	Ferrari	+1 lap
6. Schumacher	Mercedes	+1 lap
7. Rosberg	Mercedes	+1 lap
8. Heidfeld	Renault	+1 lap
9. Perez	Sauber-Ferrari	+1 lap
10. Kobayashi	Sauber-Ferrari	+1 lap
11. Petrov	Renault	+1 lap
12. Di Resta	Force India-Mercedes	+1 lap
13. Sutil	Force India-Mercedes	+1 lap
14. Buemi	Toro Rosso-Ferrari	+1 lap
15. Maldonado	Williams-Cosworth	+1 lap
16. Alguersuari	Toro Rosso-Ferrari	+2 laps
17. Barrichello	Williams-Cosworth	+2 laps
18. Trulli	Lotus-Renault	+2 laps
19. Glock	Virgin-Cosworth	+3 laps

| 20. D'Ambrosio | Virgin-Cosworth | +3 laps |
| 21. Karthikeyan | HRT-Cosworth | +4 laps |

Drivers' Championship Standings

1. Vettel	118 pts
2. Hamilton	77
3. Webber	67
4. Button	61
5. Alonso	51
6. Rosberg	26

Constructors' Championship Standings

1. Red Bull-Renault	185 pts
2. McLaren-Mercedes	138
3. Ferrari	75
4. Renault	46
5. Mercedes	40
6. Sauber-Ferrari	11

If Ferrari technical director Aldo Costa had felt a sense of foreboding when he made his whistle-stop trip home after the Malaysian Grand Prix, he was right to be concerned. In May it was confirmed that his overly cautious approach to the 2011 Ferrari had cost him his job.

Here we had the most senior technical man at the most famous team in F1 being sacked because he couldn't keep up with the cars produced by an energy drinks company. As a statement of the state of play in F1 it was stark. He also became the second F1 technical director to resign in a month, after Sam Michael.

It was also not a great advert for Ferrari's policy in the post-Ross Brawn, Jean Todt, Rory Byrne era of promoting Italian talent. Filling Costa's shoes was his deputy, an Englishman and a former senior engineer with Ferrari's arch-rivals, McLaren.

Ferrari put confidence in Pat Fry as Costa falls on his sword
24 May 2011

Four years after Ross Brawn left the team, Ferrari has once again decided to put its faith in an Anglo Saxon technical director.

Aldo Costa, who was long groomed as Brawn's successor, has been relieved of his post to be replaced by ex-McLaren engineer Pat Fry. The 47-year-old Englishman was brought in over the winter as deputy technical director. He was previously one of the senior engineers and designers at McLaren and he now assumes overall control of the chassis side of the technical operation. Luca Marmorini stays on as boss on the engine side and Corrado Lanzone is head of production.

Ferrari has lacked flair and imagination in its design recently and it is likely that Fry will now look to strengthen the design office.

Costa oversaw the 2007 world championship victory for Kimi Raikkonen with a car designed by his team under Brawn's management, and then his team came close in 2008 with Felipe Massa. But the title eluded them and has done so ever since as independent teams Brawn (ironically) and Red Bull stepped up to championship status.

Last year they narrowly missed out on the world title with Fernando Alonso, who led going into the final round, and a disappointing start to this season dogged by aerodynamic correlation problems caused by an upgrading of the wind tunnel, has led Ferrari's management to act.

The car lacks downforce and struggles to generate temperature and grip from harder compound tyres, a long-time Ferrari problem. Costa said last weekend that Ferrari had a significant upgrade to the car coming for Montreal, but he will not be around to see whether it works. Ferrari should be more competitive in the next three races anyway: Monaco, Montreal and Valencia, as they are tracks which call for soft compound tyres, which suit Ferrari better.

Although team principal Stefano Domenicali came up through the ranks with Costa and served alongside him for many years, the performance in Spain, where Alonso fell backwards and was lapped after a heroic effort in qualifying and at the start of the race, was clearly the final straw. The Ferrari is off the pace, Red Bull is getting away and a difficult decision needed to be made.

With Williams' Sam Michael resigning earlier this month, technical directors are becoming like football managers, who carry the can when the team fails to make the grade.

Under Brawn and ultimately Jean Todt, the Ferrari technical team was very stable, with Rory Byrne as chief designer. In the four years since they left the technical side has promoted and then dispensed with Luca Baldisserri and Chris Dyer, who performed senior operations roles, and now with Costa.

With Alonso signed up for five years, Ferrari is clearly hoping that he and Fry can form a new dynasty and restore stability and excellence on the technical side. They worked together well at McLaren in 2007.

Ferrari president Luca di Montezemolo said at the launch of the 150 Italia that this year the Scuderia "have to win" but with its lead driver already over 60 points behind Sebastian Vettel, it is going to require a massive turnaround to get Alonso back into the title fight like last year.

Vettel holds on to win 'red flag' race in Monaco
29 May 2011

Sebastian Vettel won the Monaco Grand Prix after the race was red flagged and then restarted with only six laps to go. Fernando Alonso was second and Jenson Button third.

It was a fascinating three-way battle for the victory, with three completely different race strategies creating tremendous tension and excitement. From about 15 laps before the end, these three drivers were all together, separated by half a second in what was shaping up to be a thrilling showdown. But the race was stopped after 72 laps following a heavy accident involving a group of cars. Vettel held on at the restart to take his fifth win of the season and his first at Monaco.

There was a space left on the grid by Sergio Perez, who was unable to start the race after being hospitalised by a heavy accident in qualifying. The Mexican suffered severe concussion and was kept in for observation.

At the start, Vettel got away cleanly, Button cut across Webber from second on the grid and Alonso also managed to pass the Australian into third place. Behind them Schumacher lost five places to tenth, but managed to re-pass Lewis Hamilton for ninth. However, as Schumacher's rear tyres went off, Hamilton forced his way past on lap 10, though by then he was already 26 seconds adrift of the leaders.

At the first round of stops both Red Bulls lost time, Vettel came in first and a delay on his stop meant that the team wasn't ready for Webber. The only one of the leaders on supersofts, Button did a fast out-lap and took the lead from Vettel, while Alonso pitted a lap later and rejoined third. Button then used his tyres to open a gap from Vettel. By lap 28 it was up to 13 seconds.

Button made his second stop on lap 33 and took another set of supersofts. Then he had some very bad luck. Multi-stop strategies are always a risk in races where a safety car is likely – at Monaco the risk of a safety car is 71 per cent, with the likelihood of a second one. Sure enough, Hamilton and Massa collided at the hairpin on lap 35 and Massa crashed heavily in the tunnel shortly afterwards. This brought out the safety car. Hamilton was later given a drive-through penalty for causing the accident.

The race restarted on lap 39 with Vettel leading from Button and Alonso. On lap 47 McLaren told Button that it was looking unlikely that Vettel would pit soon so that he would have to overtake Vettel to make his strategy work. Instead Button pitted for soft tyres on lap 49, put himself in position to undercut Vettel at the Red Bull's next stop but lost a place to Alonso. The Spaniard remained the big question mark – could he make his tyres last to the end from lap 36?

As Vettel went past the 40-lap mark on his set of soft tyres, still lapping in the 1m 19s, he proved it could be done. Vettel had nothing to lose by staying out. If he pitted he would finish third anyway. Meanwhile, Kobayashi forced his way past Sutil for fourth place on lap 66.

On lap 69 a crash involving Hamilton, Alguersuari, Sutil and Petrov happened right in front of the leaders as they came through. A safety car was deployed and it gave Vettel some respite from the pressure. The race was red flagged, the drivers were allowed to change tyres before the restart, and Vettel held on to win.

"It was not a straightforward Monaco Grand Prix. I'm really happy. It's a great honour, surely one of the best Grands Prix of the year," said Vettel. "If there had been no safety car it would have been hard to beat Jenson because he was so far ahead, but there was a safety car. The race was not easy, doing around 60 laps on one set of tyres."

**Monaco Grand Prix
Monte Carlo 78 laps**

1. Vettel	Red Bull-Renault	2h09:38.373
2. Alonso	Ferrari	+1.138
3. Button	McLaren-Mercedes	+2.378
4. Webber	Red Bull-Renault	+23.100
5. Kobayashi	Sauber-Ferrari	+26.900
6. Hamilton	McLaren-Mercedes	+27.200
7. Sutil	Force India-Mercedes	+1 lap
8. Heidfeld	Renault	+1 lap
9. Barrichello	Williams-Cosworth	+1 lap
10. Buemi	Toro Rosso-Ferrari	+1 lap
11. Rosberg	Mercedes	+1 lap
12. Di Resta	Force India-Mercedes	+2 laps
13. Trulli	Lotus-Renault	+2 laps
14. Kovalainen	Lotus-Renault	+2 laps
15. D'Ambrosio	Virgin-Cosworth	+2 laps
16. Liuzzi	HRT-Cosworth	+3 laps
17. Karthikeyan	HRT-Cosworth	+3 laps
18. Maldonado	Williams-Cosworth	+5 laps

Drivers' Championship Standings

1. Vettel	143 pts
2. Hamilton	85
3. Webber	79
4. Button	76
5. Alonso	69
6. Heidfeld	29

Constructors' Championship Standings

1. Red Bull-Renault	222 pts
2. McLaren-Mercedes	161
3. Ferrari	93
4. Renault	50
5. Mercedes	40
6. Sauber-Ferrari	21

The month ended with the FIA trying to bring in a ban on teams using the off-throttle production of exhaust gases to blow the diffuser and create downforce in the corners. It was a hideously complex thing to explain to audiences and it proved equally difficult for the FIA to impose the ban. It was supposed to happen in Barcelona, but was then withdrawn because Red Bull said it would cause reliability issues. The wording of the ban was changed several times, briefly creating an uneven playing field around the time of the British Grand Prix at Silverstone where the cars ran to a unique set of rules that didn't apply to any other race in 2011. Finally, in Germany it was put to bed for the rest of the season and – this being F1 and very forward looking – no one mentioned it again.

Chapter Six
June 2011

One of the more embarrassing stories of 2011 for F1 was the saga of the Bahrain Grand Prix. As the uprisings of the Arab Spring raged across the Gulf it was clear that a motor sport series had no business blundering into the region to pitch its tents and put on its show. As protesters died in the streets at the hands of security forces, F1 surely had to make the right call on whether the race should go ahead or not.

The race was postponed initially, but on 3 June the FIA's World Motor Sport Council reinstated it. The FIA was confident of its decision. Following the lifting of the state of emergency in time for the WMSC meeting, it conducted a fact finding mission to Bahrain which concluded that it was both safe and desirable for the Grand Prix to take place on 30 October in a spirit of "reconciliation" after the the uprisings. But was the country ready for reconciliation or was there just a temporary suspension in the process of change?

"On the one hand, Formula One isn't respecting human rights, but on the other it's a good chance for the people to express how they feel on television worldwide," Mohammed Al-Maskati, head of the Bahrain Youth Society for Human Rights, told Bloomberg TV at the time.

At the same meeting, the FIA also announced a 2012 calendar with Bahrain as the first race on 11 March.

This was a strange episode that made F1 and the FIA look out of step with moral opinion. A week later the Bahrainis and the FIA accepted that the race could not go ahead.

Bahrain accepts that 2011 race is off
10 June 2011

Last night the organisers of the Bahrain Grand Prix issued a statement accepting that it will not be possible to stage the race this year and focusing their efforts on getting ready to host the sport in March 2012.

In many ways this is what the organisers and the government there should have done from the outset, rather than push for an autumn date this season. With so much going on, and with uncertainty in the outside world as to the extent of the troubles, it was always going to be problematic to try to hold the race this year. It was surprising that the Bahrainis got as far as a positive vote in the FIA World Motor Sport Council last week.

Following a vote the teams put their foot down and made it clear to the organisers, the commercial rights holder and the FIA that they would not accept the disruption and the extension of the schedule into December to accommodate the change.

Now Bahrain has nine months – twice the length of time that has elapsed since the initial uprising in the country – to pursue discussions with the opposition groups and find a way forward which will create a stable enough society for "normal" activities, such as F1, to return.

The Chairman of Bahrain International Circuit, Zayed Alzayani, said, "Whilst Bahrain would have been delighted to see the Grand Prix progress on 30 October in line with the World Motor Sport Council's decision, it has been made clear that this fixture cannot progress and we fully respect that decision.

"Bahrain has absolutely no desire to see a race that would further extend the calendar season and detract from the enjoyment of F1 for drivers, teams or supporters. We want our role in Formula One to continue to be as positive and constructive as it has always been, therefore, in the best interest of the sport, we will not pursue the rescheduling of a race this season… We look forward to welcoming teams, their drivers and supporters back to Bahrain next year."

Speaking at the FOTA Fans' Forum in Montreal last night, McLaren boss Martin Whitmarsh – whose team is 40 per cent owned by the Bahrainis – said: "We've been going to Bahrain for many years and they've done a great job," he said. "But we have to recognise that we are a sport, not a political organisation. FOTA made its position clear in a private letter. But what we have to be careful of is, is it for us to decide on human rights, whether we should be going to China or Russia?

"We have to be very careful if we then start to be this moral arbiter of what country has the right level of human rights and we'll only go there. It was difficult for Jean Todt and the FIA, he went into a process, there was a unanimous decision, Jean is trying to run the sport in an orderly manner."

This was an awkward moment for Whitmarsh as the Bahrainis are powerful shareholders in the McLaren business. By signing the letter from all the teams saying that they would not go, he was acting against the interests of those shareholders, but he took the view that this was the right thing to do for the sport, regardless of the personal risk to him as CEO of McLaren.

Whitmarsh was now in his second term as chairman of FOTA and has always been a keen backer of the Fans' Forum initiative, which JA on F1 conceived and took to the teams as a fan connectivity project. The Montreal event was a big success with a dynamic crowd of US and Canadian F1 fans putting their questions and points of view to the big names from the world of F1. At one stage we had US fans telling the team bosses how to market their sport in America ahead of the return there in 2012 with the race in Austin, Texas.

We did three FOTA Fans' Forum events in 2011, with an event at McLaren's HQ in Woking shortly before the British Grand Prix and another at Pirelli's factory in Milan in September.

Meanwhile, Canada produced one of the most extraordinary races of the season, with appalling weather conditions contributing to the longest race in F1 history.

Jenson Button wins chaotic, rain hit Canadian GP
12 June 2011

Jenson Button won an astonishing Canadian Grand Prix with a last lap pass on Sebastian Vettel. After two high-pressure finishes in Spain and Monaco where he held on, Vettel made a mistake under pressure this time and you could tell that it hurt him. He extended his championship lead to 60 points, with Button moving into second place in the table, but it was scant consolation; everything has been going right for Vettel so far this year, but today he came unstuck.

It was Button's tenth career victory and his first since China last year. He described it as the "best race" of his career, before going off to speak to the stewards about his part in collisions with his teammate and with Fernando Alonso. Mark Webber finished third after battling with Michael Schumacher in the closing stages. The seven-times champion had his best race since his comeback, looking like he might get a podium at one point.

The race featured five safety car restarts and was stopped by race director Charlie Whiting after 25 laps due to torrential rain. The delay lasted two hours. It also featured more controversy for Lewis Hamilton who again tried to force the issue in a furious opening five laps that ended in him crashing out.

It had rained on and off all morning in Montreal, but it wasn't raining on the grid where a warm wind was blowing. The race started behind the safety car, a cautious decision but one that reflected the lack of understanding the competitors had about the Pirelli wet tyres.

Aggressive right from the start, Hamilton connected with Mark Webber going into Turn 1. "Lewis thought the chequered flag was in Turn 3," said Webber ironically. Then he had a battle with Michael Schumacher before smashing into the back of teammate Jenson Button, a collision that ended his race and brought out the safety car. Button moved over to the left, following the line most drivers were taking between the final corner and the kink at the start line. Not aware of how close Hamilton was he squeezed him into the wall. Both drivers apologised for the incident after the race.

Button pitted for intermediate tyres on lap 9. He rejoined in the queue behind the safety car in P12. But he was given a drive-through penalty for speeding behind the safety car. This dropped him to the back of the field. From here he fought back to win the race.

At the restart, Vettel was able to pull away quite easily from Alonso in second place at around a second a lap, Massa was tucked in behind. On lap 17 Button set a lap over a second faster than Vettel indicating that intermediate tyres were the ones to be on.

Ferrari reacted immediately, bringing Alonso in for intermediates and getting him out just ahead of Button. But it was a bad call as he was in again a few laps later, along with Button, when the rain fell hard. Kamui Kobayashi stayed out and rose to second place as the safety car came out again for the heavy rain.

Vettel described conditions on the main straight as "undriveable" and urged the race director via radio not to consider restarting the race because it would be too dangerous for the cars behind him. Charlie Whiting agreed and stopped the race on lap 25.

After a two-hour wait, the safety car led the 23 remaining cars around in preparation for a restart but, by the time it came, the track was ready for intermediate tyres. Schumacher made up places by coming straight in, as did Di Resta and Heidfeld. Most drivers followed suit. Alonso lost time in his stop and when he went out he was racing Button, who ran up the inside him into a chicane and they collided, putting Alonso out of the race. Button got a puncture.

At the front, Vettel pulled away from Kobayashi and Felipe Massa. On lap 41 Heidfeld and Di Resta collided at the final chicane, damaging the front wing of the Force India car. Schumacher pounced for fifth place.

By lap 49 a drying line started to appear and drivers started thinking about slicks. Webber was the first to jump – a worthwhile gamble as it brought him a speed advantage and gave Red Bull a chance to pick the perfect moment to pit Vettel.

The closing stages featured an exceptional battle between Schumacher, Webber and Button. Button got ahead of both and chased after Vettel in the closing laps. With the chequered flag being readied for Vettel once again, Button's presence was enough to force the Red Bull driver to brake too late and slide wide enough to allow the McLaren to sweep through.

"As we always say, it's the last lap that counts," said Button. "A great race. To fight my way through from last position. It's definitely my best race."

Vettel was down after the race, "It was a long race, with a long break. All in all I can be satisfied, but at the moment the impression I've got is I'm disappointed. To make a mistake on the last lap is not very sweet. I have no problem to admit I went a bit wide, outside the dry line. I got away with second.

"I could tell Jenson was quicker than us. I should have pushed a bit hard to open up a gap after the safety car. I was too cautious."

Canadian Grand Prix
Montreal 70 laps

1. Button	McLaren-Mercedes	1h23:50.995
2. Vettel	Red Bull-Renault	+2.709
3. Webber	Red Bull-Renault	+13.828
4. Schumacher	Mercedes	+14.219
5. Petrov	Renault	+20.395
6. Massa	Ferrari	+33.225
7. Kobayashi	Sauber-Ferrari	+33.270
8. Alguersuari	Toro Rosso-Ferrari	+35.964
9. Barrichello	Williams-Cosworth	+45.100
10. Buemi	Toro Rosso-Ferrari	+47.000
11. Rosberg	Mercedes	+50.400
12. De la Rosa	Sauber-Ferrari	+1:03.600
13. Liuzzi	HRT-Cosworth	+1 lap
14. Karthikeyan	HRT-Cosworth	+1 lap
15. D'Ambrosio	Virgin-Cosworth	+1 lap
16. Glock	Virgin-Cosworth	+1 lap
17. Trulli	Lotus-Renault	+1 lap
18. Di Resta	Force India-Mercedes	+3 laps

Drivers' Championship Standings
1. Vettel   161 pts
2. Button   101
3. Webber   94
4. Hamilton   85
5. Alonso   69
6. Massa   32

Constructors' Championship Standings
1. Red Bull-Renault   255 pts
2. McLaren-Mercedes   186
3. Ferrari   101
4. Renault   60
5. Mercedes   52
6. Sauber-Ferrari   27

One of the most surprising themes of the 2011 season was the erratic performance of Lewis Hamilton. Canada was a race that seemed to sum up a season that he describes as his worst in F1. He was involved in a tangle during the race with another car – his teammate – and missed an opportunity for a win as a result. In complete contrast, Button picked his way intelligently through the chaos to win.

The extent of Hamilton's lifestyle change was there for all to see in Montreal, with an array of American music and sports stars in the McLaren hospitality area as guests of the 2008 world champion and his pop star girlfriend Nicole Scherzinger. As the results failed to come for him and he got involved more and more with other cars on track inevitably the criticism arose that he was distracted by his off-track life, criticisms he refuses to accept.

Having watched Hamilton change from a boy to a man, I wrote this reflective post after the race in Montreal.

Hamilton needs to ride out the storm
13 June 2011

As the rain lashed the Montreal circuit yesterday, forcing the race to be stopped, all the leading drivers knew that there was an opportunity for the taking. Canada often presents them. Although Red Bull's Sebastian Vettel was in the driving seat when the race was held up, with constantly changing conditions, safety cars and chaos, there was a chance to make something happen. Just as Jenson Button did.

But by that stage Lewis Hamilton already had no chance to affect the outcome, having had another messy race after which Emerson Fittipaldi's verdict that he is "too aggressive when he tries to overtake, he needs to respect the other drivers," will have been ringing in his ears.

During the weekend Hamilton was surrounded by a glamorous crowd in the McLaren hospitality area. With pop stars like Rihanna and Ice T, NBA basketball players towering over other guests, this was like a night at the MTV Awards rather than a race meeting. Ron Dennis looked on quizzically at all the bling. "That's where Lewis's head is at right now," said one seasoned F1 insider as we stood together surveying the scene.

Who knows where his head is. Certainly he seems to be going about his business in a different way from before, no less intense, but somehow desperate at times, impatient and clearly frustrated. He's a brilliant entertainer, but he's fluffing his lines at the moment, unlike the 2009 and 2010 seasons where he took every half chance that was going.

Despite all the criticism, I think Niki Lauda goes too far when he says of Hamilton, "You cannot drive like this any more, someone is going to get killed." At a time when the poignant movie about Ayrton Senna plays to huge audiences in Europe, it is a comment that seems out of joint, inflammatory, tabloid.

Hamilton knows that he had the equipment to win three of the last four races; and in Montreal he was clearly the fastest man on the track in the brief period at the start before he crashed out. He said he had calmed down after the clamour of Monaco but, if anything, he was even more hyped up in Canada.

The outcome is that he falls to fourth in the championship. Talk is one thing; actions are another.

Having set himself up for the win with pole positions and then measured performances, Sebastian Vettel has found himself under intense pressure at the end of each of the last four Grands Prix and he's only won two of them. He is beatable. Hamilton got him in China; Button got him spectacularly yesterday and in Spain Hamilton almost had him in the closing stages, while we were robbed of the attacks of Alonso and Button in Monaco by a red flag. Though Vettel has ridden his luck, he has made things happen for himself.

And in the end all that counts is results.

Around the middle of June it became clear that due to the freezing of its licence fee the BBC was unlikely to continue with its level of expenditure on Formula 1. With the stories of a News Corp bid for the sport still in circulation, the Murdoch owned media – Sky News and the Sunday Times *in particular – made much of this, raising the spectre of F1 moving towards a pay TV model in the UK (it has been on pay TV in many countries for some time already).*

FOTA chairman Martin Whitmarsh had spoken on this issue before. His position at that time was very clear – that F1's current business model relies on the mass-market reach of free-to-air TV, particularly for the sponsors and manufacturers. A switch to a pay TV model would require a change of emphasis for teams, with more of their income shifting to their share of the commercial revenues (of which TV is a part) and less from sponsorship. While this would make it easier for teams in one sense, as multi-million dollar sponsors are not easy to find, it would also place an even greater emphasis on getting the teams' share of revenues up to the right level, which is what the current Concorde Agreement negotiations are about.

"It's crucial to the commercial model of Formula 1 that TV coverage should remain free-to-air, and therefore universally accessible, widely consumed and enjoyed by large numbers of viewers – and the BBC delivers that in the UK," said Whitmarsh. That comment would prove a hostage to fortune.

Almost halfway through the season and already almost 100 points behind Sebastian Vettel in the championship, the season was far from being as Ferrari and Fernando Alonso had hoped. Chances to win were there but had not been taken. Ferrari's two big problems were its lack of qualifying pace and the poor performance on the first laps out of the pits on the harder compound tyres. Both problems were really hurting them.

Alonso: "We're having a very bad year"
24 June 2011

On the eve of the European Grand Prix at Valencia, Fernando Alonso said all is not lost in his and Ferrari's quest to win the world championship this year, but admitted that the team was having "a very bad year".

After a slow start where he qualified fifth in the first four races, Alonso had a chance to win both the last two races, in Monaco and Canada, where he qualified second, but he wasn't able to make it happen.

Speaking on Thursday he said, "I think we need to have the best car. If we have the best car we can win the title because there is plenty of time and plenty of races to recover. If we are fifth or sixth, as we normally are in qualifying, it's very difficult because you cannot get the pace that everybody is doing.

"I think the championship is long. We need to concentrate, race by race. We will try to be on the podium, we will try to win every race we do. Obviously this is sometimes very difficult or impossible but this is our aim.

"This is also some pressure that you have when you are at Ferrari. You need to win every race that you do, you need to win every championship that you do and despite these seven races when I think I drove the best seven races of my career, with the best qualifying laps, compared to my teammate, compared to last year, comparing different years, the starts, everything… In some ways I agree that we are having a bad season. I think we need to understand and respect our rivals and to work harder than them and to close that gap in the near future."

Alonso didn't want to raise hopes that the changes in the off-throttle diffuser rules from Silverstone and the engine mapping changes this weekend in Valencia will put the Red Bulls behind the Ferraris. He sees it that Red Bull have the performance to be able to push when they want to and take it easy at other times. "I don't think it [the rule change] will massively change qualifying. I think Sebastian was quickest in qualifying [in Montreal]. It's true that it wasn't one second, it was 0.2 seconds, but he was the quickest in wet conditions at the start of the race.

"We were following him and he was nearly 0.8 or 0.9 seconds quicker than us on Sunday with race mapping. We saw a superior car at that moment, a dominant car, the Red Bull, in qualifying and in the race as well. It seems that sometimes they push a little bit more, sometimes a little bit less. Because of that, in races you seem a little bit closer."

Vettel in dominant form as he wins in Valencia
26 June 2011

Sebastian Vettel dominated the European Grand Prix in Valencia – his sixth win from pole of the 2011 season – and extended his championship lead to 77 points. A week short of his 24th birthday, he gave himself a present of pole position, the fastest lap and a win. He has the championship in his hands. It was a great response to the critics after his rare mistake on the last lap in Montreal two weeks ago.

He also became the first man to finish either first or second in the first eight races of the season. He has only dropped 14 points this year. What's also helped him build his massive championship lead is that there is no single main challenger this season: in the six races he has won four different drivers have finished second.

It was the German's 16th victory in 70 Grand Prix starts. He beat off a determined challenge from Ferrari's Fernando Alonso, who managed to get the better of Vettel's Red Bull teammate Mark Webber through a mixture of overtaking and strategy. Webber's third place gave Red Bull its 50th podium in F1.

Track temperatures were 47°C at the start of the race, the hottest they had been all weekend. Only Petrov and Perez decided to start the race on the medium tyres. The rest of the field went for the softs and the leading drivers ended up making three pit stops.

Vettel got away well as did Webber, while Massa shot past Alonso and Hamilton but then got boxed in on the inside of Webber, allowing Alonso to go around the outside of him into third place. Rosberg also had an excellent start up to sixth place, but Jenson Button was faster in the early stages and was able to pass him on lap 6. Alonso looked faster than Webber in the battle for second place but couldn't make the DRS wing count to overtake him.

The first stops came on laps 13–15 with Hamilton and Webber coming in first and Vettel, Alonso and Button reacting. Hamilton's early stop got him into fourth place ahead of Massa who pitted four laps later. Schumacher's race was compromised when he broke his front wing smashing into one of the Renaults on his out-lap from the pits.

On lap 21 Alonso was finally able to use the DRS wing to pass Webber and move up to second place. Vettel responded immediately, setting his fastest lap of the race to that point. He kept the gap on Alonso to 3 seconds.

Webber pitted on lap 29 for the second time and took another set of soft tyres. Ferrari reacted to the move bringing Alonso in, but he had lost time on that extra lap and Webber went past him, back into second place.

Meanwhile, McLaren did its best to slow Hamilton down, his rear tyre temperatures were high. "I can't go any slower," said a frustrated Hamilton. McLaren seemed to be using its rear tyres up more than the opposition.

Massa stayed out the extra lap again and Webber passed him, as did Alonso. Massa lost 5 seconds in his pit stop with a left rear problem. This gave Jenson Button a chance, but he couldn't take it as his KERS wasn't working.

Vettel pushed to open a gap to Webber in the third stint as only Alonso's Ferrari could match them for pace. The McLarens were a second a lap slower, as was Massa. Vettel eased away from Webber as he took less out of the rear tyres lap after lap.

Webber pitted on lap 43 for medium tyres, as did Hamilton. On the used softs, Alonso was faster than Webber. He was 19.9 seconds clear, not enough to make a stop and rejoin ahead. He delayed a lap and pulled it off, pitting on lap 47 and holding second place.

Alguersuari put in an excellent performance, running much of the race in the top ten, making a set of soft tyres last longer than most. He started 18th but his two-stop strategy got him up to eighth place, ahead of Adrian Sutil. After three consecutive poor qualifying sessions this was his best race result of the season and a good response to the pressure on his drive from reserve driver Daniel Ricciardo.

Although expected, it was a tremendous win for Vettel, who could now afford to take a holiday from the next three Grands Prix and still be leading the championship after the summer break. It wasn't as dramatic a race as the first seven this season, but it was an improvement on recent races at this track as the DRS and Pirelli tyres made a difference. It was also a day of astonishing reliability, with all 24 cars finishing the race, though Webber had to nurse a gearbox problem in the closing stages.

It was a better day for local favourite Alonso, who managed to match the pace of the Red Bulls for much of the race, though Vettel was always able to keep him at arms' length, opening a gap when he needed to without taking too much out of his tyres.

However, it wasn't a good day for McLaren or Mercedes: they simply didn't have the race pace and Lewis Hamilton sounded despondent at times on the radio, unable to go slower when his tyres were overheating, or to speed up when another set had lost grip. He finished over 45 seconds behind the winner. Meanwhile, Rosberg's Mercedes was 100 seconds behind Vettel.

European Grand Prix
Valencia 57 laps

1. Vettel	Red Bull-Renault	1h39:36.169
2. Alonso	Ferrari	+10.891
3. Webber	Red Bull-Renault	+27.255
4. Hamilton	McLaren-Mercedes	+46.190
5. Massa	Ferrari	+51.705
6. Button	McLaren-Mercedes	+1:00.000
7. Rosberg	Mercedes	+1:38.000
8. Alguersuari	Toro Rosso-Ferrari	+1 lap
9. Sutil	Force India-Mercedes	+1 lap
10. Heidfeld	Renault	+1 lap
11. Perez	Sauber-Ferrari	+1 lap
12. Barrichello	Williams-Cosworth	+1 lap
13. Buemi	Toro Rosso-Ferrari	+1 lap
14. Di Resta	Force India-Mercedes	+1 lap
15. Petrov	Renault	+1 lap
16. Kobayashi	Sauber-Ferrari	+1 lap
17. Schumacher	Mercedes	+1 lap
18. Maldonado	Williams-Cosworth	+1 lap
19. Kovalainen	Lotus-Renault	+2 laps
20. Trulli	Lotus-Renault	+2 laps
21. Glock	Virgin-Cosworth	+2 laps
22. D'Ambrosio	Virgin-Cosworth	+2 laps
23. Liuzzi	HRT-Cosworth	+3 laps
24. Karthikeyan	HRT-Cosworth	+3 laps

Drivers' Championship Standings

1. Vettel	186 pts
2. Button	109
3. Webber	109
4. Hamilton	97
5. Alonso	87
6. Massa	42

Constructors' Championship Standings
1. Red Bull-Renault   295 pts
2. McLaren-Mercedes   206
3. Ferrari   129
4. Renault   61
5. Mercedes   58
6. Sauber-Ferrari   27

The month ended with the FOTA Fans' Forum at McLaren's Technology Centre in Woking. This was the biggest event so far, with a panel of top names from the F1 teams including Lewis Hamilton, Kamui Kobayashi, Martin Whitmarsh and Ross Brawn and an audience of about 300 F1 supporters.

Fans were very concerned about News Corp's interest in F1 and the growing suggestions of the sport being on pay TV. Again Whitmarsh sought to calm fears by saying that free-to-air TV was the business model of the sport. "All the FOTA teams believe in free-to-air television," he told the audience. "There will be parts of the market where there's some differentiated service offered, but if you think about the business model of F1 teams, which is all about attracting brands and giving them brand exposure, they require us to have a large audience. Historically, that meant being on free-to-air. Our current contracts require that it remains on free-to-air and the teams, through FOTA, are clearly going to safeguard their business interests and the interests of the fans in this regard. But it isn't as simple as 'is it on BBC or ITV?'

"Fans want a lot more information. We're in a very data-rich sport: we have a lot of telemetry data and strategic information, and lots of modelling and simulation that every team is doing. We're an ideal sport to feed the real fans additional information, as well as the traditional TV feed. We've got to try and unscramble that, and it isn't as simple as 'we must stay free-to-air'. The media is really multifaceted and we've got to ensure that there's a mass free entry through which to see Grands Prix. But there's an awful lot of people

who want extra information that you won't get through a free-to-air route.

"There's speculation surrounding News Corp's interest in the sport and let's be clear: the teams are working together and this sport isn't going anywhere without the teams. If we stay together, we can control the direction of the sport and we're not trying to do that for any other reason than what's in its best interests."

Hamilton and Kobayashi entertained the crowd with analysis of their best overtaking moves. Both drivers agreed that of the three aids to overtaking introduced to F1 this season; KERS, Pirelli short-life tyres and DRS, the latter is the most powerful and interesting.

"I love the new tyres, Pirelli have done an amazing job," said Hamilton. "The DRS is probably the most unique part. It makes it easier to get closer to people. The DRS gives you the opportunity to catch them up and overtake, so that's been cool. Before we had it it was very difficult to overtake. What we're trying to achieve with it is to put drivers in a position where they are able to make the manoeuvre. Of course, there are some opportunities when you can breeze past someone before you get to the braking zone. I passed Michael last weekend and was able to move back onto the racing line, so it was way too easy. I watched the replay and Eddie Jordan said it was a special move. Just shows what he knows about it!"

Kobayashi agreed. "DRS is a cool system. At the start of the season we were worried because it was new and we didn't know if it was safe. After a couple of races we see that it's unique. Psychologically it's important because it's not just for overtakes, sometimes we need to use it well, like when you catch a backmarker."

A straw poll of fans taken before this discussion showed that the majority were prepared to give the DRS a chance and didn't find it artificial. However, around a quarter of the 300 people present said they found it made overtaking "too easy".

Chapter Seven
July 2011

Is Daniel Ricciardo making a big mistake starting his F1 career with HRT?
5 July 2011

Just before the weekend Hispania Racing Team (HRT) confirmed that the Australian driver Daniel Ricciardo will race for them starting at Silverstone in place of Narain Karthikeyan. HRT is around 4 seconds a lap off the pace in qualifying this season, an improvement of 1.5 seconds over last season. In Canada Tonio Liuzzi qualified 0.1 seconds faster than Timo Glock, but in Valencia the gap was a second and in Barcelona it was 0.5 seconds.

The 22-year-old Red Bull sponsored Ricciardo has been doing the Toro Rosso Friday testing duties, but it is clear that Red Bull driver mentor Dr Helmut Marko wanted to accelerate the programme with him. It always looked tricky to find a way into the Toro Rosso race set up, and when Jaime Alguersuari put in back-to-back career best results in the last two races, another route was needed.

Marko is also close to Sebastien Buemi, having backed him since childhood, while Alguersuari's father is a man of significant money and influence. I will be very interested to dig into this situation and see whether he had some hand behind the scenes in brokering with the Spanish-owned HRT team to take Ricciardo. I suspect not, but you never know.

Ricciardo himself doesn't seem to have had much to do with the process, only finding out shortly before the announcement that this was his next career move. He is going to continue with his season of World Series by Renault in parallel, which is a real tester for him.

Certainly, going by what HRT owner Jose Ramon Carabante said, he is hoping there will be more to come in terms of helping Red Bull develop drivers, though they already have Toro Rosso for that, of course. "This agreement is a reward for all the hard work Hispania Racing has shown since we started in Formula One last year," Carabante said. "We're proud that the Formula One world champion team has trusted us to help develop their drivers. Let's hope that this is just the start of a fruitful relationship."

Hispania is undergoing some changes at the moment. The team has been acquired by Thesan Capital, a Spanish investment firm, which has taken on Carabante's stake. Carabante appeared to be one of those F1 team owners who underestimated the costs involved in taking the team on. HRT has the smallest budget of all the F1 teams. There have also been suggestions that Dr Colin Kolles may be moving on from his role as team leader.

So the question remains, is Ricciardo making a terrible mistake in jumping at the first F1 race seat that comes his way? Will this opportunity be a good thing for the Australian, or will it create a bad impression to see a young driver who's tipped for the top being lapped three times, as the HRTs were in Valencia, setting a fastest lap some 6 seconds slower than the race-winning Red Bull car. Silverstone always shows up a bad car and, although he knows it well from his British F3 winning season, this weekend he will be looking in his mirrors as much as at the track ahead.

On the upside, Ricciardo will get some F1 race experience and will have a good benchmark against Tonio Liuzzi, whom some F1 observers rate pretty highly. At Force India he was not as strong as Adrian Sutil, who is now struggling to beat Paul di Resta.

Not every promising young driver can start in a race-winning car, as Lewis Hamilton did, for example, in 2007. Fernando Alonso started in a Minardi in 2001, doing a full season in the back of the grid team. He started dead last at Silverstone that year, qualifying over 4 seconds off the pole time. In the race he was lapped three times. But he always says that year was a great time to learn out of the spotlight. I remember many occasions that year being impressed at the speed with which the Minardi was being driven and he certainly did enough to earn his move through the ranks with Renault. Flavio Briatore was steering that process, as Marko is with Ricciardo. In this respect it was similar to Ayrton Senna's first F1 season with Toleman in 1984.

So it can work out, but it's crucial for him to do what both Senna and Alonso did in their apprentice seasons and stand out in a poor car. We will quickly see what Ricciardo is made of and he will have ten races (it is thought Karthikeyan will race in India) to make his mark before Marko makes a decision on the next step for him.

It took Ricciardo a while to get on top of Liuzzi, but from Monza onwards he generally had the measure of the Italian. However, in the relentless conveyor belt of F1, another Red Bull-backed driver looking for a way into F1 emerged in the form of Jean Eric Vergne. Marko likes to keep pressure on his drivers. One senses that he would like to move Mark Webber out of the way and release the logjam of drivers building up, probably by promoting Alguersuari. But Webber's close relationship with Red Bull owner Dietrich Mateschitz meant that the Australian has renewed his contract for 2012.

One of the most interesting things to come out of Ricciardo's debut for me was learning that there is an art to "backmarkerdom", which drivers in that position must learn. Basically, if you drive a Hispania or one of the other slower cars, you are going to be lapped several times by the leader and others during a race. The art is in not losing too much time in the process. Ricciardo will have spent as much time looking in his mirrors for Red Bulls, Ferraris and the rest as he will looking at the track.

I'm told by insiders that by moving off-line, getting the tyres dirty and cleaning them up again, which takes a few corners, he was losing around 4 seconds every time a car lapped him (relative to what he would have done on a clear lap). In comparison, his teammate Tonio Liuzzi has now got being lapped down to a fine art and at Silverstone lost only around 0.8 seconds each time. As a result Ricciardo was a long way behind Liuzzi at the end of the race.

Around this time Williams announced that it was getting back into partnership with Renault, and rumours about Lewis Hamilton's meeting with Red Bull boss Christian Horner were finally put to bed. The meeting in Montreal, where Hamilton had dropped in on Horner quite publicly, had started rumours that Hamilton would join Red Bull. The idea was given credibility because Red Bull is a maverick brand and Hamilton's edgy style would give them appeal in markets that they are keen to reach. However, with Vettel under contract for three more years Red Bull do not need Hamilton from a racing point of view. There would also clearly be risks of destabilising the team by having two champion drivers, as has happened in the past.

What was interesting about this episode was that both sides let the story hang there for a while. But then Horner took the opportunity to say what common sense always suggested: "A Hamilton-Vettel combination, on paper, would look very attractive to any team," he said. "However, what you have to look at is the dynamics of any partnership like that and it's difficult to see how two sportsmen at the absolute top of their game could work in harmony under one roof.

"That's where the dynamics within a team are so important. History demonstrates more often than not whether you look at Prost and Senna or Mansell and Piquet, that it doesn't tend to work."

Much ado over blow diffusers leaves media and public baffled
9 July 2011

This afternoon Formula 1 served up a war of words, which is hard to describe, much less explain. It's hard for even the specialist media to understand, much less convey to F1 fans. Nor does it do great service to the sport or to the people at the centre of the argument. F1 thrives on intrigue and hype, but this is one confrontation that would perhaps have been best left behind closed doors.

McLaren boss Martin Whitmarsh and Red Bull boss Christian Horner got worked up and battled it out in an FIA press conference, arguing over how much percentage the throttle should be allowed to be open when the driver lifts off the accelerator pedal.

As sporting narratives go "off-throttle exhaust blown diffusers" are not exactly Ali versus Frazier or a Maradona's "Hand of God" goal. It's a very obscure point in a sport which is already complicated enough to explain.

In a nutshell, there are two methods of blowing the diffuser to create extra downforce worth around 0.4 seconds per lap when the driver lifts off the accelerator. One involves introducing fuel into the system, which is the Mercedes way; the other does not, this is the Renault way. The FIA tried to impose a blanket rule on all engines that the throttle could be no more than 10 per cent open, but Renault objected saying that this left Mercedes' system at an advantage. Renault argued that it needs to be allowed to have the throttle open 50 per cent when the driver lifts off as it is an important part of cooling the engine and has reliability implications. The FIA changed the ruling today to give Renault 50 per cent, believing that this makes the relative penalty to both engines the same. This was a surprise to McLaren and Ferrari.

After the press conference I interviewed both men for TV and even they were having problems explaining concisely what the argument is about. Horner was indignant, unhappy that the FIA's change of ruling is being painted by Whitmarsh and others as a performance advantage for Renault and his team.

Whitmarsh said that the ruling was a "surprise" to him and other teams and meant that they would have to follow suit, changing the way the Mercedes engine operates to allow them the same 50 per cent throttle opening as Renault.

In fact, talking to engineers tonight, it seems that Mercedes is allowed to operate 68 per cent open if it does not inject fuel, which allows for the differences in throttle mechanism between engines. And it gets worse: these engines and maps are so clever that they switch from one method of blowing to another depending on the corner.

Whitmarsh describes today's ruling as a "very substantial performance benefit" for Renault and compared it to asking the FIA to be allowed to run a car 100 kilos lighter because the brakes can't cope with the loads. Horner has a different view, "Let's not make any mistake here," he said. "Firing on over-run, the thrust that that generates through the exhaust, generates a bigger effect. Let's just be absolutely clear on that."

One of the most important things in any competitive sport is that whatever the rule, it has to be the same for everybody. To my mind, it would have been better for the FIA to avoid confusing mid-season changes and simply say that all blown diffusers are banned at the end of 2011 (which they are) and until then teams can carry on with what they are doing. No one was complaining before about equivalence, but they are now.

On Saturday morning at Silverstone the FIA announced that, after overnight consultations, they were reverting to the previous ruling that only 10 per cent throttle opening is permitted, much to the annoyance of Red Bull and Christian Horner.

It led to Silverstone being a one-off race, a real anomaly, won by Fernando Alonso and Ferrari, as teams ran to a different set of rules from the other races. After Silverstone the teams agreed to go back to what they were doing before, as per the race in Valencia, the only difference being that they would not be allowed to change engine maps between qualifying and the race.

It was an unfortunate episode, which again showed a lack of consistency in direction from the governing body. In fairness to them, however, it was the thorniest and most complex of technical issues and it's essential to get these things right, as they come up all the time in F1 and are usually a key performance differentiator, dictating the sporting picture the fans and media see.

In the run up to Silverstone I had interviewed F1's commercial supremo Bernie Ecclestone at length, and as always he was good value. Looking back on the interview now the passage that stands out was one in which we discussed the potential News Corp bid for F1. At the time the phone hacking scandal surrounding the News of the World, *a Murdoch-owned paper, was beginning to escalate. Ecclestone dismissed the News Corp bid, stressing his strong conviction that free-to-air TV was the bedrock of F1 TV distribution. The following month he did a deal with Sky to take F1 TV in the UK onto a pay platform for the first time.*

News Corp/Exor came out recently and said they're interested in buying F1's commercial rights. Have they been in touch with you about their plans?

"I don't think they have any plans."

Are they appropriate people to run F1?

"Most of the people that are involved in F1 think that it would be wrong to have something as strong as the Murdoch group, which is obviously very strong, involved because we built the business up through free-to-air TV and I think the minute we moved away from that we might find ourselves in trouble. We'd have to wait and see. Also it would be wrong to have Exor, who basically own Ferrari, in there because they'd have a big influence over the rules."

Would News Corp's involvement in the phone hacking scandal in the UK be a problem here?

"It's nothing to do with us. They are not hacking our phones! We have nothing they'd want to hack for!"

Could a new owner of F1 take the content and create more revenue streams on new media?

"I've no idea what they would do. Anything that could be done, we're doing it. We've looked into it. All these different methods of broadcasting. The minute we allow other people to broadcast by other means it would upset the people we've got contracts with."

Fernando Alonso wins British Grand Prix as Red Bull slip up 10 July 2011

Fernando Alonso won a thrilling British Grand Prix at Silverstone ahead of the Red Bull pair of Sebastian Vettel and Mark Webber. Vettel lost the lead to Alonso when his second pit stop went disastrously wrong. He lost further time behind Lewis Hamilton and could not bridge the gap to the Ferrari driver.

It was Alonso's first win of the season, the 27th of his career and his second at Silverstone. Earlier in the day he had driven the Ferrari that won this race 60 years ago and was proud to have delivered the win on such an important anniversary, which underlines how long Ferrari have been in F1.

There was heavy rainfall in the hour before the start, particularly around the old pits building and the complex of corners leading to Copse. So wet was the track, with Perez losing control on the formation lap, that intermediate tyres was the only choice for the start.

Sebastian Vettel won the start against his teammate, the pole sitter Mark Webber. Vettel got a perfect getaway while Webber was bogged down. Starts have been a consistent problem for Webber all season and the initiative he had gained in qualifying was lost in the first 200 metres of the race. Button got a good start up to fourth from fifth on the grid, as did Lewis Hamilton, who made up four places on the opening lap.

Schumacher was the first to take the soft slick tyres on lap 11, he was forced to stop after sliding into Kobayashi and losing his nose cone. As he set fastest sector times, Button switched too, with Alonso and Webber coming in a lap later, as did Hamilton. Vettel had the luxury of taking an extra lap before making his stop as he had a 6-second lead before the stops. Afterwards it was down to 3.3 seconds.

The McLaren worked well on slick tyres on a damp track; Button passed Massa for P5 and shortly afterwards Hamilton passed Alonso on the wettest part of the circuit for third place. Webber closed up on his teammate on the slick tyres. Hamilton's tyres began to drop off and Alonso was able to re-pass him using DRS on the Wellington Straight.

Paul di Resta was going very well in seventh place, lapping faster than the cars behind including Rosberg's Mercedes, but a disastrous stop on lap 26 cost him a lot of time, before his race was ruined following contact with a Toro Rosso. Another disastrous pit stop, on lap 28, cost Vettel the lead to Alonso. On a track still damp in parts the lesson was that old tyres up to temperature were faster than brand new tyres. Alonso and Hamilton used this to undercut Webber and when Vettel had his problem, both men found themselves ahead of the world champion.

As Alonso drove away from them, Vettel was faster than Hamilton and had to try to make a pass. Alonso was almost two seconds a lap faster than Hamilton around lap 32. Still Vettel didn't try a move on him.

Red Bull had to wait until lap 37 to pit Vettel – because any earlier and he may not have made the finish – and he duly undercut Hamilton for second place. Alonso pitted a lap later and maintained his 10-second lead. Button pitted at the same time but as he emerged his front right wheel fell off and ended his race.

The new interpretation on engine mapping for blown diffusers meant a change in fuel consumption for the race and with 15 laps to go Hamilton had to go into fuel saving mode, allowing Webber to close on him and pass for a podium place with five laps to go.

At the front Alonso was able to continue to drive away from Vettel, who fell into the clutches of Webber at the end. But the Australian was told by the team to "maintain the gap" and did not try a pass. Meanwhile Toro Rosso's Jaime Alguersuari got into the points from the lower third of the grid for the third race in a row.

British Grand Prix
Silverstone 52 laps

1. Alonso	Ferrari	1h28:41.194
2. Vettel	Red Bull-Renault	+16.511
3. Webber	Red Bull-Renault	+16.947
4. Hamilton	McLaren-Mercedes	+28.986
5. Massa	Ferrari	+29.010
6. Rosberg	Mercedes	+1:00.665
7. Perez	Sauber-Ferrari	+1:05.590
8. Heidfeld	Renault	+1:15.542
9. Schumacher	Mercedes	+1:17.912
10. Alguersuari	Toro Rosso-Ferrari	+1:19.108
11. Sutil	Force India-Mercedes	+1:19.712
12. Petrov	Renault	+1:20.600
13. Barrichello	Williams-Cosworth	+1 lap
14. Maldonado	Williams-Cosworth	+1 lap
15. Di Resta	Force India-Mercedes	+1 lap
16. Glock	Virgin-Cosworth	+2 laps
17. D'Ambrosio	Virgin-Cosworth	+2 laps
18. Liuzzi	HRT-Cosworth	+2 laps
19. Ricciardo	HRT-Cosworth	+3 laps

Drivers' Championship Standings
1. Vettel   204 pts
2. Webber   124
3. Alonso   112
4. Hamilton   109
5. Button   109
6. Massa   52

Constructors' Championship Standings
1. Red Bull-Renault   328 pts
2. McLaren-Mercedes   218
3. Ferrari   164
4. Mercedes   68
5. Renault   65
6. Sauber-Ferrari   33

After the Silverstone race there was a familiar debate about Red Bull's decision to tell Webber to hold station as he closed in on teammate Vettel in the final laps of the race. The whole point of running different strategies is that it gives you a chance to be there at the end. But Red Bull denied Webber the opportunity to capitalise.

After the 2010 Brazilian Grand Prix, Red Bull owner Dietrich Mateschitz had articulated his philosophy of why his drivers would be allowed to race each other right to the end and the team would not intervene: "Let the two drivers race and what will be will be," he said. "If Alonso wins we will have been unlucky. I predict a Hollywood ending. Worst case scenario we don't become champion? We'll do it next year... But our philosophy stays the same because this is sport and it must remain sport. We don't manipulate things like Ferrari do."

At the time Mateschitz's attitude seemed noble and full of Corinthian spirit, but at Silverstone Red Bull's instruction to Webber to "maintain the gap" behind teammate Vettel made the words seem pretty hollow.

Webber had ignored instructions from his own engineer Ciaran Pilbeam and was shaping up for a move, but heeded the instructions after team boss Christian Horner intervened. He made his feelings clear afterwards at the press conference, where he said he was "not all right about it" as he felt that he should be entitled to fight for an extra place. As he pointed out, if anything had happened to the leader Fernando Alonso, he would have been fighting for the win.

Team orders are now legal in F1, but the team faced serious accusations of hypocrisy while Mateschitz's credo was ignored. On one level it was not a big deal; it was only for three points. But on another level it was huge because Red Bull has given up the moral high ground, and even worse, has shown that its values were fine when Vettel was the one being given a chance, but that the same doesn't apply the other way around. Was it a worthwhile sacrifice for three points?

Team boss Christian Horner said that they had done it because they feared the drivers might take each other off. This seems unlikely given Vettel's lead in the points table and his obvious intelligence.

In fact, it led once again to accusations that Red Bull favours Vettel, a weapon critics use to diminish his achievements. In my mind he should be allowed to race Webber. Results like this look manipulated and needlessly undermine a set of values that Red Bull worked hard to establish last season.

Ecclestone denies wrongdoing as former F1 bank chief is charged
22 July 2011

F1's commercial supremo Bernie Ecclestone has admitted paying £27 million to a former colleague but says it was not a bribe. The 80-year-old said that he has done nothing wrong and will clear his name, as prosecutors in Germany allege that he paid bribes of $44 million (£27 million) to Gerhard Gribkowsky, who was the lead banker responsible for the 2006 sale of the sport to current owners CVC.

Prosecutors further allege that Mr Ecclestone received $41.4 million (£25.4 million) in commissions from the bank, as well as a large payment to Bambino Holdings, the family trust. The prosecutor has told my colleagues at the *Financial Times* that Ecclestone "remains under investigation".

Gribkowsky, who has been in jail in Munich since January, was formally charged with "corruption, embezzlement and tax evasion" yesterday. The prosecutor alleges that his former employer, Bayerische Landesbank (BayernLB), incurred damages of $66 million as a result of Gribkowsky's actions. The prosecutor said that Gribkowsky sold his bank's 48 per cent of F1's commercial rights without an updated valuation in return for payments in the form of "fake consulting contracts", which were paid into Gribkowsky's Austrian companies and on which he did not pay tax.

Speaking in the *Daily Telegraph* Ecclestone subsequently admitted that he did pay the money to Gribkowsky but only because Gribkowsky was threatening to go to the Inland Revenue in connection with the Ecclestone family trust. He said that the money he received from BayernLB was a commission on the sale of the stock to CVC, amounting to 5 per cent of the purchase price, and that he had already given this information to the prosecutors when he visited them in Munich in April.

Under German law a court must now decide whether Gribkowsky should face trial. This appears to be a formality and it is possible that a trial could start before the end of this F1 season. It is not clear at this stage whether Ecclestone will face any charges, but the *Daily Telegraph* suggested that prosecutors may wait to see the outcome of the likely trial before deciding on further actions.

This could all have a very interesting effect on the ongoing discussions with teams and the FIA over the 2013 Concorde Agreement, not to mention the possible sale by CVC of its interests in F1. Although the private equity firm claims that it has no interest in selling, behind the scenes they are believed to be keen to exit. However, to get the best price they must wait for the negotiations to be concluded and for the situation in Germany to be resolved with Ecclestone still as CEO.

Meanwhile, the word is that although News Corp is going through some significant challenges of its own with the phone hacking scandal in the UK, it remains interested in F1. Time will tell whether any possible changes in management as a result of the scandal alter that view.

The Gribkowsky trial began in late October and was set to run on into the New Year. Ecclestone was not charged with anything, but was requested to appear as a witness. It was a matter of the utmost importance to the sport because until this matter was settled negoti-ations between the teams, F1's commercial owners CVC Capital Partners and the FIA over a new Concorde Agreement could not move forward.

Hamilton beats Alonso in closely fought German Grand Prix
24 July 2011

Lewis Hamilton won a tense three-way battle for victory in the German Grand Prix, beating Fernando Alonso and the pole sitter Mark Webber. It was Hamilton's second win of the season and the 16th of his career.

It was a great weekend for Hamilton, the result set up by a stunning qualifying lap and a great start, where he took the lead from Webber on the run down to Turn 1. And the victory was topped off by his overtake on Alonso after the Spaniard had emerged ahead of him from his second pit stop. "If we keep pushing these are the kind of results we can get," said a delighted Hamilton over the radio on the slowdown lap. "It couldn't have been any better; we didn't expect this. I feel great. It was one of the best races I've ever done."

It was another tense and exciting race with Webber, Hamilton and Alonso all competitive, closely matched and enjoying themselves. There were some great battles between them that brought the race alive. In contrast, it was one of runaway leader Sebastian Vettel's more low-key races, he lost out in a battle with Alonso, then got undercut by Massa at the first round of pit stops. Brake problems were clearly part of the reason.

It was a chilly day, the track temperature just 15°C. Drizzle had been in the air intermittently in the morning and a few minutes before the start rain was falling. But it wasn't enough for the drivers to go with anything other than soft slick tyres.

Webber has a poor start record this season and again, as at Silverstone, he lost the lead off the start line. Lewis Hamilton took the lead into Turn 1, while behind Webber, Alonso and Vettel battled over third, passing and re-passing each other several times on the opening lap.

Paul di Resta and Nick Heidfeld dropped to the back of the field after an incident. Heidfeld took the blame but was unable to serve his subsequent penalty as he was taken out by Buemi who didn't see him as they went into the chicane on lap 10. Rosberg got a great start up to fifth ahead of Massa, whose engineer Rob Smedley radioed his driver that he had to get past the Mercedes or his race would be "ruined".

Alonso attacked Vettel repeatedly and got past him on lap 8, clearly using KERS and drafting down the inside into Turn 1. Soon afterwards Vettel made a mistake, spinning off the track and losing 7 seconds in the process.

Massa got past Rosberg on lap 12 and a lap later the leaders got stuck in to each other. Hamilton ran wide at the chicane and Webber passed him into the final corner, but Hamilton used KERS and the McLaren's straight line speed advantage to re-pass him on the pit straight. This allowed Alonso to join the fight and the top three battled hard.

Webber pitted on lap 15 and managed to undercut Hamilton who waited two laps to react. Alonso also pitted on lap 17 and he rejoined third. Vettel was passed by Massa and came into the pits. He rejoined behind Massa who stopped a lap later. Webber tried to open a lead over Hamilton and Alonso, but wasn't able to. At the halfway stage the leading trio of Webber, Hamilton and Alonso were within 1.6 seconds of each other.

Webber pitted on lap 31, Hamilton came in a lap later and undercut him. As Webber tried to re-pass, Hamilton gave him a little nudge to the outside, which was enough to knock his momentum. Alonso pitted a lap later and came out ahead of Hamilton, but the Englishman pulled off the pass around the outside of Turn 2, the same move that Webber had failed to make on him. It was a classic Hamilton move and really caught Alonso napping.

Button was on a two-stop strategy, his race having been somewhat compromised by poor qualifying and a poor start, but just as he was making some progress, passing Rosberg for sixth place, he had to retire the car with a hydraulics failure.

Petrov was the first to go onto the slower medium Pirelli tyres, followed by Kobayashi. When Petrov began setting personal best lap times and the Japanese driver went immediately quicker than his teammate on the older softs, the picture was clear.

Hamilton went for mediums first, Alonso followed but had a messy in-lap and stayed behind his old rival, while Red Bull gambled by leaving Webber out on the old soft tyres, but as his tyres had been on since lap 31 they didn't have enough left in them and he rejoined third almost eight seconds behind second-placed Alonso.

Massa and Vettel played cat and mouse over coming in for medium tyres right up to the final lap. They came in with Massa ahead, but a faster stop for Red Bull meant that Vettel came out ahead and took fourth place.

German Grand Prix
Nürburgring 60 laps

1. Hamilton	McLaren-Mercedes	1h37:30.334
2. Alonso	Ferrari	+3.980
3. Webber	Red Bull-Renault	+9.788
4. Vettel	Red Bull-Renault	+47.921

5. Massa	Ferrari	+52.252
6. Sutil	Force India-Mercedes	+1:26.208
7. Rosberg	Mercedes	+1 lap
8. Schumacher	Mercedes	+1 lap
9. Kobayashi	Sauber-Ferrari	+1 lap
10. Petrov	Renault	+1 lap
11. Perez	Sauber-Ferrari	+1 lap
12. Alguersuari	Toro Rosso-Ferrari	+1 lap
13. Di Resta	Force India-Mercedes	+1 lap
14. Maldonado	Williams-Cosworth	+1 lap
15. Buemi	Toro Rosso-Ferrari	+1 lap
16. Kovalainen	Lotus-Renault	+2 laps
17. Glock	Virgin-Cosworth	+3 laps
18. D'Ambrosio	Virgin-Cosworth	+3 laps
19. Ricciardo	HRT-Cosworth	+3 laps
20. Chandhok	Lotus-Renault	+4 laps

Drivers' Championship Standings
1. Vettel   216 pts
2. Webber   139
3. Hamilton   134
4. Alonso   130
5. Button   109
6. Massa   62

Constructors' Championship Standings
1. Red Bull-Renault   355 pts
2. McLaren-Mercedes   243
3. Ferrari   192
4. Mercedes   78
5. Renault   66
6. Sauber-Ferrari   35

BBC and Sky drop broadcast bombshell, F1 on pay TV in UK
29 July 2011

This morning's announcement by the BBC and BSKYB that they are to share the coverage of Formula 1 in the UK has come as a bolt from the blue to the F1 paddock and to fans of the sport. It is clear that the teams and sponsors have not been consulted and it remains to be seen how they will react when they learn the details of the arrangement. And it could start a trend across the international broadcast landscape of F1.

The teams are likely to resist any deal which reduces the audience number. Whereas the BBC currently enjoys audiences of between 6 and 7 million per race, the SKY audiences for Premier League football suggest that they might get an F1 audience of around 1 to 2 million on their pay sports channel, far less when the race is also on BBC at the same time.

Until recently it had appeared that the BBC was likely to drop the expensive contract it signed in 2008 as the BBC Trust looked to make significant savings. The word in the TV sports industry was that Channel 4 was a possible destination. But with ITV not in the running and no other competitive free-to-air offer on the table, F1's commercial supremo Bernie Ecclestone clearly wasn't satisfied with the money on offer from Channel 4. He has struck a bold deal, one which doesn't completely go against his and the teams' stated credo that F1 should stay on free-to-air TV, but instead offers a rather awkward compromise for fans and sponsors, whereby half the races stay on the BBC with the mass audience, while the whole season will be covered in great depth and with significant resources thrown at it by Sky Sports.

Although half the races will be free-to-air, the dedicated fan will still need to buy a Sky dish or sign up to a Sky package at around £40 per month on BT Vision, Freeview or Virgin Media to get full race coverage. The fact that fans will have to pay the full monthly subscription for only half the races seems an awkward sell to me.

There is some good news, however. Under the deal, Sky Sports would cover all the races, qualifying and practice sessions. They have also confirmed that unlike their coverage of other long-form sports, like cricket, they will not run ads during the 90 minutes of the live race.

The BBC will continue to broadcast F1 in its current format but for only half the races. The only races they confirmed were Monaco, Silverstone and the final round. The intention was to save about 60 per cent of their existing budget, reducing the cost dramatically while maintaining a footprint in the sport until the end of 2018. The original deal was due to end in 2013 and would not have been renewed.

Coming just days after Rupert and James Murdoch appeared in front of a Parliamentary Select Committee, this was a typically bold deal by Murdoch and a strong forward move in the teeth of adversity. To me it felt like it had been coming for some time as far as Sky and the sport were concerned. F1 fans will provide new money for the Sky coffers in a business which always needs to generate new lifeblood.

Foreign broadcasters active in F1 were becoming resigned to their own networks looking at this deal and seeing a way forward for the future. Who said the revolution will not be televised?

There was instant and strong reaction to the principle of this deal among F1 fans in the UK. We did a poll and 82 per cent of a sample of 5,000 readers said that they would not watch F1 on Sky. It's normal to get an angry reaction and time will tell whether fans will vote with their feet and do something else on Sunday afternoons. But the strength of feeling against the Sky move was strong. The BBC was viewed as the culprit for having failed to carry out its plans to cover F1, therefore opening the door to this compromise.

When the full picture of BBC cutbacks was announced in October, it was clear that they had tried to "salami slice" budgets across all areas, rather than get rid of any individual items. This approach was criticised – many people felt that the BBC has become too multi-headed as an organization and should have focused on excellence in the traditional areas rather than cutting across the board.

But the BBC saw it as a trend in sport brought about by escalating rights costs and felt that the future was about partnerships such as this one with Sky. F1 had enemies and detractors within the BBC that made it unsustainable, although those people had been happy enough to watch the Sports department commit over £50 million a year in rights and production back on 2008 when ITV was forced to drop its contract.

There was confusion at the time about whether the BBC would be showing highlights of the races they did not cover live, or would show the whole race tape delayed. Ecclestone said the former; the teams' association chairman Martin Whitmarsh said the latter. The picture remained fuzzy for some time.

Jenson Button rises above the rest to win Hungarian Grand Prix
31 July 2011

On his 200th Grand Prix start and the fifth anniversary of his maiden victory in Hungary, Jenson Button drove a perfectly judged race to take the 11th victory of his career and his second of the season. The win takes him to fourth place in the all-time points scorers list behind Schumacher, Alonso and Prost.

As in Button's most recent victory, in Canada, it was Sebastian Vettel who followed him home. Once again it was a great outcome for the German driver's championship challenge as it extended his lead to 85 points, the largest margin at any point this season. Fernando Alonso finished third despite a series of mistakes by himself and strategy mistakes by the team. He was only ten seconds behind at the end.

"It's good to have a couple of weeks break because it could take me that long to get over tonight. My 200th race, I don't know why I like these conditions so much, a great call by the team not to go to the intermediate tyres. We go into the break on a nice high," said Button.

It was a tricky race, and with a record 88 pit stops it was a day for not making mistakes. Button once again showed his cool head to rise above it. He also had another amazing wheel-to-wheel battle with his teammate Lewis Hamilton.

The race started in unexpectedly drizzly conditions, which made the track slippery, and a further brief rain shower later in the race caused some strategy mistakes. As all the running up to race day had been dry, the first few laps saw the drivers finding the grip level and braking points of the intermediate tyres on the damp track. At the start Vettel got away well from pole as Button attacked Hamilton for second place. The two Mercedes cars made great starts with Rosberg up to fourth and Schumacher following him.

Alonso passed Schumacher and then Rosberg on the second lap as the leaders were slithering around on a surface that looked as grippy as ice, particularly in Turn 2 where Vettel, Alonso and Massa all had moments. Hamilton put huge pressure on Vettel on lap 4 and at that point the FIA said that the DRS wing was enabled. Alonso made a mistake allowing Rosberg back past him. Another mistake allowed Massa to pass, though Alonso re-passed him soon after.

With the lap times over 20 seconds slower than in qualifying, the McLaren was clearly faster than the Red Bull in the treacherous conditions. On lap 6 Hamilton forced Vettel to run wide and swept past him into the lead. He immediately began pulling away at 3 seconds a lap.

On lap 11 Webber and Massa were the first drivers to come in for slick tyres. Effectively the number two drivers for both teams, they were used to gain information on the dry tyres for their more competitive teammates. Meanwhile, Alonso set the fastest laps to that point and had reduced the gap to Hamilton and Vettel to 10 seconds by the time they all stopped on lap 13. Schumacher stayed out and this put him into the lead for the first time since he made his comeback. He pitted straight after.

Button had a great pit stop and a very fast out-lap and this set him up for an attack on Vettel on lap 14, which he converted into a pass. Webber passed Alonso at the same time, as the Ferrari struggled on the dry tyres on a still slightly damp track, the team's weakness at not warming up the tyres – even the supersofts – very evident.

On lap 26 Heidfeld's Renault caught fire and exploded after a pit stop. There was no safety car, but Webber, Alonso and Massa pitted, with Hamilton pitting a lap later, his tyres clearly shot. This was what Jenson Button wanted to see, his tyres were in better shape and he continued, as did Alonso, another driver whose tyres were looking good at the end of the stint.

Button pitted on lap 28 while Vettel decided to stay out. He lost five seconds in the process, bringing him back towards Webber, but in time Vettel simply drove away from his teammate, who came under pressure from Alonso on lap 34.

Alonso, unable to pass Webber, pitted a third time on lap 37 trying the undercut. He managed it as he was hugely faster on his new tyres. Webber reacted, Red Bull putting him onto the soft tyres, which he would take to the finish. Vettel went for the same strategy, as did Button. Button got the tyres up to speed straight away and was faster than Hamilton who was on the supersofts.

On Lap 47 Hamilton spun and Button passed him as rain began falling again at the back of the circuit only. The McLarens stayed out, Alonso pitted for softs, having realised the mistake they'd made at their third stop.

The rain began to make life difficult for the drivers on lap 50 with lap times 6 seconds slower than the lap before. As Rosberg and Webber pitted for intermediates, the McLarens passed and re-passed each other, but it was Hamilton in front at the crucial moment when it was time to pit for intermediates. He decided to go for them, which proved to be a mistake.

Rather than queue behind him, Button had to do another lap, and as he did so, it became clear that he didn't need to stop again. This was the decisive moment. The move to intermediates was the wrong one and it cost Hamilton and Webber dear. Hamilton also got a drive-through penalty for almost hitting Di Resta after a spin and he came out behind Massa and Webber in sixth place.

On lap 58 Webber passed Massa for fourth, and Hamilton attacked and passed him too on the same lap to move up to fifth. He then passed Webber for fourth on lap 63 as the pair negotiated traffic. Kobayashi got in their way on very worn tyres and Webber lost out. Kobayashi pitted at the end of that lap.

There were strong performances from Di Resta in seventh place, Buemi in eighth and Alguersuari tenth again for Toro Rosso. Daniel Ricciardo had a strong day in the HRT beating Liuzzi and D'Ambrosio. Both Lotus cars retired again.

Hungarian Grand Prix
Hungaroring 70 laps

1. Button	McLaren-Mercedes	1h43:42.337
2. Vettel	Red Bull-Renault	+3.588
3. Alonso	Ferrari	+19.819
4. Hamilton	McLaren-Mercedes	+48.338
5. Webber	Red Bull-Renault	+49.742
6. Massa	Ferrari	+1:17.176
7. Di Resta	Force India-Mercedes	+1 lap
8. Buemi	Toro Rosso-Ferrari	+1 lap
9. Rosberg	Mercedes	+1 lap
10. Alguersuari	Toro Rosso-Ferrari	+1 lap
11. Kobayashi	Sauber-Ferrari	+1 lap
12. Petrov	Renault	+1 lap
13. Barrichello	Williams-Cosworth	+2 laps
14. Sutil	Force India-Mercedes	+2 laps
15. Perez	Sauber-Ferrari	+2 laps
16. Maldonado	Williams-Cosworth	+2 laps
17. Glock	Virgin-Cosworth	+4 laps
18. Ricciardo	HRT-Cosworth	+4 laps
19. D'Ambrosio	Virgin-Cosworth	+5 laps
20. Liuzzi	HRT-Cosworth	+5 laps

Drivers' Championship Standings
1. Vettel   234 pts
2. Webber   149
3. Hamilton   146
4. Alonso   145
5. Button   134
6. Massa   70

Constructors' Championship Standings
1. Red Bull-Renault   383 pts
2. McLaren-Mercedes   280
3. Ferrari   215
4. Mercedes   80
5. Renault   66
6. Sauber-Ferrari   35

Chapter Eight
August 2011

Despite the calendar getting increasingly congested, with 20 races envisaged from 2012 onwards, August is the month when F1 takes a summer break, returning for its traditional appointment with the Belgian Grand Prix at Spa. But it's rarely quiet, and this year rumblings over the BBC/Sky deal kept the fans engaged.

Away from that story and always on the look out for trends in F1, I wrote an insight into the situation at Williams – halfway through its worst season for decades, in the teeth of wholesale change. The year had started with confidence and a floatation, but results on the track had simply not come through as midfield rivals surged ahead of them.

In the months that followed, the team pushed hard to put in place building blocks for the future, with Frank Williams spending many autumn weeks in Qatar trying to seal a deal which might set the team back on track for the top. At the same time the 2007 world champion Kimi Raikkonen was lined up to make a comeback in a bold move aimed at revitalising both his career and the team's future.

Williams adrift in midfield battle
9 August 2011

It's good from time to time to glance at the Constructors' Championship table and remind yourself of the big picture in terms of the state of play between the teams. There is the usual disproportionate sharing of points with the top two or three teams hogging the majority and the new teams desperate for even a sniff of a single point. But it's the midfield teams that are the most interesting at the moment.

Last year the top four teams were followed by Renault in fifth, then Williams, Force India, Sauber and Toro Rosso. This year Renault has 66 points, Sauber 35, Force India 26 and Toro Rosso 22. They are all reasonably close to each other on performance, either qualifying around the fringes of the top ten or, in Toro Rosso's case, managing to get cars regularly into the points using a particular race strategy. The odd one out is Williams, with only four points on the board, down in ninth place in the table.

The car clearly has its difficulties, not least that in races it is quite hard on its tyres and for much of the season has had a poor start performance, losing many places off the grid. Pastor Maldonado has managed to qualify it in the top ten three times since Barcelona; the problem has been converting that into points. Rubens Barrichello's two ninth places from Monaco and Canada are all the team has to show for the season so far.

I asked Barrichello over the Hungarian GP weekend whether he thought the team would be able to bridge the points gap as it did in the second half of last season: "Not if we don't improve the fundamental problem. If we keep on testing and experimenting then we are going to score points but not in that range," he said. "Unless we go to a race where there are 15 cars off and finish on the podium... The car has its problems. If we don't go down under and cure the whole situation to start growing again and we keep just changing the top then it's just like masking.

"It's not a lack of effort that Williams isn't bringing new things. They are bringing loads of new things, but they are not working. Last year some of them did work and then our year improved so much. Right now, we are trying new stuff and not feeling that it's getting there."

Last season Barrichello qualified in the top ten in nine of the last ten races and scored three top-seven finishes. That's the kind of performance Force India is showing now with its updated car. Barrichello has been keen to volunteer to test and evaluate things, such as running without KERS in Germany to see if that helped with rear tyre issues.

And he points out that the team is actually in the fortunate position of having both a new technical director focused on next year's car and the old one working on developing this year's car. "We have Mike Coughlan working on next year and Sam [Michael] is already being paid so we might just as well use him to do something for this year. In that respect we are quite lucky. We just need to improve the damn car."

Williams boss Adam Parr said at the start of the season that the team's business model required them to finish in the top five or six in the championship. Currently, sixth place Sauber is 31 points ahead and that looks like a very steep hill to climb from where the team is now.

My F1 career began in April 1990 and I well remember the weekend in August 1991 when Michael Schumacher burst onto the scene with Jordan. Schumacher is three years younger than me and I've covered his whole career, writing two books with and about him; one after the infamous incident where he rammed Jacques Villeneuve at Jerez in 1997 and the other a definitive biography after his retirement in 2006.

Although he spent three years on the sidelines, the fact was that in August this year he celebrated the 20th anniversary of his F1 debut, a remarkable achievement and one that owes much to the advances of safety in F1 as to his undoubted powers on longevity.

A special weekend for Michael Schumacher
22 August 2011

This weekend's Belgian Grand Prix at Spa marks the 20th anniversary of Michael Schumacher's F1 debut – at the wheel of a Jordan-Ford – a truly astonishing statistic.

Schumacher becomes the first F1 driver in history to still be active 20 years after his debut. He also took his first F1 win at Spa in 1992. It is also 17 years since he was disqualified from victory in the 1994 race for having worn down the plank under his floor too much, and seven years ago at Spa he clinched his seventh world title.

"Everything for me comes back to Spa. The race will certainly have a special touch to it this time, as this is where I drove my first ever Formula One race 20 years ago," said Schumacher. "It's hard to believe that it was such a long time ago. A lot has changed in those 20 years, but one thing has not: the track is still sensational. I just love the great nature of the location and the resulting layout with all the ups and downs. To me, Spa remains my 'living room', because it has been the stage for so many things which have been remarkable for my sporting career."

Spa has also many other memories for him: his astonishing battle with Mika Hakkinen in 2000, his win in 1995 from nowhere on the grid, the collision with Coulthard, the list is endless. As a six-times winner of the race and many other podiums there, it's the place that is probably most synonymous with him as a racer.

I remember his debut as if it were yesterday. He was on the pace immediately, in fact I was standing at the top of Eau Rouge with the legendary writer Denis Jenkinson and Schumacher caught his attention straight away for his commitment through the high-speed corner. In those days before it was modified and made easier, it was not a simple flat-out corner, it was a huge challenge.

At the end of Friday practice Jenks gave me what he thought was the top-five based on simply seeing the cars go through Eau Rouge, and Schumacher was among them. When we got to the press office and studied the times, his top-five order was exactly right!

There was a lot of hype around the young German, and within a fortnight he had been poached by Tom Walkinshaw and Flavio Briatore to drive for Benetton, with whom he went on to win two world titles in 1994 and 1995.

Of course, it's not been an unbroken sequence of 20 years, as he had three years of retirement before deciding to come back. He's already said that he will do the third year of his three years with Mercedes, despite a disappointing lack of results.

All eyes will be on Schumacher and his unique celebration this weekend.

Renault drops Heidfeld, confirms Senna for rest of season
24 August 2011

Less than 24 hours before the drivers are due in the Spa Francorchamps paddock for the FIA press conference, Renault has confirmed that Bruno Senna will race for the team this weekend. A brief statement said only that he would race in Spa in place of Nick Heidfeld and that he would be at the press conference. The team will announce more details in due course.

The news was first broken by BBC's Eddie Jordan on Monday and comes after a disappointing campaign for Heidfeld, who was drafted in to replace the injured Robert Kubica. Senna drove in Hungary on Friday morning as a prelude to this opportunity. Like his former HRT teammate Karun Chandhok in Germany, he is being given a chance to show what he can do over a race weekend.

There have been suggestions from team principal Eric Boullier that he would like to run Romain Grosjean in the car this year, the French/Swiss driver is managed by Gravity, which is part of the Genii group that owns the Renault team.

At the same time, Genii announced earlier this month an important strategic tie up with WWI Group, to create a $10 billion investment partnership. As the statement said, "The two companies will focus on private equity investments in energy, renewable energy, real estate, information technology, telecommunications, oil, gas and the automotive sector. Their association gives birth to the eighth most powerful private equity investment company in South America."

The idea is to get Brazilian investors to diversify their portfolios, so it's very much Brazil focused. With Bruno Senna being from such a significant Brazilian family, there must be some positive connections here, but it's not clear at this point whether he will hold on to the seat to the end of the season or whether Grosjean will get a run once he's clinched the GP2 title. For a driver, Senna is a very good communicator and an effective operator in social and business situations.

Long-term the driver situation is fluid; Renault still has to wait on Kubica who is in rehabilitation after his rally accident. There is talk of him trying out an F1 simulator in the next month to assess the repair to his damaged bones and nerves.

Heidfeld is on the sidelines again, a position he's become accustomed to. He had a great podium at the start of the year in Malaysia, but since then he's not had a great run, with five further points finishes, but retiring from three of the last five races. He has been outqualified 8-3 by Vitaly Petrov and sits two points ahead of him on 34. Renault are 14 points behind Mercedes in the constructors' championship and 31 points ahead of Sauber, so Mercedes are probably the most relieved by today's news as it makes it less likely that they will be caught for fourth place with Petrov and Senna in the Renault, even though Schumacher currently sits below the Renault drivers in the table.

This weekend marks the 50th race since Renault's last win in F1.

Mark Webber signed the long expected one-year contract renewal deal to stay at Red Bull after a summer of negotiations with team boss Christian Horner and Red Bull owner Dietrich Mateschitz. The deal was announced on the morning of his 35th birthday, during the Spa weekend.

The deal meant a sixth season with the team for the Australian who, along with David Coulthard, has played a key role in building Red Bull up to world championship level, although more recently Sebastian Vettel is the one who's taken the spoils.

Webber described the decision to add another year as a "no brainer," given the competitiveness of the Red Bull package at the moment; unbeaten in qualifying and dominating both championships

There is the feeling that 2012 will be Webber's swansong year and a new driver will come through the Red Bull driver programme to partner Vettel. That programme is managed by Dr Helmut Marko, who gives every sign of being keen to move Webber on to give his young charges a chance. But Webber's relationship is primarily with Red Bull boss Dietrich Mateschitz and loyalty counts for a lot in that association

Vettel copes with compromises on tyres to win thrilling Belgian Grand Prix
29 August 2011

Despite suffering from severe tyre blistering in the early stages, which forced him to pit twice for new tyres by lap 15, Sebastian Vettel won the Belgian Grand Prix ahead of Red Bull teammate Mark Webber and Jenson

Button, who started 13th on the grid and survived a scare when his front wing was broken early on, forcing him to stop.

Given the problems he faced, it was one of Vettel's most impressive wins to date. It was greatly helped because the Red Bull was more competitive here than it has been in recent years, but there was still a lot of work for him to do given the restrictions of the tyres. Many of the cars were set up at a certain camber angle to deal with the vertical load in Eau Rouge corner in particular, this meant that the inside shoulder of the tyres was blistering on many cars, but especially the Red Bull. This doesn't necessarily affect lap times, but it does raise safety questions as there is always the chance of a failure.

It was Vettel's seventh win of the season and the 17th of his career, and his grip on the world title was even more secure when Lewis Hamilton crashed out of the race. Vettel's win extended his lead at the top of the championship to 92 points with only seven races to go. At this rate he could wrap up his second world title by the Indian Grand Prix in October. Surprisingly, it was only Red Bull's second one-two finish of the season.

Race morning saw plenty of behind-the-scenes action with some teams, including Red Bull, asking the FIA for dispensation to get new fronts to deal with the tyre problems. This did not happen. "We had a lot of concern going into the race given the damage on the tyres so we took quite a risk," said Vettel. "We [he and Webber] both stopped early and the target was to see how the tyres ran and not think too much about the outcome. There was more management than usual, but the car worked brilliantly. I'm very happy with how we managed the tyres."

There were some fantastic performances throughout the field with Webber recovering from a poor start to finish second, Jenson Button making up ten places from his grid slot and Michael Schumacher coming through from last place to fifth at the finish.

The track was dry at the start and everyone except Michael Schumacher and Jenson Button started on the soft tyres. Nico Rosberg made an electric start, up to second on the first corner from fifth on the grid. There was quite a bit of contact in the first corner with Alguersuari, Senna and Kovalainen all suffering some damage and Senna, who hadn't raced for a while, was given a drive-through penalty. Rosberg went ahead on the Kemmel Straight but Vettel retook the lead on lap 4.

Webber and Button both pitted on lap 5, Webber's tyres already suffering.

Alonso and Massa attacked Rosberg and we had a sequence of fantastic racing, as Alonso passed Massa and as the Brazilian tried to resist, Hamilton went through as well.

Vettel pitted on lap 7, reporting vibrations on his first set. He rejoined in ninth place. This early switch to new tyres was critical to the outcome of the race as he was able to lap very fast and build a margin, while others were still trying to make their qualifying tyres last.

Alonso passed Rosberg for the lead, great progress from his eighth place on the grid. Meanwhile, Hamilton was starting to see blisters on his front tyres but still managed to pass Rosberg using DRS on lap 8, for second place. However, when Hamilton passed Kobayashi the pair collided with Hamilton hitting the barriers hard and going out of the race.

The safety car was deployed on lap 15 and as some cars came into the pits, Webber found himself in second place behind Alonso, the difference being that Webber had got his medium tyre phase out of the way, Alonso had not. Vettel pitted for the second time under the safety car.

The race restarted on lap 16. Alonso held the lead, but Vettel passed Webber on the straight and set about Alonso, using his fresh tyres. He got ahead, but Alonso seemed to be managing the tyre wear, apparently planning to make one less stop. Button was making great progress at this stage, having already got his medium tyre phase out of the way early on. He passed Sutil and Massa in quick succession.

Vettel was trying hard to avoid making an extra stop at the front on his third set of tyres. He managed it and only pitted for the medium tyres when Alonso did so on lap 30. He had coped very well with the compromise enforced by the blistering early on, a tough job but one he and the team managed superbly. Understanding and working the tyres just right seems to be one of his strongest traits, as he also showed in the final part of qualifying.

In the closing stages the main interest was Webber trying to catch Alonso, both on the medium tyres, but the Red Bull was much faster.

Michael Schumacher had a great day to celebrate his 20th anniversary. Starting at the back of the grid he used an inverted strategy starting on and running mainly mediums with soft tyres at the end to get into the top six and fight with his teammate Rosberg, who started fifth. Rosberg was told to "save fuel" in the closing stages and Schumacher passed him for fifth place.

Meanwhile, Button – on the soft tyres – was catching Alonso at a second a lap with six laps to go. He passed him with four laps remaining and took the final podium spot.

Belgian Grand Prix
Spa Francorchamps 44 laps

1. Vettel	Red Bull-Renault	1h26.44.893
2. Webber	Red Bull-Renault	+3.741
3. Button	McLaren-Mercedes	+9.669
4. Alonso	Ferrari	+13.022
5. Schumacher	Mercedes	+47.464
6. Rosberg	Mercedes	+48.674
7. Sutil	Force India-Mercedes	+59.713
8. Massa	Ferrari	+1:06.076
9. Petrov	Renault	+1:11.917
10. Maldonado	Williams-Cosworth	+1:17.615
11. Di Resta	Force India-Mercedes	+1:23.994
12. Kobayashi	Sauber-Ferrari	+1:31.976
13. Senna	Renault	+1:32.985
14. Trulli	Lotus-Renault	+1 lap
15. Kovalainen	Lotus-Renault	+1 lap
16. Barrichello	Williams-Cosworth	+1 lap
17. D'Ambrosio	Virgin-Cosworth	+1 lap
18. Glock	Virgin-Cosworth	+1 lap
19. Liuzzi	HRT-Cosworth	+1 lap

Drivers' Championship Standings
1. Vettel   259 pts
2. Webber   167
3. Alonso   157
4. Button   149
5. Hamilton 146
6. Massa   74

Constructors' Championship Standings

1. Red Bull-Renault   426 pts
2. McLaren-Mercedes   295
3. Ferrari   231
4. Mercedes   88
5. Renault   68
6. Sauber-Ferrari   35

Chapter Nine
September 2011

In 2010 Felipe Massa went missing, particularly after the furore over the Ferrari's team orders switch with Fernando Alonso in the German Grand Prix. He blamed many things for his decline in competitiveness, but mainly the Bridgestone tyres.

This season was little better: in a poor qualifying car, the Brazilian managed to outqualify his teammate on several occasions, but he was always slower in the race and Alonso's chances of a podium generally hinged on whether he got ahead of Massa early enough in the race. In Korea, in October, his failure to do so, and Ferrari's failure to instruct a switch, led the Spaniard to say "I give up" shortly before the end of the race.

Many felt that Massa had been indulged by Ferrari's management when in 2010 they gave him a new two-year contract and rumours about possible replacements never ceased to swirl. Had Robert Kubica not been injured, it's quite possible Ferrari's option on Massa for 2012 might not have been taken up and the Pole might have been drafted in.

Approaching Ferrari's most important appointment of the year, in Monza, Massa sat on less than half the points of his teammate, a pale shadow of the man who fought for the 2008 world championship.

Massa: If I felt I'd lost Ferrari's support, I'd quit
6 September 2011

There's an awkward interview with Felipe Massa in *El Pais*, the leading Spanish daily paper, which was done during the Spa weekend and which slipped under many people's radar.

Reading it through, the set up all seems very familiar; a newspaper goes to interview the underachieving teammate of its national hero and asks him how he feels about being beaten by their man. For Massa in this scenario you could insert any driver down the years who has found himself paired with an ace.

However, Massa is slightly different in that he was once a contender: 11 times a Grand Prix winner, he almost won the 2008 world championship – in fact, he believed he had for about 30 seconds after victory in the Brazilian Grand Prix finale, until Lewis Hamilton scrabbled past Timo Glock into the fifth place he needed to snatch the title away from him.

Massa's dignity in defeat that day was the most impressive memory of the whole occasion for me. And so it is today, faced with a Spanish journalist wanting to know what has changed since that 2008 season when Massa won six races. "Nothing, I am exactly the same," says the 30-year-old Brazilian. "It is true that I have not got the results since then, but I have the same ambition and determination."

Of course, two significant life changing things have happened since then: he had a huge accident where a spring from another car hit him in the face, taking him out for the second half of 2009, and then he became a father for the first time. Massa says that neither of these things has slowed him down. "These two things give you a lot of experience, but none of it affects me when I get into the car – at that point you do not remember anything. I forget about my son, my wife, my father and mother. Michael [Schumacher] won many titles as a parent. People talk about it too much – although it is true that these two years have been the most intense of my life."

Massa says that he feels he has the "full support" of Ferrari and that the moment he feels he no longer has it, "I will quit immediately," he said.

The fact is that the last two races have seen an upturn in Massa's fortunes, certainly in terms of finding his speed. He qualified ahead of Alonso in Hungary and Spa, although on both occasions he's gone on to finish behind the Spaniard – in Spa a puncture spoiled his race.

One of the more bizarre stories of the year was the news that Iran was building an international racetrack. The Middle East power-broker, whose president has an eye for controversy, became the latest country to see motor sport as a vehicle for positive growth and international prestige.

The project is being put together by the TSI Group, based in Tehran, which laid out details of the new facility, which is apparently already under construction just outside the capital city. Called iLand, it is a multi-purpose facility with a motor racing circuit at its heart. The facility has not been designed by F1's favourite architect Herman Tilke, but rather by a UK agency called Apex Circuit Design.

The press statement says, "The iLand Race Resort will comprise a 5-kilometre race circuit built in the style of the classic 'naturally contoured' circuits such as Spa-Francorchamps (Belgium), the Nürburgring Nordschleife (Germany) and Donington Park (UK). It is to be built on a parcel of land of 75 hectares that is 1,100 metres above sea level, with a natural topography range of 22 metres. It will be serviced by a country club, expo centre and road safety training school and will be linked to the wider nearby development through the iLand Central Business District. Initial groundworks have commenced for construction and Phase 1, the West circuit, is scheduled for completion in 2012, with full construction and operation anticipated in 2013."

The circuit's initial aim is to be granted an FIA Grade 2 license, which would allow it to host events for everything bar Formula 1. So this would include GP2 and Indycar. There will also be a kart circuit capable of hosting international events.

I'm a big advocate of motor sport reaching new frontiers, but it is hard to imagine the international motor sport community going to Iran any time soon.

The advice from the UK Foreign Office regarding Iran is that "British travellers to Iran face greater risks than nationals of most other countries. There is therefore a risk that British nationals could be arbitrarily detained, despite their complete innocence.

Independent travellers, especially if going off the beaten track, face greater risk than those in tour groups or business visitors."

Furthermore, "The Iranian authorities have in many cases failed to meet their international obligations to notify the relevant embassies immediately that their nationals have been detained. There have been occasional cases of independent travellers detained for more than a month without access to anyone outside the Iranian system."

And we thought going to Bahrain this year might be risky...

On arrival in Monza, one of the most welcome pieces of news was the appearance in the paddock of Robert Kubica's manager to say that his client was on the mend and was set to make a recovery from his horrific injuries. Although he stopped short of predicting a successful return to F1 racing, he did say that doctors had told Kubica he would recover, despite partially severing his right hand.

Kubica's manager: "no doubts" he will recover from injuries
9 September 2011

Daniel Morelli, the manager of Polish driver Robert Kubica, has just delivered an upbeat assessment of his condition, saying, "We have no more concern on the final outcome of the recovery."

Pressed to explain what exactly he meant by that, he said that he had "no doubts" that the Pole would recover fully from the nerve damage to his right hand sustained in his rally accident in February.

There were some concerns about the range of movement he might have prior to the most recent operation on his right elbow. But, having gained full mobility as a result of the intervention, neurosurgeons now say the way

is clear for him to recover. The next steps are that he will undergo four more weeks of intensive therapy to help build muscle strength in his right arm: he is currently doing five to six hours a day, seven days a week.

The target is for Kubica to drive either in an F1 simulator or in some kind of racing car in October and then if he feels that he is able to move forward, the team has said it will organise a test in a 2009 F1 car, which is permitted under the testing restriction rules. This would continue until the new season's testing begins on 7 February 2012.

Morelli made it clear that although Kubica does not have a contract with the Renault team for 2012, he has had assurances from team boss Eric Boullier that there is a seat for him if he is able to perform at the same level as before. "Lotus Renault GP has given us assurances that a seat for Robert is definitely available," he said. That seat is currently occupied by Bruno Senna, having replaced Nick Heidfeld from Spa onwards. Senna is in for the rest of the season. Morelli said that Kubica will not make a return to the F1 paddock this season and will only do so when he is "in a helmet" ready to race again.

"It's good news," said Morelli. "Now we need nature to do its work. The nerves must complete their recovery. But it's just a question of time. He will decide when his condition will be OK to drive. He has never lost the feeling that he will be back."

His functionality and movement is still restricted: he is able to hold objects in his right hand, but not squeeze them, though he has been able to use his hands to play video games.

Vettel wins Italian Grand Prix – a win in Singapore and he could be champion
11 September 2011

At the age of 24 Sebastian Vettel is now potentially just one race away from being crowned world champion for the second year in a row. A win at Singapore could guarantee him the title. He won his eighth race of the season on a track where Red Bull was not considered one of the favourites, thanks to a bold pass on Fernando Alonso in the early stages of the race.

It was Vettel's 18th career win, his second at this circuit and Red Bull's first at Monza. Behind him there were intense battles featuring Hamilton, Button, Alonso and Schumacher, making it an entertaining race. Button finished second, with Alonso holding off Hamilton in the closing stages to take a seventh podium of the season.

"It's very emotional," said Vettel, who was in tears after the race. "It's the best podium in the world. The only thing that could make it better would be wearing a red suit, but it was great. The car was fantastic. We are very disciplined as a team; make very few mistakes. We act as a team and we all remain calm. As for the championship, we're in a great position. It's over when it's over and not before."

The warm weather Ferrari had been hoping for certainly came through, it was a muggy 29°C, when the cars formed up on the grid. At the lights Alonso got the dream start he had hoped for, squeezing past Hamilton and Vettel and into the lead from fourth on the grid. Behind them all hell broke loose when Liuzzi came sailing in sideways as the midfield went through the chicane, taking out Rosberg and Petrov. Liuzzi blamed Kovalainen for causing him to lose control.

The safety car was deployed and, at the restart, Hamilton was not ready and found himself a second behind Vettel as they crossed the line. Schumacher passed him for third.

Alonso and Vettel battled for five laps, before Vettel pulled off a sublime pass on the Ferrari driver into the second chicane, his left wheels on the grass at one stage. He described Alonso as "an animal", albeit jokingly. "He didn't leave much room," he explained.

Webber tangled with Massa, losing his wing, and as he hurried back to the pits, he lost grip in the Parabolica and crashed out. Amazingly, it was the first retirement of the season for a Red Bull driver.

At the front Vettel quickly pulled away from Alonso, with Schumacher and Hamilton battling for third place. Button joined in, the DRS bringing the three cars very close together. Button got ahead, while Schumacher stayed ahead of Hamilton at the stops.

Vettel was 12 seconds clear by lap 24, totally in control of the race, while Button pulled away from Schumacher and Hamilton. He closed in on Alonso, but couldn't pass him.

Perez, Alguersuari and Maldonado had benefitted from the chaos at the start to get into the top ten in the opening stint. Perez and Alguersuari stayed there after the first stops, Maldonado couldn't and slipped to 11th behind Buemi. Perez later retired.

Making no headway against Alonso, Button decided to pit on lap 35 to try the undercut, but Barrichello blocked his way in. Ferrari reacted, bringing Alonso in and he stayed ahead. However, Ferrari's problems with warming up the harder tyres struck again, Button able to pass Alonso on his first lap out of the pits. He opened a gap of 2 seconds.

Senna's tactic of starting on the medium tyres and pitting under the safety car started to pay off as he fought with Buemi for ninth place. Senna was on soft tyres, Buemi on medium. He passed him on lap 48. Schumacher finished fifth, Massa sixth, Alguersuari again made a name for himself with seventh, while Di Resta got a strong eighth place ahead of Bruno Senna who scored his first world championship points.

Italian Grand Prix
Monza 53 laps

1. Vettel	Red Bull-Renault	1h20:46.172
2. Button	McLaren-Mercedes	+9.590
3. Alonso	Ferrari	+16.909
4. Hamilton	McLaren-Mercedes	+17.471
5. Schumacher	Mercedes	+32.677
6. Massa	Ferrari	+42.993
7. Alguersuari	Toro Rosso-Ferrari	+1 lap
8. Di Resta	Force India-Mercedes	+1 lap
9. Senna	Renault	+1 lap
10. Buemi	Toro Rosso-Ferrari	+1 lap
11. Maldonado	Williams-Cosworth	+1 lap
12. Barrichello	Williams-Cosworth	+1 lap
13. Kovalainen	Lotus-Renault	+1 lap
14. Trulli	Lotus-Renault	+2 laps
15. Glock	Virgin-Cosworth	+2 laps

Drivers' Championship Standings
1. Vettel	284 pts
2. Alonso	172
3. Webber	167
4. Button	167

5. Hamilton   158
6. Massa   82

Constructors' Championship Standings
1. Red Bull-Renault   451 pts
2. McLaren-Mercedes   325
3. Ferrari   254
4. Mercedes   108
5. Renault   70
6. Force India-Mercedes   36

The mystery over where outgoing Williams' technical director Sam Michael would end up was resolved shortly after the Monza weekend, when McLaren announced him as their new sporting director. The post had been vacant since Dave Ryan stepped down from the job at the Malaysian Grand Prix of 2009.

The role of sporting director can mean many things in F1. For some teams it is a kind of glorified team manager, for others it can be more engineering-led. However, one thing they usually have in common is an in-depth knowledge of the FIA Sporting Regulations rulebook. So when something happens in a race where interpretation is required, the sporting director will be the one arguing the toss with the race director. This requires an understanding of all areas of the racing business, from engineering to strategy to rules to logistics.

At Mercedes the vastly experienced Ron Meadows holds the role, Jonathan Wheatley does a similar job at Red Bull. Dave Ryan was in the same mould, with huge experience of all kinds of situations in F1. This wisdom is vital when dealing with stewards and with situations that arise out of the blue, where a cool decision under pressure is needed.

Sam Michael has plenty of the right kind of experience: firstly as a race engineer to Heinz Harald Frentzen at Jordan, after which he was promoted to senior operations engineer. He then took that role to Williams. When BMW partnered with Williams he was promoted again, in his thirties, to technical director. As Williams has adjusted to life as an independent team, Michael has worked with the resources available, though not always with happy outcomes.

His new role at McLaren – in overall control of both technical and operational matters at the racetrack, roles in which he was most effective at Jordan and Williams – will essentially play to his strengths.

McLaren aims to be a billion dollar business
23 September 2011

Ron Dennis was in confident mood at the launch of McLaren Automotive Asia in Singapore today. Taking the stage with his local partner, entrepreneur Peter Lim, he said that his vision for McLaren is to make it a company that measures its turnover in billions of dollars.

Among confident predictions of how McLaren will press on into the Asian market, he also confirmed that in the near future the USA is going to be the company's leading market and that it is likely to start a racing programme there to support its sales drive, "You will see a McLaren presence in some form of motor sport in America," he said.

McLaren Automotive's plan is for 42 per cent of the cars to sell in the USA, 35 per cent in Europe and the rest in Middle East and Asia. Although he didn't speak at the event, Talal al Zain, the powerful CEO of Bahraini investment vehicle Mumtalakat, a key McLaren shareholder and partner in its push for growth, was sitting in the front row.

Dennis said that in five years' time, McLaren will carefully examine the possibility of an IPO in the various markets, but that he would rather encourage shareholders to take money as dividends. "My ambition for the group is that in ten years F1 will be bigger, but only 10 per cent of our business," he said. "Growth is not just automotive but also applied technologies. Planning went in last week for two new factories. We intend to have turnover in the billions and we will achieve it," he said confidently.

Asked how his plans might cope with the looming financial crisis Dennis said, "No company can say, 'I'm immune to what's happening in the world'. However, I am averse to debt. We have a model that is driven by an out-of-balance ratio of equity to debt. But any company that doesn't react to the markets is foolish. Asia isn't immune to a global slowdown, but it is pretty robust."

McLaren's analysis of the high-end sports car market is that before the 2009 slowdown this sector was selling 140,000 cars a year and that when new cars come in the market grows. "It's about creating more choice," said Dennis. The slowdown took the market down to 80,000 cars a year and today it has climbed up to 100,000. McLaren aims to have a 4 per cent share of the high-end sports car market, which Dennis described as "conservative", while acknowledging that the market is dominated by Ferrari.

"Our ambitions are driven by the desire to be exclusive," he said. "When we are fully mature we will be making 4,000 cars a year. There will be three models and variants of them, in different segments of the price market."

Dennis explained that it's not good to have waiting lists in excess of a year because the customer becomes frustrated. However, if the waiting list is less than one year the value depreciates quickly. Value is held up by waiting lists. At the moment the waiting list is two years, which he described as "not good".

Building a brand that people admire is one thing, building one that people love is quite another and its something very few companies achieve. It will be interesting to see how McLaren evolves in this area.

Raikkonen poised to return to F1 with Williams
23 September 2011

Kimi Raikkonen is on the verge of signing a deal to return to F1 with Williams. The 2007 world champion has been in discussions with the team for several weeks, following a visit to the factory in Grove. Sources suggest that discussions are going the right way and they are now close to a deal.

It is understood that the Finn, who will be 32 next month, is keen to get back into F1 competition after two years on the sidelines in rallying. The timing is significant on both sides. Williams are on the look out for a bold move to boost the team and Raikkonen can see that the F1 driver land-scape is likely to change a lot at the end of 2012 and that a strong season, reminding everyone what he can do, might open some doors.

Michael Schumacher's comeback is both a positive example and a warn-ing to the Finn as it took the seven-times champion some time to get up to speed. Raikkonen has kept sharp by competing in world rally for the past two seasons, but at the same time he will have to work hard with the Pirelli F1 tyres. All his rivals will have had a year's experience on them.

From the Williams point of view, team boss Adam Parr is keen to move on after a season to forget in 2011. He has hired a new technical team, led by Mike Coughlan, with Dr Mark Gillan (who is in Singapore ahead of this weekend's race) in charge of race operations and Jason Sommerville as chief aerodynamicist. Of course, he has plenty of other options. He could retain Rubens Barrichello, hire a known quantity like Heikki Kovalainen or go for a rookie alongside Pastor Maldonado. Alternatively, he could wait to see whether a Robert Kubica comeback might dislodge Bruno Senna from Renault. Rumours of a connection with Adrian Sutil have been firmly denied on both sides.

One thing is for sure, Williams are likely to finish ninth in the Construc-tors' Championship this year and that will mean a shortfall in prize money and sponsor bonus money. However, most major sponsor contracts have a clause where they pay more if a world champion comes to the team and that may be another factor to encourage the Raikkonen move, particularly if his wage demands are reasonable.

Hiring Raikkonen would be a very bold statement from Williams as he is a world champion and an 18-times race winner. He certainly has the speed and the skills to compete with the best in F1, is likely to get some eye-catching results and his name might also help attract a sponsor or two, although he is not known for being keen on promotional appear-ances. For F1 it would mean that there would be six world champions in a field of 24 drivers, which has never happened before in the sport's 61-year history. The feeling in the paddock is very positive.

One possible question mark against Raikkonen is motivation, something he seemed to have run out of in his final season with Ferrari in 2009. Driving what is likely to be a midfield car, even if it is a regular points challenger, he might be seeking to prove a point rather than win races.

One key relationship he will not have to develop from scratch is with new Williams technical director Mike Coughlan who worked with the Finn at McLaren from 2002 until his move to Ferrari in 2006. They know each other well.

To me the return of Raikkonen was an inspired move by Williams. The risk was that they would appear desperate, but they needed something to inject energy and momentum into the team and this looked like an ideal route.

Paying for it was the key and Sir Frank Williams spent a month in Qatar working on a massive sponsorship deal with Raikkonen at the heart of it. Williams already has a significant partnership with Qatar, basing a technology centre there to develop its flywheel hybrid technology.

Williams knew the risk was that Raikkonen would do one season and then move onto Red Bull or Mercedes, but they didn't appear to mind that too much. The important thing was to get a really good season out of a great driver with a point to prove, to get loads of coverage and to inject some energy and life back into the Williams brand.

Unreachable Vettel within touching distance of title after Singapore Grand Prix win
25 September 2011

Sebastian Vettel is just one point away from clinching the world championship after another dominant performance in the Singapore Grand Prix. Only Jenson Button stands in his way, but a single point from any of the remaining five races will do it for him.

It was Vettel's ninth win of the season and he joins Michael Schumacher and Nigel Mansell as the only drivers who have won nine races in an F1 season. It was also the 19th of his career. Amazingly, having led almost 600 laps this year this was the first time this season he has led a race from start to finish. Jenson Button had another strong weekend with second place, which consolidates his position behind Vettel in the drivers' championship and takes him further ahead of teammate Lewis Hamilton in the points race.

Button, who jumped Webber for second place at the start and was untroubled thereafter, was reeling Vettel in at the end, but he didn't really have a chance to attack the champion, especially after being held up earlier by Kobayashi, who didn't observe the blue flags and was given a drive-through penalty. He also lost time at the end behind the two Williams cars that were battling for position.

"I was in control," said Vettel of the closing stages. "Obviously I faced the traffic first, had to slow down, but then Jenson has the same problem once I'm through. I found myself on the last lap with 5 seconds lead. We had turned the engine down towards the end of the race. Jenson looked like he was flat out, nothing to lose, but we were in control."

Mark Webber finished third after a good battle with Fernando Alonso. But once again he was left ruing a poor start, losing two places off the line to Button and Alonso, albeit he did start from the dirty side of the grid. Paul di Resta also had an outstanding night, choosing a different strategy as the highest placed driver on the grid to start on soft tyres. It set him up for a career-best sixth place, with Force India's joy being completed by Adrian Sutil who picked up more points in eighth place.

Force India knew they didn't have the pace to compete with Mercedes in qualifying, but believed they could get from lights to flag faster than the Silver Arrows using the two types of tyre available. So it proved, Di Resta beating Rosberg, who once again was not able to finish ahead of his grid position.

Ferrari saw Alonso come in fourth on a day when technical director Pat Fry admitted that their car didn't have the pace on either tyre compound. This is a big disappointment for Ferrari, who were very competitive in Monaco on the same compounds.

And it was another of "those" races for Lewis Hamilton who lost four places at the start, then had a collision with Felipe Massa in which he broke his front wing and for which the stewards gave him a drive-through penalty. In total Hamilton passed through the pits five times, though he fought back through the field with a series of overtakes and claimed fifth place at the end.

1

2   **3**

1 › **Red Bull** became
the team to beat and
as such became more
secretive and less
friendly. We've seen
it many times before.

2 › The **RB7** was
the class of the field
in 2011 with a record
number of pole
positions. In Vettel's
hands it was dominant.

3 › Design genius
Adrian Newey
dominated the sport
with Williams in the
early 1990s, McLaren
in the late 1990s and
is now in the form of
his life with Red Bull
Racing.

4

7

5   6

4 › Although the championship was one sided, the colour and thrill of F1 continued to excite millions.

5 › Pirelli re-entered F1 and quickly changed the game, producing tyres with high wear rates which made strategy a key factor in the races once again.

6 › Jenson Button had a wonderful season for McLaren, with wins, podiums and many charging drives. Even his teammate was forced to admit Jenson was on it in 2011.

7 › Sebastian Vettel dominated the season, taking his second world title and setting new records for achievement at the age of 24. The scary part is he's still getting better.

8   10

9   11

8 › Fernando Alonso expected a winning Ferrari in 2011 but it wasn't to be. The car was poor on some of the Pirelli compounds, but the Silverstone win was a highlight.

9 › Bernie Ecclestone had a high pressure year once the Gribkowsky fraud trial got underway in Germany.

10 › Lewis Hamilton described it as his worst year in F1 and he seemed distracted and weighed down at times. He also had a lot of collisions in a scrappy year.

11 › Evergreen **Michael Schumacher** got his smile back in the second half of 2011 when he put in some very strong race performances. He wants to win again in 2012.

12   14   15

13   16   17

12 › The name Senna returned to the F1 grid in 2011 after the Renault team replaced Nick Heidfeld with Ayrton's nephew **Bruno Senna**.

13 › Mercedes were in a race of their own, ahead of the midfield, but not fast enough to race at the front.

14 › It was a tricky season for Renault with lead driver Robert Kubica sidelined by a horrific rally accident and substitute **Nick Heidfeld** not meeting requirements.

15 › Mark Webber
found himself in some
great fights with his
rival Fernando Alonso –
there's a lot of respect
between them.

**16 › Asian entrepreneur
Tony Fernandes**
fought against Group
Lotus and went to
court twice to resolve
legal issues. He has
demanded a more
competitive car next
season.

**17 › Sauber's rookie
Sergio Perez** had some
strong performances,
especially in qualifying
and had to show
character to bounce
back from a horror
crash in Monaco.

18

19   **20**

18 › *JA on F1* continued its groundbreaking fan engagement work on FOTA Fans' Forum, with events in Montreal, Milan and at McLaren's HQ in Surrey.

19 › The **Senna** movie was a huge hit at the box office and on DVD, bringing new audiences to the sport.

20 › *JA on F1* hosted a premier event in London with film makers Manish Pandey and Asif Kapadia.

Massa lost out hugely in the incident; he had a puncture and had to tour slowly back to the pits. He was furious with Hamilton after the race and confronted him privately, but Hamilton rebuffed him. So he raised his objections in front of the TV cameras and later lambasted the Englishman, "He cannot use his mind," said Massa. "He could have caused a big accident. He is paying for that, that's the problem. He doesn't understand, even paying for a problem." Following the confrontation, Hamilton did not face the media for comment.

As usually happens here, the race once again featured a safety car around half distance – possibly as a result of tyre wear and driver fatigue – and maintains the circuit's 100 per cent safety car record. It was annoying for Vettel in one sense, as he had built an 18-second lap, largely thanks to a mesmerising opening stint. But in another sense it was helpful to him as traffic was a big problem for everyone today and by bunching up the field behind him, it meant that he didn't have to lap as many cars as he might have done in the second half of the race.

The safety car was triggered by an accident for Michael Schumacher, who misread the body language of Sergio Perez' Sauber and hit him. Perez was able to continue and scored a point for tenth place.

Singapore Grand Prix
Marina Bay Circuit 61 Laps

1. Vettel	Red Bull-Renault	1h59:06.537
2. Button	McLaren-Mercedes	+1.737
3. Webber	Red Bull-Renault	+29.279
4. Alonso	Ferrari	+55.449
5. Hamilton	McLaren-Mercedes	+1:07.766
6. Di Resta	Force India-Mercedes	+1:51.067
7. Rosberg	Mercedes	+1 lap
8. Sutil	Force India-Mercedes	+1 lap
9. Massa	Ferrari	+1 lap
10. Perez	Sauber-Ferrari	+1 lap
11. Maldonado	Williams-Cosworth	+1 lap
12. Buemi	Toro Rosso-Ferrari	+1 lap
13. Barrichello	Williams-Cosworth	+1 lap

14. Kobayashi	Sauber-Ferrari	+2 laps
15. Senna	Renault	+2 laps
16. Kovalainen	Lotus-Renault	+2 laps
17. Petrov	Renault	+2 laps
18. D'Ambrosio	Virgin-Cosworth	+2 laps
19. Ricciardo	HRT-Cosworth	+4 laps
20. Liuzzi	HRT-Cosworth	+4 laps
21. Alguersuari	Toro Rosso-Ferrari	+5 laps

Drivers' Championship Standings

1. Vettel	309 pts
2. Button	185
3. Alonso	184
4. Webber	182
5. Hamilton	168
6. Massa	84

Constructors' Championship Standings

1. Red Bull-Renault	491 pts
2. McLaren-Mercedes	353
3. Ferrari	268
4. Mercedes	114
5. Renault	70
6. Force India-Mercedes	48

Ecclestone: Vettel is the best driver on the grid
29 September 2011

Today on *F1.com* there is the transcript of a chat between F1 commercial boss Bernie Ecclestone and Red Bull racing supremo Christian Horner. The interview includes two eye-catching quotes: the first is Ecclestone's blunt assessment that championship leader Sebastian Vettel has now grown into the best driver on the grid and is still improving, and the second is a swipe at FOTA, which Horner, an FOTA member, seems to endorse.

"In my view Sebastian is the best driver on the grid right now... " says Ecclestone, who has always taken a close interest in the young German's career. Horner concurs saying that Vettel is "getting better with every bit of experience that he gains ..." Ecclestone adds, "and there is no end in sight to that curve. There is still a lot to come from him."

"Sebastian has an absolute will to succeed but has stayed very grounded," continues the 80-year-old impressario. "No win, however big, will stop him being grounded. That is immensely important in this business. Seb is relaxed and will always remain true to himself – that is why things come easy."

There is a swipe at Ferrari when the conversation turns to whether Vettel should switch to drive for the Italian team at some point in his career. Ecclestone is then asked whether Vettel really should consider such a move: "Well, seeing the situation as it is now it would be an appropriate means to slow him down..."

But the biggest swipe is at FOTA, the teams' association, which is evolving, three years after its formation and has just taken on a new general secretary, Oliver Weingarten, replacing Simone Perillo, who has gone into Italian politics with Ferrari president Luca di Montezemolo's Italia Futura movement. Ecclestone says that FOTA "is an unnecessary association of people who should put their sole emphasis on getting competitive cars on the grid. It's just more of what they don't have to think of. I look after that so there are enough financial resources."

Interestingly, in the same passage Horner says of FOTA, "I also don't spend too much time thinking in that direction."

Although Horner has always stayed quite close to Ecclestone through all F1's twists and turns and has served on FOTA working groups, this is the first time I can recall him publicly distanced himself from the association.

It's an interesting development in a multi-layered jigsaw puzzle, which we will not see as a finished picture for some time.

The month ended with JA on F1 *launching the search for a Fan Ambassador to go to Abu Dhabi to take part in an event organized by our partner Shell. This is the second year we have created this programme and it capped off a great year for* JA on F1 *connecting the fans with the sport.*

Chapter Ten
October 2011

October began with a wobble in the progress of the "Circuit of the Americas" near Austin, Texas, as a Grand Prix venue with news that all was not well on the promotional side of the event. One year away from its debut race, there was an article in the Austin American-Statesman *newspaper suggesting that some changes might be afoot in the management and promotion of the 2012 US Grand Prix.*

The Statesman *had seen a letter sent by the Texas state comptroller Susan Combs to F1 commercial boss Bernie Ecclestone, which details a transfer of ownership rights to the US Grand Prix in the promoter contract. The letter indicates that Ecclestone personally bestowed the rights to Tavo Hellmund rather than to the major investors in the Austin project, which includes billionaire entertainment impressario Red McCombs. At the same time a "slowdown" was noted in building work at the site, possibly linked to the change.*

Soon after it was announced that New Jersey would host a street race starting in 2013, with Manhattan as a skyline. This has been a dream of Bernie Ecclestone for many years. As is his way he had moved on quickly from the groundbreaking deal with Austin and no one was quite sure if the New Jersey deal was a good or bad thing for the city.

Meanwhile, in the aftermath of Singapore and yet another tangle between Lewis Hamilton and Felipe Massa, the officials ran a race edit featuring a radio clip of Massa's race engineer Rob Smedley urging his driver to: "hold Hamilton as much as we can. Destroy his race as much as we can, c'mon boy!" The Daily Mail *worked that up into a story and many others piled in behind them.*

It was Smedley who delivered the infamous words to Massa last season in Germany, "Fernando is faster than you, do you understand?" – possibly the most demotivating words Massa has ever heard on his radio during a race, as they were a code for him to move over.

What was most interesting about Smedley's choice of words in the latest incident was that he felt that the best way to motivate Massa is to get him to see that "destroying" Hamilton's race is a positive thing to do. It's a very aggressive attitude, but it speaks to that part of Massa's psyche which has not forgiven nor forgotten the loss of the 2008 world championship to the Englishman, largely due to the pit lane debacle during the safety car in Singapore, which was triggered by Nelson Piquet's deliberate accident. Massa has called for that race result to be annulled, describing the incident as a "robbery".

Button commits future to McLaren
5 October 2011

Jenson Button has committed himself to a long-term contract at McLaren, ruling out a move any time soon to any of the team's rivals. McLaren team boss Martin Whitmarsh describes him as "one of the most capable and respected drivers we've ever had."

Button is in the form of his life at the moment, lying second in the drivers' world championship, with a chance to become the first F1 teammate to beat Lewis Hamilton in the points standings – he is currently 17 points ahead – and he is thoroughly enjoying his racing. He's stood on the podium nine times in 14 races including two top-drawer wins in Canada and Hungary.

Although he'd enquired about a seat at Red Bull and was also on Ferrari's radar, Button always said that his preferred option was to stay at McLaren. He was hoping for a better deal financially than the one he signed when he left Brawn in 2009 and now the situation has been resolved in a multi-year deal. "Multi-year" means more than two, but doesn't specify exactly how long. There will be options and clauses for when he stops racing and becomes an ambassador for the expanding McLaren brand and particularly the road car operation.

Button speaks enthusiastically about the new deal, but it's noticeable that he does not say that he will finish his career at McLaren, leaving the door open, in other words. He will not, however, be part of the driver merry-go-round which is likely to take place this time next year with possible seats at Ferrari and Red Bull coming up, as well as Mercedes. Massa, Webber and Schumacher all have deals expiring at the end of 2012.

"I've never felt more at home at a team than I do at Vodafone McLaren Mercedes," said Button. "I've won four of the greatest races of my life here, I'm currently lying second in the drivers' world championship, and I feel that I'm driving better than ever.

"You can only achieve that with the right level of support – and I truly believe that the passion and determination to win are stronger here at Vodafone McLaren Mercedes than anywhere else. As a Grand Prix driver, those are incredibly powerful feelings to share and be part of, and they've only reinforced my desire to commit my long-term future to this team.

"I've made no secret of my ambition to continue winning races and world championships, and I fully believe this is the place where I can achieve those aims... We at Vodafone McLaren Mercedes know how to win, and we're busy refining an organisation that will enable us to keep on doing that for years to come."

Whitmarsh later let slip that the deal was for at least three years as a driver, plus the time after as an ambassador for the McLaren brand. Button had really got his feet under the table at McLaren and there were signs in the final quarter of the season that this was getting to his teammate Lewis Hamilton. As Hamilton kept missing opportunities and failing to score the big points, Button kept racking up the results – six podiums in seven races from Hungary to India, for example, with a blend of consistency, speed and canniness. He was driving with more confidence than at any stage of his career so far. Behind Vettel, he was undoubtedly the season's top performer.

Following the Indian Grand Prix later in the month, Whitmarsh came out with some very interesting comments that did not fulfil the usual function of smoothing the way, but rather poured more fuel on the fire. He suggested that part of the reason for Lewis Hamilton's poor form and niggly attitude towards many people in F1 was that he wasn't enjoying being beaten by his teammate. "Lewis will be feeling under pressure because of the great performances from Jenson at the moment," said Whitmarsh.

"Lewis, the great, exciting driver that he is, will not like being beaten by Jenson. I don't want him to enjoy being beaten by his teammate.

I want him to try to beat Jenson, just as I want Jenson to try to beat Lewis."

Whitmarsh didn't need to say this, but Hamilton's form is causing him some concern and the team has to face up to this issue to get the best out of their two drivers. Many people, including myself, thought Button was making a mistake when he went to McLaren in the winter of 2009, as Hamilton seemed clearly the faster of the two. But this year the pressure was on the young superstar to match up to the older, wiser man.

With the new contract in his pocket Button excelled himself in Japan, taking the win, ahead of Hamilton, as Vettel slipped to third place in a careful display which brought him his second world title.

Vettel is world champion again as Button wins Japanese Grand Prix
9 October 2011

Sebastian Vettel became the youngest double world champion in the history of F1 today, the 24-year-old finishing third in the race and wrapping up the title with four races still to go.

"To win the championship here is fantastic," said an emotional Vettel. "I'm so thankful to everyone in the team, working day in and day out pushing hard. We found ourselves in a strong position and it's great to achieve our goals. This year we have always been one step ahead. There is no secret; it's step by step. The hardest thing after winning is to go out and do it again. I needed all the support from the team, from Mark, from everyone working for me."

The top four cars finished just eight seconds apart, but the race was won in some style by Jenson Button, his 12th Grand Prix victory. Button was the only driver able to match Vettel's pace in the early stages and both he and Alonso, who finished second, took advantage of some rather conservative strategy designed by Red Bull to ensure Vettel got a podium rather than push the limits in search of the race win as well.

It was Button's fifth win with McLaren, the first in fully dry conditions and surely one of his best. He extended his lead over teammate Lewis Hamilton in the championship to 32 points. "This circuit is very special. We love this place so to get a victory here means a lot," said Button.

Strategy was critical and pre-race predictions from Pirelli suggested that the soft tyres were degrading at around 0.2 seconds per lap. It was felt that some cars starting the race on used soft tyres could be pitting as early as lap 7 or 8 and the strategy engineers were very much playing a watching and waiting game. Nevertheless, many of the cars outside the top six who had the choice of tyres at the start went for the softs too.

At the start Vettel pushed fellow front row starter Jenson Button onto the grass in an uncompromising move that forced Button to back out of the throttle. This allowed Hamilton to pass him around the outside for second place. The stewards looked into it but decided not to give Vettel a penalty. However, in the cool down room before the podium Button picked him up on it saying, "Is this how we're racing now then?" Vettel did not respond.

Paul di Resta got a good start from 12th up to 8th, Sutil gained two places from 11th to 9th, while Kobayashi lost four places, much to the disappointment of the crowd.

Vettel settled into his usual rhythm early on, opening a gap over Hamilton, while on lap 6 Alonso sailed past teammate Felipe Massa, who had outqualified him. Massa didn't put up much of a fight, Alonso was using the DRS which was very powerful on the pit straight today.

Hamilton let Button past as he had a puncture, which brought him into the pits first. This ultimately caused him to lose a track position to Alonso. Vettel followed him into the pits on lap 10, Button and Alonso pitted a lap later and made up 3 seconds on Vettel in the process.

Hamilton and Massa tangled again on lap 21, but the stewards took no action. Massa's car had some damage on the left side front wing and floor. Webber undercut Massa for P4 and really came into the race on lap 24 when the safety car was deployed for debris on the track, this allowed all the cars who had only made one stop to pit.

On lap 28 the race was restarted with Button leading from Vettel, Alonso, Webber, Massa and Hamilton. On lap 34, Vettel became the first of the front-runners to pit for medium tyres, Webber did the same a lap later, still coping with a front wing which was missing some vital parts. Vettel emerged in traffic behind Rosberg and Sutil, and was a second a lap slower than leader Button, which gave Alonso a chance. Button pitted on lap 37 and Alonso came in a lap later, jumping Vettel in the process for second place.

Schumacher led the race for a while, by virtue of making one less stop and helped by the safety car. When he rejoined after his third stop he'd got ahead of Massa.

In the closing stages Alonso closed in on Button as once again the Ferrari proved faster at the end of a stint. However, Button soaked up the pressure and kept his car out of DRS range to finish first.

Japanese Grand Prix
Suzuka 53 laps

1. Button	McLaren-Mercedes	1h30:53.427
2. Alonso	Ferrari	+1.160
3. Vettel	Red Bull-Renault	+2.006
4. Webber	Red Bull-Renault	+8.071
5. Hamilton	McLaren-Mercedes	+24.268
6. Schumacher	Mercedes	+27.120
7. Massa	Ferrari	+28.240
8. Perez	Sauber-Ferrari	+39.377
9. Petrov	Renault	+42.607
10. Rosberg	Mercedes	+44.322
11. Sutil	Force India-Mercedes	+54.447
12. Di Resta	Force India-Mercedes	+1:02.326
13. Kobayashi	Sauber-Ferrari	+1:03.705
14. Alguersuari	Toro Rosso-Ferrari	+1:04.194
15. Maldonado	Williams-Cosworth	+1:06.623
16. Senna	Renault	+1:12.628
17. Barrichello	Williams-Cosworth	+1:14.191
18. Kovalainen	Lotus-Renault	+1:27.824
19. Trulli	Lotus-Renault	+1:36.140
20. Glock	Virgin-Cosworth	+2 laps
21. D'Ambrosio	Virgin-Cosworth	+2 laps
22. Ricciardo	HRT-Cosworth	+2 laps
23. Liuzzi	HRT-Cosworth	+2 laps

Drivers' Championship Standings
1. Vettel   324 pts
2. Button   210
3. Alonso   202
4. Webber   194
5. Hamilton   178
6. Massa   90

Constructors' Championship Standings
1. Red Bull-Renault   518 pts
2. McLaren-Mercedes   388
3. Ferrari   292
4. Mercedes   123
5. Renault   72
6. Force India-Mercedes   48

After clinching his second title, it was only fitting that we should pay tribute to Sebastian Vettel, especially as I had noticed from the extensive number of comments received on the site that many fans like to underestimate his skills as a driver. Because he sits in the best car, there is a widespread view that this is the factor making him win and that any other leading driver in the same car would beat him.

Having initially not been sure about Vettel when he first came into F1 as a 19-year-old, I have spent quite a bit of time with him, watched him develop and mature to the point where there is no doubt in my mind that he is a very complete driver with a fantastic brain who has earned his place among the greats.

If nothing else he's achieved more at 24 years of age than any other driver in F1 history. This was my tribute to him after his triumph in Japan.

Sebastian Vettel: So much so young
10 October 2011

Some say he's going to win as many titles as Schumacher, others say he's still improving as a driver, while others still say it's all because of the car

125

JAMES ALLEN ON F1

and that Vettel cannot overtake. But the fact is that no other 24-year-old driver has achieved more – two world titles, 19 wins and 27 pole positions.

And now Fernando Alonso has challenged him to a contest to see who can be the youngest ever three times world champion – one of them is likely to beat Ayrton Senna's record of 31 years of age. Alonso has been waiting five years for his third title.

Whatever the hype, the hyperbole or the criticisms swirling around this morning, the fact of the matter is that Sebastian Vettel is now a two times world champion, the youngest of the nine drivers who have achieved that feat.

And he thoroughly deserves it. He wanted to clinch it in style yesterday with victory in Suzuka, but when it became clear that the Red Bull's tyre wear was going to make that impossible and Jenson Button had him covered, pragmatism took over and he settled for a place on the podium and a smaller trophy to clutch as he celebrated his historic achievement.

Of course, many F1 fans don't like Vettel: they don't like the finger he waves around when he comes first in a qualifying session or race, they don't like the fact that he has the fastest car when he hasn't struggled enough in his early life to deserve it – the dreaded "entitlement" argument so regularly trotted out against Lewis Hamilton. And they don't like some of the things he does on the track like the chop on Button at the start yesterday, or the whirly finger "loony" gesture after he'd collided with teammate Mark Webber in Turkey last year.

I do like Vettel. I like him very much as a person and as a racing driver, and I respect him because he is true to his craft. He's the perfect combination of fast, intelligent, focused and hard working. Apply those criteria to the other drivers on the grid and see how many tick all four boxes. Chances are the ones that do will be the most successful, and that's the way it's always been at the top level of F1.

This season has gone pretty much as expected. Coming off the back of last season, the signs were all there that the confidence which that unlikely title win in Abu Dhabi gave to both Vettel and the technical team at Red Bull would mean that they would come flying out of the traps in 2011. The fast car they produced gave them pole position at every race, but winning the races has proved more difficult. McLaren and Ferrari were able to challenge them at most places on race day. The rivals beat them six times, but it could easily have been more.

I don't think Vettel will match Schumacher's seven titles because he's around at the same time as some formidable talents and the likelihood is that McLaren and Ferrari will get their act together soon and build a car which can fight for the title. When they do, both teams have the drivers to take on Vettel.

It may be next year, it may be 2013, but it will happen.

Some fans believe he would not beat Alonso or Hamilton if they were his teammates. Maybe, but it's a moot point and we'll never know because it makes no sense for a team to try an experiment like that while F1 history shows how counterproductive it is to employ two drivers with a voracious appetite to win.

In the meantime, it's time for fans of every persuasion to set aside any partisan feelings and accept that this year Vettel has been superb. He's hardly put a foot wrong all year: a few crashes in practice sessions, the spin on the last lap in Montreal. And he's also given us some great moments: several perfect laps in qualifying, the pass on Alonso in Monza among them.

F1 is about being the best of the best in every department; "competing to win" as Senna used to put it. And few people have a real understanding of what it takes to win in F1. While rivals have missed opportunities, missed a trick on car design or put in a botched pit stop, the fact is that this year Vettel and his Red Bull team have given a textbook example of how it should be done.

There had been rumours that Force India boss Vijay Mallya was looking to sell his team due to financial problems. He strenuously denied them. But soon after Japan, he confirmed that he had sold 42.5 per cent of the F1 team to Sahara India Pariwar, described as "a leading promoter and patron of sports in India." The fee was US$100 million

The deal therefore valued the team at $235 million (£150 million), a significant uplift on the price Mallya paid to buy the team known as Spyker. This is the same Silverstone based team that was originally known as Jordan and founded by BBC pundit Eddie Jordan.

Rather than offer Mallya a partial exit, the investment was said to be going into developing the team to take it to the next level. Force India in 2011 was roughly where Red Bull Racing was five years ago, so why shouldn't they follow in RBR's footsteps if they make the right moves?

The investment is also an important indicator of the impact F1 is likely to have in India. It came just a fortnight ahead of the inaugural Indian Grand Prix at Buddh International Circuit, near Delhi. Business buy-in like this is critical to the future success of the sport. This is what didn't happen in Korea, Turkey and other "failed" races. Sahara is a big mover in sports in India, they are currently shirt sponsors of the Indian cricket team and owners of the Pune Warriors IPL franchise.

Red Bull clinch constructors' championship as Vettel wins Korean Grand Prix
16 October 2011

Sebastian Vettel may have clinched the 2011 world championship, but it hasn't dented his motivation as he again out-raced and out-thought his opponents, despite the race not working out the way Red Bull had thought it would in terms of tyre strategy. Pole sitter Lewis Hamilton battled with understeer all race and finished second.

It was Vettel's tenth win of the season, making him the only driver apart from his fellow-countryman Michael Schumacher to win ten or more races in a season. It was the 20th victory of his career and, with Mark Webber's third place, it gave Red Bull the constructors' championship for the second year in a row. It was also Red Bull's 25th F1 victory. The first was in 2009.

"It's good to see that the whole team keeps on pushing," said Vettel. "The car was fantastic, fun to drive. I managed to get a bit of a gap because those guys were fighting. It's great after last week winning the drivers' championship now to get the constructors' championship."

It was a race that summed up the season in many ways; without Vettel it would have been a close and thrilling battle between Hamilton, Button, Webber and Alonso.

After five races of finishing behind his teammate Jenson Button, Lewis Hamilton was satisfied to get back in front again. It was only his second podium in the last 11 races, while it was Button's first time off the podium for six races. And there were some stunning performances from drivers lower down, most notably Jaime Alguersuari who finished seventh, equalling his career best.

At the start, Hamilton was faster off the line, but Vettel passed him at the end of the back straight. Behind them the other McLaren was also struggling as Massa, Webber and Alonso got ahead of Jenson Button. The rest of the opening stint was uneventful, but the worn supersoft tyres lasted longer than anticipated, which required a change of plan for Vettel at the first stop.

Button closed up on the Ferraris and tried the undercut them at the first stops, but Mercedes brought Rosberg in at the same time and faster pit work put him ahead. The two passed and re-passed using the DRS zone, with Button keeping the upper hand.

Schumacher jumped Alonso in the first pit stops, but then a promising race was wrecked by Petrov who misjudged the braking zone and smashed his rear wing. It was the third time this year that the pair have collided. This brought out the safety car.

At this stage Vettel and the McLarens were on a second set of supersofts, while Webber and Alonso were on softs. Red Bull's plan to use up new supersoft tyres in Q1 and save soft tyres for the race had clearly not worked out as expected, so they had to make the most of what they had. This is a good example of how adaptable they are as a team; they still managed to come out on top even though Plan A had not worked. A fast car helps, but it's also about staying calm and improvising. This is something they've done a lot this year.

The race restarted with Vettel leading Hamilton, Webber, Button, Rosberg, Massa, Alonso and Alguersuari. Alonso was still behind Massa at this stage, there was no easy breeze past as we saw in Japan.

Webber, on the soft tyres, was able to open a gap of 5 seconds over Button on supersofts and closed in on Hamilton in the second stint. By lap 32 Webber's failure to pass the Englishman was playing into Vettel's hands and he pulled away, removing any possibility of his losing the race and of

Webber winning it. Alonso pushed very hard at the end of the stint on used softs and jumped teammate Massa in the second stop, begging the question why did Webber not try the same thing on Button and run a lap or two longer? It also begged the question about what might have happened if Alonso had been able to get ahead of Massa earlier in the race?

Webber and Hamilton battled all the way to the finish, Webber got ahead briefly on lap 49 as the pair lapped a Lotus, but Hamilton was able to steam back past him on the straight.

It was another good day for Toro Rosso with Alguersuari challenging Rosberg for seventh place on much newer tyres as Buemi passed Di Resta for ninth place. They have had some very good races this season, using imaginative strategy, and they thoroughly deserved the points they scored.

There were three fights to resolve in the closing stages: Webber vs Hamilton, Alonso vs Button and Alguersuari vs Rosberg. Then on lap 54 Alonso said, "I give up," possibly a bit of gamesmanship, possibly a message to the Ferrari team that a good result had been jeopardised by him spending so much time behind Massa early on. Alonso said afterwards that this was not the case and that he simply wasn't fast enough in the early stages of the race.

Vettel finished the job off with a flourish, setting the fastest lap on the final lap.

Korean Grand Prix
Yeongam 55 laps

1. Vettel	Red Bull-Renault	1h30:01.994
2. Hamilton	McLaren-Mercedes	+12.019
3. Webber	Red Bull-Renault	+12.477
4. Button	McLaren-Mercedes	+14.694
5. Alonso	Ferrari	+15.689
6. Massa	Ferrari	+25.133
7. Alguersuari	Toro Rosso-Ferrari	+49.538
8. Rosberg	Mercedes	+54.053
9. Buemi	Toro Rosso-Ferrari	+1:02.762
10. Di Resta	Force India-Mercedes	+1:08.602
11. Sutil	Force India-Mercedes	+1:11.229
12. Barrichello	Williams-Cosworth	+1:33.068

13. Senna	Renault	+1 lap
14. Kovalainen	Lotus-Renault	+1 lap
15. Kobayashi	Sauber-Ferrari	+1 lap
16. Perez	Sauber-Ferrari	+1 lap
17. Trulli	Lotus-Renault	+1 lap
18. Glock	Virgin-Cosworth	+1 lap
19. Ricciardo	HRT-Cosworth	+1 lap
20. D'Ambrosio	Virgin-Cosworth	+1 lap
21. Liuzzi	HRT-Cosworth	+3 laps

Drivers' Championship Standings
1. Vettel 349 pts
2. Button 222
3. Alonso 212
4. Webber 209
5. Hamilton 196
6. Massa 98

Constructors' Championship Standings
1. Red Bull-Renault 558 pts
2. McLaren-Mercedes 418
3. Ferrari 310
4. Mercedes 127
5. Renault 72
6. Force India-Mercedes 49

Soon after the Korean Grand Prix came the tragic news that Dan Wheldon, a childhood friend of Jenson Button and Anthony Davidson, had been killed in a "dash for cash" Indycar race at Las Vegas.

Wheldon was a two times Indy 500 winner, including this year's event, and IRL series champion. This race, only his third start this season, was a challenge organised by the Indycar series to try to win the race from 34th and last place on the grid in pursuit of a $5 million prize fund. He got caught in a multi-car pile up.

"It will be pure entertainment. It's going to be a pack race, and you never know how that's going to turn out," Wheldon had written in a blog entry before the race.

Dario Franchitti, who was in the race with Wheldon, said "I could see within five laps people were starting to do crazy stuff. I love hard racing but that to me is not really what it's about. One small mistake from somebody . . .

"One minute you're joking around in driver intros and the next he's gone. He was six years old when I first met him. He was this little kid and the next thing you know he was my teammate. We put so much pressure on ourselves to win races and championships and today it doesn't matter."

After the event everyone roundly criticized the organizers for allowing 34 cars to race on a 1.5-mile oval. David Coulthard said that standards of safety in Indycar are 20 years behind F1. A week later Moto GP racer Marco Simoncelli was also killed when he fell from his bike in the Malaysian Grand Prix and was hit by two other bikes, one of which was ridden by Moto GP legend Valentino Rossi.

At the next F1 Grand Prix in India the drivers paid tribute to their fallen colleagues.

Vettel wins colourful first Indian Grand Prix and pays tribute to fallen racers
30 October 2011

Sebastian Vettel made more history today as he won the first Indian Grand Prix, setting a new record for most laps led in a season in the process. The German went past Nigel Mansell's 692 laps led from the 1992 season.

It was his 11th and most comfortable win of the season and the 21st of his career. He won from pole, led every lap and set the fastest lap time. "I'm very proud to be the first winner of the Indian Grand Prix," said the world champion, "It's a great country, great people, they don't have much but they are happy and we can learn a lot from them. I find it inspiring.

"Jenson was at some stages very strong today. We were in a comfortable position, always controlling it, but with Jenson in my mirrors we had push to the end. I have mixed emotions with two tragic weekends for everyone who is a fan of motor sport. We have to pay respect to Dan Wheldon and Marco Simoncelli who lost their lives, young and committed race drivers."

Vettel opened up a gap early on over Jenson Button and managed it to the end, making his pit stops calmly and keeping out of reach of the McLaren, which had another strong race after a troubled qualifying session. Fernando Alonso grabbed the final podium spot after a race long battle with Mark Webber.

At the start Button dived up the inside from P4 on the grid and went past Alonso, he then passed Webber on the long straight for the first time. Behind them Trulli, Barrichello, Glock and Kobayashi got into trouble with various incidents and had to pit on lap 1. Lewis Hamilton got a poor start, losing a place to Felipe Massa, finding himself behind the second Ferrari as he has quite a bit recently. Michael Schumacher got a great start up to eighth, right behind his teammate Rosberg.

Webber came back at Button on lap 5 using the DRS wing and trying a move at the end of the long straight; Button squeezed him out.

Alonso, Webber and Hamilton all stopped on lap 16, Alonso falling behind Schumacher as he exited the pits. This cost him time in his battle with Webber. But he was able to pass the German a lap later.

Button pitted on lap 19, Vettel a lap later. Hamilton had closed on Massa by 3 seconds, pitting a lap earlier through the first round of stops. Hamilton attacked Massa for fifth place and got alongside, but Massa turned into him, yet another coming together between the pair. This time it was definitely Massa's fault, the clash damaging the McLaren's front wing. Hamilton had to pit for a new one, dropping to ninth.

"We had the one minute silence before the start of the race and me and Felipe were standing next to each other," said Hamilton. "He hasn't spoken to me in a long, long time so I put my arm around him and just said 'good luck for the race'.

"But in the race I tried to overtake and I tried to come out of it because it didn't look like he was going to give me any space, and we collided."

Massa got a drive-through penalty and a lap after serving it, when he was just 6 seconds ahead of Hamilton and all set for a second round battle, Ferrari pulled him in for a tyre stop and front wing change. He rejoined but retired soon afterwards with a broken front suspension having hit a kerb at a bad angle.

In the battle for third place, Webber was struggling with higher tyre wear than Alonso and when he suddenly lost a second a lap he was forced to pit and take the hard tyres. Alonso stayed out and was able to jump him when he came in for hard tyres soon after.

The two Mercedes drivers had a great battle for fifth and sixth places, Schumacher recovering well from a poor qualifying session to take the fight to Rosberg. He got ahead of the younger man in the second round of pit stops. He was told, "You are free to race, but keep it clean." He held off Rosberg to the end.

Vettel set the fastest lap of the race near the end to round out a perfect day.

Indian Grand Prix
Buddh International Circuit 60 laps

1. Vettel	Red Bull-Renault	1h30:35.002
2. Button	McLaren-Mercedes	+8.433
3. Alonso	Ferrari	+24.301
4. Webber	Red Bull-Renault	+25.529
5. Schumacher	Mercedes	+1:05.421
6. Rosberg	Mercedes	+1:06.851
7. Hamilton	McLaren-Mercedes	+1:24.183
8. Alguersuari	Toro Rosso-Ferrari	+1 lap
9. Sutil	Force India-Mercedes	+1 lap
10. Perez	Sauber-Ferrari	+1 lap
11. Petrov	Renault	+1 lap
12. Senna	Renault	+1 lap
13. Di Resta	Force India-Mercedes	+1 lap
14. Kovalainen	Lotus-Renault	+2 laps
15. Barrichello	Williams-Cosworth	+2 laps
16. D'Ambrosio	Virgin-Cosworth	+2 laps
17. Karthikeyan	HRT-Cosworth	+3 laps
18. Ricciardo	HRT-Cosworth	+3 laps
19. Trulli	Lotus-Renault	+4 laps

Drivers' Championship Standings

1. Vettel   374 pts
2. Button   240
3. Alonso   227
4. Webber   221
5. Hamilton   202
6. Massa   98

Constructors' Championship Standings

1. Red Bull-Renault   595 pts
2. McLaren-Mercedes   442
3. Ferrari   325
4. Mercedes   145
5. Renault   72
6. Force India-Mercedes   51

Chapter Eleven
November 2011

One of the noticeable trends of the second half of the season was the ever-improving performance of Toro Rosso. The team had taken a big step forwards since introducing new technology around the time of the Japanese Grand Prix. Were they doing it alone, or was there some help from sister team Red Bull Racing, especially once the championship was wrapped up?

I'd been very impressed with the imaginative strategies of Giorgio Ascanelli and his team of engineers, which made the most of the car's easy action on the Pirelli tyres. But there were some commercial reasons why moving Toro Rosso up the grid was of the utmost importance

What's pushing Toro Rosso up the grid so quickly?
3 November 2011

The performance of the Toro Rosso cars at the weekend underlined how much progress the team has made in the second half of the season. But where is the boost coming from and is there a back-story to it?

Jaime Alguersuari and Sebastien Buemi both qualified in the top ten in India and Alguersuari raced strongly to another points finish. In the last five races the team has scored 29 points, while rivals Sauber in the same period have scored 6 and Force India 19.

Since Suzuka, in particular, the Toro Rosso has been making huge strides. In Singapore the delta in qualifying from Toro Rosso to the pacesetter Sebastian Vettel was 4 seconds, which equates to 4.1 per cent of the lap time. In Japan, where they tested the exhausts, it was 3.1 per cent, then in Korea it came down to 2.4 per cent and in India it was 2 per cent. Meanwhile, Alguersuari drove away from Adrian Sutil in the middle stint of the race in India. So how have they done it?

They've done it with new aerodynamic parts like wings and floors, but particularly by getting the most from the exhaust blown diffuser in a very short space of time – and this is where it gets interesting. As I write the F1 Commission meeting today is discussing among other things the degree of technical collaboration allowed between teams. It's interesting to look at Toro Rosso, who under the Concorde Agreement regulations are not allowed to simply get a car or even parts of one from sister team Red Bull. But they are allowed to share ideas, and rival teams believe that they have been getting advice on the key areas to focus on in developing the blown diffuser, and this has given them a short cut to getting it right.

Most established teams now have some form of blown diffuser but it's a fiendishly difficult thing to get right. Red Bull pioneered it with engine partner Renault last season, but this season it has really come into its own and contributes a massive amount of downforce.

Even teams with huge resources like McLaren and Ferrari took their time to get it right. For the midfield teams, whose resources are more limited, this process can take even longer and some pointers in understanding the system and how to optimise it would be very helpful in getting quick results.

This is fair enough and does not breach the current rules, but it's a huge advantage. As to why Red Bull as a company might do it… the answer is money. The difference between eighth place where Toro Rosso were, and sixth place which is now within reach in the final two races, is worth around €7 million.

But there is a wider game at play too, as Red Bull owner Dietrich Mateschitz has already hinted that he would consider selling a stake in Toro Rosso to the right partner. He has entered into an agreement with IPIC, the Abu Dhabi-based investment company. Among other brands, IPIC owns CEPSA, the Spanish oil company and Falcon Bank, both of whom are now Toro Rosso sponsors. Such a positive growth curve in performance is bound to play well next week when the parties meet at the Abu Dhabi Grand Prix, especially if a partial sale is on the agenda.

Returning to the F1 Commission meeting today, the nub of the issue is that grey and even incomplete areas were left in the rules on technology sharing in the last Concorde Agreement. It is in the interests of the sport, the big teams and the small teams, for technology sharing like that between

McLaren and Force India or Red Bull and Team Lotus. It brings the smaller teams up and makes the midfield really competitive.

For the next Concorde Agreement, due to start in 2013, the stakeholders want clarification of how much Intellectual Property transfer should be allowed and how to regulate it. With a change of engine formula in 2014, powertrain manufacturers will want to have a "works team" and a customer team and this is the right moment to discuss how much further technology sharing goes in that relationship.

Inevitably among competitive people there is suspicion, but this is an area where the sport can easily sort that out by learning from the defence industry, where there are strict protocols and guidelines in place for IP sharing and problems are avoided.

After a row lasting well over a year and with two hearings in the High Court, the battle over which entity was the real Lotus in F1 was resolved when the Team Lotus had its application to rebrand as Caterham F1 team accepted by the F1 Commission, while Renault took over the right to call its chassis Lotus. At the same time Virgin disappeared from F1 as the Russian brand Marussia took over. Having covered this story extensively and been the first to report that Tony Fernandes' Team Lotus was going to rebrand as Caterham, I took a tongue-in-cheek approach by writing the following post on the day the changes were announced.

Lotus, Renault and Virgin teams all change names
3 November 2011

"And so it came to pass that in Milton Keynes in the shire of Buckingham, Stewart GP begat Jaguar, which begat Red Bull, which smote everyone into submission.

"While Tyrrell begat BAR, which begat Honda which begat Brawn which begat Mercedes which chased furiously after the Red Bulls."

Name changes in Formula 1 are as old as the hills; it's a business and takeovers are an essential part of business life. They aren't always allowed, as Tom Walkinshaw found when he tried to turn Arrows into TWR, but generally where it's in most people's interests to see strong brands with staying power in F1, the powerbrokers don't stand in the way.

Today the F1 Commission met in Geneva and sources confirm that the three teams seeking to change names have been allowed to do so, without any loss of earned income under the Concorde Agreement rules. Virgin's ill-starred, two-year adventure has come to an end. The brand has gradually reduced its presence as Marrussia's has increased and now the small volume Russian car company is the brand that billionaire scientist Andrei Cheglikov has decided to use for the team he now controls. It's a smart move to get it done now, while Team Lotus is still looking for approvals to make its changes.

Meanwhile, the Lotus vs Lotus battle has ended with Tony Fernandes also rebranding his team around a sports car brand. Caterham F1 Team, probably with Air Asia tacked on the front as title sponsor next year, will be the platform for an ambitious strategy of marketing low-cost sports cars to Asia, linking in with Fernandes' other sporting asset – Queens Park Rangers Football Club.

The Lotus-Renault GP team meanwhile also has the right to change its chassis name away from Renault to Lotus, should it choose to do so. Group Lotus is a sponsor at present, but the agreement with Genii has clauses under which it could become an equity partner. Renault sold its interest in the team to Gerard Lopez's Genii concern at the end of 2009 and since then has moved to focus solely on engine supply.

The new five-year deal signed with Red Bull makes it clear that RBR is Renault's "works" team from now on, which makes it effectively a manufacturer-backed team, as far as engines go at least.

The net cost to Renault of taking this route of supplying other customer teams is less than a third of what it was when it ran its own team. Like other manufacturers who pulled out in 2008-9, Renault found that owning an F1 team means you have to win or lose funding when economic times get tight. Ironically, now they are engine suppliers to Red Bull Racing, they are winning everything, as they did when they were engine suppliers to Williams and Benetton in the mid-1990s.

Times change, names come and go, but some things remain the same.

As the teams headed out to Abu Dhabi for the penultimate race of the season and some decisive meetings about the way forward for their association, the FOTA, Bernie Ecclestone was in Munich giving evidence in the Gribkowsky trial. It seemed like a process had begun so I wrote this overview post looking at some of the trends I thought would be important.

Behind-the-scenes intrigues set path towards new Formula 1
9 November 2011

Behind the scenes in F1 at the moment there is movement everywhere as things start to click into gear in a process that will ultimately lead to a change of ownership of the sport and a new way of operating it.

Today and tomorrow in Munich, Formula 1's commercial boss Bernie Ecclestone will give evidence in the fraud trial of Gerhard Gribkowsky, a former banker and chairman of F1's holding company. Clearing up this matter and getting to the bottom of what happened when CVC bought the sport from Gribkwosky's bank, BayernLB, is crucial to the hopes of CVC, the sport's current commercial rights holders, getting its assets in a position to sell and exit the sport with a large profit.

Also vital to this process is getting the Formula 1 teams, including Ferrari, to sign a new Concorde Agreement, and this weekend, in Abu Dhabi, the teams will reconvene to discuss the best way forward for FOTA. It is passing through a delicate moment, struggling to balance the diverse needs of its members within the cost saving RRA framework it established in the teeth of the financial crisis of 2008-9. There are outside and inside forces at work trying to pull that group apart, but all members know that they must stick together to get a satisfactory outcome from these negotiations.

Meanwhile, behind the scenes in the wider business world, stories are emerging from Bloomberg and colleagues elsewhere in the business media that the interest of News Corp and the Agnelli family investment firm Exor in buying the sport is still very much alive. James Murdoch, son of News Corp scion Rupert, is sidetracked at the moment as he prepares to give further evidence before a British parliament select committee into phone hacking at the *News of the World*. But sources insist the F1 dossier is open and work is ongoing.

It is a tangled web of separate but ultimately connected threads, and over the course of the next 18 months, as these threads resolve themselves, we will see the Formula 1 of the future emerging. Trying to second-guess the outcome is hard, but I do see some trends and patterns beginning to emerge.

With Ecclestone fighting several fires at once – the Gribkwosky trial and possible resulting investigations by the UK Inland Revenue into his family trust – now is the moment for the teams and the FIA to find reasons why an alliance would be in both of their interests.

The FIA owns the sport, the teams participate in it and both sides want more of the revenues which spring from it and which are currently contracted to, and exploited by, Ecclestone and CVC. By working together the teams and the FIA would provide a formidable competitive challenge to Ecclestone. Some F1 team insiders believe that the only way that they will be able to get a satisfactory outcome to the negotiations is by presenting a game changing united front with the FIA.

As for News Corp/Exor, there are challenges ahead to them taking over the sport, as there are a number of other serious potential buyers out there. Qatar is getting closer to the sport via Williams and has put itself on a world sporting stage by winning the rights to host the FIFA World Cup in 2022. Acquiring sports rights like F1 would fit perfectly with that strategy. But I've always believed that the most likely buyers for F1 are the people who will host this weekend's Grand Prix – Abu Dhabi.

They understand the sport: they have a stake in it as a race promoter, as a shareholder in the Mercedes team and as a sponsor of Toro Rosso. Their influence is growing and through ownership of Manchester City Football Club the Executive Affairs Authority, which manages all their major projects like F1 and football, is learning a great deal about the global exploitation of sporting rights.

There are many twists and turns ahead, but it feels as though we are now on a trajectory towards a new Formula 1.

Sun sets on Vettel as Hamilton wins in Abu Dhabi
13 November 2011

Lewis Hamilton won the Abu Dhabi Grand Prix after a close battle with Fernando Alonso. It was Alonso's 73rd podium and his first trophy from this event, so he now has a complete set of trophies from every track he's raced on in F1. Jenson Button finished third.

It was Hamilton's 17th career victory and his third of this season and although he said he felt "fantastic" he was also pretty humble in his post-race statements, saying that one win hadn't necessarily put him back on track.

It was a day when the Red Bull team was less than the flawless outfit we have seen all season: Sebastian Vettel had a puncture, which led to a suspension breakage on the way back to the pits on the opening lap, and Mark Webber's first pit stop was very slow and took him out of contention in the battle with Jenson Button for the podium. But the Australian lit up the second half of the race with some bold overtakes as he took on a very ambitious three-stop strategy to successfully jump Felipe Massa. However, it was the first time in 20 races that a Red Bull driver has not stood on the podium.

In contrast to last year's event, where there were only 11 on-track passes, this race featured plenty of spectacular overtaking throughout the field, although most of it down to DRS. The double DRS zone made things difficult for some drivers who passed their opponents in the first zone and were then re-passed in the second.

That said there were a lot of problems with backmarkers costing the leaders time, the stewards looking into several examples with Pastor Maldonado being a leading culprit. He was given a penalty for blocking.

The track temperature was 31°C when the race started, similar to the start of qualifying. Vettel, on pole, immediately had a failure of his right rear tyre, which pitched him into a spin, he returned to the pits but it wasn't safe to continue.

Vettel's retirement left Hamilton out in front with Alonso moving impressively from fifth to second on the opening lap, past Webber and Button, who also swapped places a couple of times. Schumacher and Rosberg also had a ferocious scrap on the opening lap, Rosberg getting ahead in the early stages.

Di Resta's pace on the medium tyres was impressive in the first stint, lapping faster than teammate Sutil who was on soft tyres by lap 7.

By lap 13 Webber had got close enough to Button to activate the DRS and started attacking. Button was struggling with a KERS problem that meant not only did he lack the power boost it gives, but also his braking was affected.

On lap 17 the three leaders came in, Hamilton, Alonso and Button, while Mark Webber stayed out, but a slow stop spoiled his chances of jumping Button for third place and he fell behind Felipe Massa into fifth.

Webber and Massa had a double DRS battle on lap 31, the Australian taking advantage of a mistake by Massa to pass in the first zone, but overshooting the braking zone as he tried to stay out of Massa's way, Massa sailed back past him in the second zone.

The second stops came from lap 36 onwards, with Webber taking a third set of soft tyres, requiring another pit stop to run the mediums. Alonso came into the game when Hamilton lost time behind traffic, but Alonso found Ricciardo coming in ahead of him, it was close as the Spaniard exited the pits but Hamilton stayed in front.

Webber's bold three-stopper called for him to build a 22-second gap over Massa before a final stop at the end. He was helped in this by Massa picking up some debris from a Williams on lap 46 and a spin on lap 50. The Brazilian has yet to register a podium finish in 2011.

"When I was doing the in-lap I was thinking this was one of my best wins," said Hamilton. "With all the doubt that's been around me, and it's my mum's birthday so that makes it even better.

"This weekend I've been clearer in my mind, I've had less weighing on me. I was able to drive clearly. In the last race I had that mistake, but here I didn't make a mistake. I feel fortunate to have finished and not got in any trouble."

The only dark cloud on Hamilton's day is that the gap between him and Button is now 28 points, meaning that he will definitely finish behind a teammate for the first time in his F1 career. Alonso's ninth podium of the season means that he is now only ten points behind Button and has a chance to finish second in the world championship.

Abu Dhabi Grand Prix
Yas Marina Circuit 55 laps

1. Hamilton	McLaren-Mercedes	1h37:11.886
2. Alonso	Ferrari	+8.457
3. Button	McLaren-Mercedes	+25.881
4. Webber	Red Bull-Renault	+35.784
5. Massa	Ferrari	+50.578
6. Rosberg	Mercedes	+52.317
7. Schumacher	Mercedes	+1:15.900
8. Sutil	Force India-Mercedes	+1:17.100
9. Di Resta	Force India-Mercedes	+1:40.000
10. Kobayashi	Sauber-Ferrari	+1 lap
11. Perez	Sauber-Ferrari	+1 lap
12. Barrichello	Williams-Cosworth	+1 lap
13. Petrov	Renault	+1 lap
14. Maldonado	Williams-Cosworth	+1 lap
15. Alguersuari	Toro Rosso-Ferrari	+1 lap
16. Senna	Renault	+1 lap
17. Kovalainen	Lotus-Renault	+1 lap
18. Trulli	Lotus-Renault	+2 laps
19. Glock	Virgin-Cosworth	+2 laps
20. Liuzzi	HRT-Cosworth	+2 laps

Drivers' Championship Standings
1. Vettel	374 pts
2. Button	255
3. Alonso	245
4. Webber	233
5. Hamilton	227
6. Massa	108

Constructors' Championship Standings
1. Red Bull-Renault	607 pts
2. McLaren-Mercedes	482

3. Ferrari	353
4. Mercedes	159
5. Renault	72
6. Force India-Mercedes	57

The cost of competing in Formula 1
17 November 2011

The leading F1 teams are in the thick of an argument at the moment about how much money they should be allowed to spend every year to go racing, with Red Bull out on a limb, taking a different view from other FOTA members about the next phase of the Resource Restriction Agreement.

If it all goes wrong, as some predict, this could lead to a new "arms race" in F1 with Red Bull, Ferrari and Mercedes able to spend more than McLaren (which no longer has Mercedes factory backing as it did in the last arms race) and far more than the midfield teams. Let's hope it doesn't come to that because everyone loses in that scenario.

Against this backdrop, it seems like a good opportunity to review some quotes which came to light during the preparation of a *Financial Times* Special Report on F1 on which I helped last week. My colleague John Reed spoke with Jean Francois Caubet, who manages Renault's F1 engine programme, and he spelled out the amount Renault used to spend on the sport and how that compares with what they outlay now, being just an engine supplier. He also confirms that Renault threatened to quit the sport completely this summer over the 2014 engine rules.

"We have a total cost of around €120 million," said Caubet, explaining how much they spend on the existing engine programme. "The net cost – total cost minus sales – is €60 million. For €60 million you have a big exposure in the world."

This is interesting for a number of reasons. It shows that the costs are still high: Renault still spends €120 million a year even though the V8 engines are frozen from a development point of view. The company supplies 16 racing engines a year plus test engines to Red Bull, Lotus Renault and Team Lotus (soon to be renamed Caterham). Next year they will add Williams to the roster.

This is a huge saving compared to the time when the French car maker ran its own team, which it sold at the end of 2009. "In the past the total cost of the team was between €250 million to €280 million. [But after deducting] sponsorship and TV rights, net cost about €180 million," explained Caubet.

In other words Renault is now spending a third of the amount it spent to run its own team in 2009. It has won the world championship for the last two years with Red Bull Racing. This arrangement seems to be working well.

"We have a five-year deal with Red Bull. In the past it was difficult to have a long-term strategy, because the strategy was linked to results. For a car maker, you can't explain what's your budget in five years on a team," added Caubet.

"Also we have a long-term strategy on advertising – Renault will do more advertising, more PR and more communications.

"When you control the team, you must win. And if you don't win, the cost is so high. If you have a crisis, the sponsorship stops like BMW, Toyota, Honda. Because you are a car maker, you need to win. If you don't, the board asks the question."

Caubet also confirms that Renault threatened to pull out of F1 altogether if the new generation 2014 engine wasn't introduced, "We pushed the FIA to conclude on the new regulation [it concluded in June]. Either the new regulation is clear and we will stay in F1 or we keep the same engine and Renault will stop," he said.

The 2014 engine is very important to Renault because it wants to scale down road car engines and push towards turbo hybrids, which is what the F1 engines will be. Just as Renault pioneered turbo engines in F1 and then took them to road cars, now turbo hybrids will tie F1 to the consumer market.

"It will be downsized, fuel efficiency, and a big part on the electric side," he said. "We think in 2015 to 2020, probably 80 per cent of all the engines in the world will be downsized, probably turbo, and with hybrid or electric power.

"We took the decision to stay in F1 only if the new engine was relevant and the new regulation was relevant… We now start the race with 170kg of fuel. In 2014 we will start the race with 130kg – nearly 35 per cent less. Each year we are pushing to decrease the fuel consumption by 5 per cent. It's difficult to reach this goal.

"Today the engine is more of a commodity; in three years, it will be the key thing that makes you win or lose the race."

It will be fascinating in 2014 when engines become performance differentiators again, something they have not been since the V8 engines were frozen.

Vettel takes record 15th pole of the season
26 November 2011

World Champion Sebastian Vettel scored his 15th pole position of the season, setting a new record that beats the one set by Nigel Mansell that has stood for almost 20 years. It was Vettel's 30th pole position in just 81 Grands Prix.

It was a scintillating lap by Vettel, only 0.1 seconds faster than teammate Mark Webber, but a perfect summing up of the season in many ways, as the German put everything together in one lap. The Red Bull's prowess in the middle sector was the decisive factor in keeping them ahead of the McLaren of Jenson Button, who edged out teammate Hamilton with a very strong performance.

"These numbers are made for ever. I said to myself going into qualifying that I must get everything out of the car. It's all about putting everything into one lap. Fortunately we had some great Saturdays and this feeling now is very special," Vettel said.

Vettel acknowledged that he beat Mansell's record with three more races in the season, but it still clearly means a lot to him.

Rain showers had been forecast, but as the qualifying hour got underway the track was dry and the ambient temperature was high, though the wind was increasing in force. Nevertheless, everyone went out early to get a lap in as the weather was hard to predict.

Rubens Barrichello did a fantastic lap to get into Q2 0.5 seconds ahead of teammate Maldonado who was eliminated along with the new teams. Heikki Kovalainen was only 0.4 seconds slower than the Williams, the best of the season, thanks to the new rear wing. Meanwhile, the HRT cars both outqualified the Virgin cars, Liuzzi ahead of Ricciardo for the first time since Korea.

In Q2, Paul Di Resta failed to make the most of a quick Force India car, ending up 11th, 0.3 seconds behind teammate Sutil as he has been all weekend. "I really struggled. We have a top speed issue which gave away some lap time to the opposition," he said. Barrichello did an excellent job to get the Williams up to 12th when their expectation had been that they'd be in the lower reaches of Q2. "The people pushed, I used the power of the people," said the delighted Brazilian. Bruno Senna did a great job to get his Renault into the top ten.

In Q3, Vettel set the pace in the first runs, 0.3 seconds ahead of Webber and 0.4 seconds up on Button. In his second run he broke through into the 1m 11s, with a perfect lap.

Button edged out Hamilton for the seventh time this season and the younger man was forced to admit he was beaten for pace, "Jenson was massively quick today," said Hamilton candidly. "I ended up a couple of tenths away from him, so clearly I could have gone a bit faster, but the fact is that although I didn't make any mistakes on my best lap I just wasn't quite quick enough on the day."

Webber finally gets his win in Brazil season finale
27 November 2011

Mark Webber won the Brazilian Grand Prix for the second time today, the seventh victory of his F1 career. It was his first win of the season and came about because of a rare technical problem for his teammate Sebastian Vettel.

"It's a bit of a relief, the feeling is nice," said Webber. "In this sport you take them as they come. I can only control what I'm doing. With ten laps to go I thought it's nice to finish the season with a win and another win in Brazil, always been a good track for me."

The world champion rolled in second, having survived most of the race with a gearbox problem. Jenson Button came through, after an intense race-long battle with Fernando Alonso, to claim his 12th podium finish of the season and the eighth in nine races since Hungary. The second half of the season saw Button score 161 points to Vettel's 176, a much closer ratio than the first half. It confirmed him in second place in the championship.

At the start, the top three got away cleanly, while Hamilton lost fourth place to Alonso, another strong getaway from the Ferrari driver. Massa also gained a place at the expense of Rosberg. Further back, Kovalainen got a flying start, gaining four places. The big loser off the line was Barrichello, possibly starting his last race, who lost seven places.

In the opening stint Vettel pulled away from Webber, while Button's McLaren didn't have the pace to live with them. Instead, Button had to deal with Alonso, who passed him on lap 12. On the same lap Senna and Schumacher tangled, with damage to both cars. Schumacher punctured a tyre and debris was strewn around the track.

Vettel's tyres started blistering at this point and then he developed a gearbox problem.

Button pitted on lap 15 with Alonso and Hamilton coming in a lap later and the order stayed the same. Vettel pitted on lap 18 and Webber a lap later. This cost Webber time in the battle with Alonso, who gained 3 seconds on him through this phase. Massa delayed his stop until lap 22, coming in five laps later than his teammate.

Vettel's gearbox problem got steadily worse through the second stint and Webber closed right in as Vettel had to short shift every corner of every lap. He let Webber past him on lap 29, as Alonso closed in at a second per lap.

Tyre wear was worse than expected – compelling most teams to go to three stops. Button was in for a second stop on lap 32, switching to the medium tyres. This strategy was pretty bold. Intended to gain him pace, which it did, he would have been vulnerable if it had rained and everyone were to pit for wet tyres.

Hamilton pitted on lap 34 and went to the soft tyres. He too developed a gearbox problem at mid-distance. Despite this, he reprised his season long battle with Massa. Massa was on worn tyres and needed to stop again, so it was up to Hamilton to judge the risk. Their pace was almost 2 seconds slower than the front-runners. Hamilton switched strategies, pitting for medium tyres, and Massa reacted and pitted a lap later, holding the place. But Hamilton's gearbox failed a couple of laps later and that put him out of the race.

Button had to stop for another set of medium tyres on lap 53, but he had enough of a margin over Massa to pit and rejoin ahead of the Brazilian. With a new set of medium tyres, Button went on the attack. Alonso pitted soon after but the Ferrari's lack of pace on the medium tyres was again evident as Button hauled him in and passed him for third place.

Adrian Sutil had a great day, running strongly and finishing ahead of Nico Rosberg's Mercedes, he was even lapping at the same pace as Massa in the final stint. Whether this was enough to save his drive with the team only time will tell. It was almost enough for Force India to catch Renault in the constructors' championship – they missed it by just four points. Meanwhile, Sauber held off Toro Rosso for seventh and Lotus confirmed a very valuable tenth place – the last of the prize money earning positions.

Webber finished off the race with a series of fastest laps, lapping everyone up to sixth place Sutil in the process.

Brazilian Grand Prix
Interlagos 71 laps

1. Webber	Red Bull-Renault	1h32:17.434
2. Vettel	Red Bull-Renault	+16.983
3. Button	McLaren-Mercedes	+27.638
4. Alonso	Ferrari	+35.048
5. Massa	Ferrari	+1:06.733
6. Sutil	Force India-Mercedes	+1 lap
7. Rosberg	Mercedes	+1 lap
8. Di Resta	Force India-Mercedes	+1 lap
9. Kobayashi	Sauber-Ferrari	+1 lap
10. Petrov	Renault	+1 lap
11. Alguersuari	Toro Rosso-Ferrari	+1 lap
12. Buemi	Toro Rosso-Ferrari	+1 lap
13. Perez	Sauber-Ferrari	+1 lap
14. Barrichello	Williams-Cosworth	+1 lap
15. Schumacher	Mercedes	+1 lap
16. Kovalainen	Lotus-Renault	+2 laps
17. Senna	Renault	+2 laps
18. Trulli	Lotus-Renault	+2 laps
19. D'Ambrosio	Virgin-Cosworth	+3 laps
20. Ricciardo	HRT-Cosworth	+3 laps

Drivers' Championship Final Standings
1. Vettel   392 pts
2. Button   270
3. Webber   258
4. Alonso   257
5. Hamilton   227
6. Massa   118
7. Rosberg   89
8. Schumacher   76
9. Sutil   42
10. Petrov   37
11. Heidfeld   34
12. Kobayashi   30
13. Di Resta   27
14. Alguersuari   26
15. Buemi   15
16. Perez   14
17. Barrichello   4
18. Senna   2
19. Maldonado   1

Constructors' Championship Final Standings
1. Red Bull-Renault   650 pts
2. McLaren-Mercedes   497
3. Ferrari   375
4. Mercedes   165
5. Renault   73
6. Force India-Mercedes   69
7. Sauber-Ferrari   44
8. Toro Rosso-Ferrari   41
9. Williams-Cosworth   5
10. Team Lotus   0

Chapter Twelve
Strategy Reports

Making the right decisions at the right time is crucial to success in F1. The race unfolds in a blur and it is very easy to make a bad decision, in the cockpit or on the pit lane.

As we saw in Abu Dhabi last year with Ferrari and Fernando Alonso, a bad strategy call during a race can cost a world championship. This season race strategy played a far more significant role in the outcome of the races and even the qualifying sessions than it has in recent years. And it needed careful planning, because things were never quite as they seemed.

This was deliberate. One of the things Pirelli wanted from its return to F1 was for the teams to have to think tactically about how to use its tyres. They deliberately designed them to wear out more quickly than the Bridgestones. Also changing the game this year was the introduction of the adjustable DRS rear wing, which was designed to make overtaking easier. This meant that strategists had a wide range of options open to them because they didn't have to be as worried as before about coming out of the pits behind a slower car and not being able to overtake.

Working together with our partner UBS, we took hold of the race strategy story in F1 and produced a series of pre- and post-race reports which reached a huge audience worldwide of over 8 million people in 8 different languages.

The F1 teams bought into the idea, because they knew that it was in their interests for fans to have a better understanding of the tough decisions they have to take during the heat of a Grand Prix. Abu Dhabi last year showed that. The groundbreaking content was produced with input and data from strategy engineers from several teams, so was 100 per cent authentic.

Race strategy adds a welcome extra dimension to Formula 1 and I find it fascinating. What follows is a compilation of the UBS Strategy Reports from the season.

With so many new variables this season, the opening round of the 2011 World Championship, the Australian Grand Prix in Melbourne, was something of an experiment for all the teams in terms of race strategy, with the tyres being the dominant factor. We had no safety car this year in Melbourne, another important influence on strategy.

But the most important factor in strategic decisions this season was the fact that the new Pirelli tyres degrade much more quickly than the Bridgestones used in recent years and that when they start to go off the performance drops very quickly and severely. Managing that process and making quick decisions was the key in Australia.

Australian Grand Prix
Melbourne, 27 March 2011, 58 laps

Before the weekend the indications were that several pit stops would be needed to complete the race at Albert Park. However, this did not turn out to be the case, partly because the track surface is very smooth.

On race day, the simulations showed that two stops was the ideal and the variations we saw were due to a brave gamble on the one hand (Perez – one stop) and a forced change of plans on the other, due to setbacks (Alonso and Webber – three stops). However, the podium finishers all stopped twice.

The key to navigating through was flexibility and a willingness to change tactics. However, at the front Sebastian Vettel showed that when you have a dominant car you can make the strategy bend to your will.

In depth case study – Sergio Perez

The 21-year-old Mexican, on his debut, was the talk of Melbourne with his bold strategy of stopping just once. After winter testing this seemed almost inconceivable, but the Sauber is the most gentle car on its tyres and Perez drove expertly to make a set of soft tyres last 35 laps.

Having qualified outside the top ten, he had a free choice of tyres on which to start the race. He was the only one to opt for hard tyres. This meant that he would run a longer first stint than everyone else. He was 14th on the first lap. His pace on the hard tyres was over a second slower than his teammate Kobayashi on the soft tyres. When the cars in front made their first stops, he moved up the order and was seventh when he made his first stop on lap 23.

At this stage he was put onto soft tyres, with the intention of stopping again for another set of softs later in the race. The expectation was that this would give him tenth place at the end.

As he drove he found that he could manage the tyres, and that contrary to expectations, the track was rubbering-in, which punished the tyres less. The team strategists decided to try to get him to the finish without stopping again, targeting a better finish than tenth by saving 25 seconds on a pit stop.

It was a very risky tactic – at any moment his tyre performance could suddenly drop off by two seconds or more, ruining his race. He managed the process brilliantly and was even faster than the cars in the top three at around three-quarter distance. As his rivals, like Kobayashi, Buemi, Sutil and Di Resta, went for their second stop he stayed out and moved into seventh place, which he held to the flag. Sadly, the Sauber's rear wing was found to be illegal and he was disqualified from the results. The team decided not to appeal.

Nevertheless, Perez's bold gamble made strategists realise that they should have spent more time doing a long run on the soft tyres in Friday practice to learn about it, rather than just testing it out briefly at the end. They were thinking that the hard and soft tyres would behave as they had in the Barcelona test in terms of relative degradation, but that wasn't the case. We will see all teams doing a long run on Friday in Malaysia as a result. And we could see more drivers "doing a Perez" as the year goes on.

Massa and Alonso: Ferrari on the back foot

Testing had indicated that the Ferrari was the second fastest car behind the Red Bull, with the Ferrari competitive on long runs. But in Melbourne the car proved to be harder on its tyres than its rivals and this pushed them down the road of having to stop three times. They will have to get on top of this problem quickly if they are to compete for the title this year.

Alonso started fifth on the grid, but lost four places at the start. He passed Rosberg and Massa and gained another place when Button was penalised for an illegal overtake. But tyre-degradation meant he suddenly lost performance around laps 10 and 11. He had to stop on lap 12, coming out behind Petrov. Despite his setback at the start he was in the hunt for a podium against Webber and Petrov, who was only going to stop twice. Normally when you have a bad start you try to stop less often than your rivals to regain track position, but that wasn't an option for Ferrari.

The three-stopper did allow him to push hard in each stint and it got him ahead of Webber at the final stop.

Renault could see what Alonso was doing, but did not react and stuck to their plan to stop twice. Alonso pushed hard, closing the gap to Petrov to 19 seconds when the Russian pitted for the second time on lap 36. Alonso's plan at this stage was to pit again, leaving him enough laps at the end to catch Petrov using the advantage of new tyres against old ones. First he had to jump Webber and he managed that by staying out one lap longer before the final stop on lap 42.

Alonso then caught Petrov at over a second a lap in the closing stages, but the plan didn't work because the soft tyres on the Renault held up well enough now that the car was running light on fuel and the track was rubbering-in and being kinder to tyres. Petrov held his nerve and Alonso ran out of laps in which to pass him.

Webber: Strategy call didn't work

Mark Webber left Melbourne with much to reflect on and analyse. Driving the same Red Bull RB7 car as race winner Sebastian Vettel, Webber finished fifth, a full 38 seconds behind his teammate. The reason was that he was very hard on his tyres and the team made a call at his first stop that didn't work out.

Third on the opening lap, he nevertheless clearly had the pace in the car to get ahead of Lewis Hamilton through strategy. But his tyre wear was savage: he was the first to pit on lap 11 after his tyres suddenly lost 2 seconds of performance on lap 10. Switching to the hard tyres, his plan was to run a long middle stint and then a final soft-tyre stint. This was also an evaluation exercise for the team so they would have some advance information on the hard tyre for Vettel's last stint.

But it proved to be the wrong decision for Webber as the hard tyres were degrading as much if not more than the softs, were hard to warm up and had no pace. He was jumped by Alonso later in the race. Webber did just 15 laps on the hards and then two more stints on soft tyres.

Malaysian Grand Prix
Sepang, 10 April 2011, 56 laps

Tyre degradation remained the challenge in Sepang, with the teams and the drivers required to react to conditions and make quick decisions. "A lot of it is getting the strategy right, which is up to the team but also the driver," said Jenson Button after the race. But the adjustable DRS wing and the difference between cars with KERS and those without was also a far more significant factor in the way the racing played out than in round one. With Sepang's long straights, it was relatively easy to overtake, especially for cars with KERS, and this contributed to strategic thinking.

With the data from Melbourne to work from, the strategies for Malaysia worked out pretty much as the simulators said it would. We had a mix of two-, three- and four-stop strategies. Those doing four stops, like Mark Webber, used five sets of tyres in the race, when the total allocation for qualifying and the race is six sets.

The total time for a pit stop was just 21 seconds, 7 seconds less than Melbourne. So if you could run unimpeded then three stops was the fastest way to go in Sepang. But only race winner Sebastian Vettel really had that luxury. For most other drivers, making three stops inevitably meant coming out of the pits in traffic at some point. Being able to overtake a car on older tyres was crucial at such moments to making the strategy work and we saw a lot of that, for example, Hamilton on Petrov on lap 26.

The three podium finishers all did subtle variations on the same strategy with three stops, using soft tyres for the first three stints and then hard tyres for the final stint. This was the winning strategy, but there were plenty of significant variations.

At its hottest the track temperature was 54°C on Friday and that did two things: it skewed people's attitudes towards tyre degradation, pushing some into planning shorter stints and more pit stops, and it also made them believe that the hard tyres wouldn't last much longer than the softs and that they were a second a lap slower. However, Mark Webber's long run on Saturday morning provided a counter argument for those willing to gamble on making a set of hard tyres last 18 laps or more.

Sauber's Kamui Kobayashi managed to do the race with just two stops, making a set of soft tyres last 19 laps and a set of hards last 20 laps. Williams was also planning two stops for both its cars. To contemplate that you needed to be able to do a minimum of 18 laps on a set of tyres; something not everyone can do.

Lewis Hamilton: Team strategy decisions questioned

Lewis Hamilton questioned some of his McLaren team's decisions after the race. He felt that he was brought in prematurely for some of his stops and it contributed to him being forced to make a fourth stop, at his request, just four laps from the end. Had he been able to stay out a little longer on his first two stints that could have been avoided. The team argued that he used up his tyres in pushing hard in the opening phases of the race to catch Vettel. It shows how finely balanced the decision-making is and how an extra couple of laps on the early stints can make all the difference at the end of the race.

Hamilton lost a place at the start to Nick Heidfeld. He was unable to pass as the Renault had the fastest car through the speed trap. Hamilton was also the victim of a slow pit stop on lap 37, which cost him a place to his teammate Jenson Button. What could have been a second place ended up being eighth place.

Running third in the opening stint he pitted relatively early on lap 12. He took a second set of soft tyres at this point and managed to undercut Heidfeld, who stopped two laps later. Now in second place, Hamilton began closing on race leader Vettel, bringing the gap down from 9 seconds to 3.9 seconds by lap 23. The team appear to have felt that he took too much out of the tyres in this quest, which hurt him later. One could argue also that it was a vain quest anyway, as Vettel was clearly not pushing his car at all and could have gone faster whenever he needed to. But Hamilton is a racer and that's the way he chose to play it.

Still catching Vettel he came in for his second stop on lap 24, prematurely he felt, and looking at the lap times you'd have to agree. He was put on the hard tyres.

Why did they do this? Several reasons: Hamilton had flat spotted a set of soft tyres in qualifying, so had fewer soft tyres available than the others. But the team was also looking at the example of Adrian Sutil in the Force India, who was running on hard tyres at this point and was going slightly faster than teammate Paul di Resta on softs.

Also, for those who noticed it, Webber had done a long run on hard tyres on Saturday morning, which was very fast. So the hard tyres maybe wasn't such a bad idea.

It was clear that Hamilton was trying to make a three-stop plan work, but he lost time at that second stop and then struggled with the balance of the car on hard tyres and started losing ground. A collision with Fernando Alonso damaged the floor of the car. Having pitted on lap 37 he felt unable to make his hard tyres last 19 laps to reach the finish. Although he was lapping in the 1m 43s, he felt that he had to stop again and in doing so he lost track positions to Heidfeld, Webber, Massa and Alonso. It was costly decision. In contrast, Button managed to make his set of hard tyres last 18 laps, and they were still fast at the end.

Mark Webber: Zigging while the others zag

Mark Webber did something different from the rest in Melbourne: stopping three times when the winning call was two stops. In Malaysia he was at it again, despite driving the fastest car in the field. So why is he having problems with strategy while teammate Vettel is cruising at the front?

In Melbourne, it was down to him being harder on the tyres than Vettel. In Sepang there was more to it. Webber's race was compromised by a poor start due to a clutch problem and then no KERS to help him. Once they hit 100 kmh after the start (the point at which they can use KERS) the cars behind him shot past: Massa, Alonso, Heidfeld, Petrov and Schumacher. From third on the grid he was ninth on the opening lap and tenth on lap 3 when Kobayashi passed him.

Without KERS to help him pass cars, he and his engineer were forced to think outside the box. If they did the same as everyone else, went the thinking, they would end up ninth. So they decided at the end of lap 1 to switch from a three- to a four-stop strategy. This allowed him to push hard in four of the five stints. But he lost a lot of time in the opening stint behind Kobayashi, who was 2 seconds a lap slower than the leader Vettel. Such is the pace of the Red Bull, however, that once in clean air, Webber was able to progress.

It paid off in the sense that he was able to recover and finish fourth: the strategy giving him either clear track to run on or new tyres with which to pass cars after his stop, helping to get him ahead of Kobayashi, Schumacher, Petrov and Massa. He pulled off some great moves on new tyres. But he was also helped by Hamilton and Alonso's problems.

Kobayashi: Sauber makes tyres last again

Kamui Kobayashi pulled off quite a feat on Sunday. He managed to be racy, overtaking cars in spectacular style, while at the same time managing to make his tyres last long enough to get away with a two-stop strategy. And that was quite impressive.

Mindful of Sergio Perez' performance in Melbourne, where he gained track positions by stopping only once, it was in the minds of a number of teams to do the minimum and stop twice in Sepang. The tyre degradation was too severe to contemplate one stop; the lap times would drop off suddenly and that would be costly. Kovalainen, Glock and Alguersuari managed it, but the most effective was Kobayashi who got a seventh place finish from a tenth place start.

However, this was more of a survival strategy by Kobayashi than anything else. Looking to go to lap 17 on his first set of soft tyres, his pace was not great in the opening stint. On the soft tyres again in the middle stint he was racing against Michael Schumacher, who was on a three-stopper. Kobayashi did well to make his final set of hard tyres last 20 laps. He made it work and got ahead when Schumacher made his third stop. He also gained a place when Lewis Hamilton was penalised after the race.

Chinese Grand Prix
Shanghai, 17 April 2011, 56 laps

So much happened in the Chinese Grand Prix, it's important to take the time to examine exactly how and why things worked out as they did. The overriding observation is that strategy was the difference between winning and losing on Sunday.

While we have seen some interesting mixtures of strategy in the first two races, the podium finishers in both Melbourne and Sepang all followed the same strategy. The Chinese Grand Prix was the first race to show variations on this. Another interesting difference from the first two races is that we had four fast cars out of their normal position on the grid: Webber 18th, Heidfeld 16th, Schumacher 14th and Petrov 10th. This meant that the two Toro Rosso cars and the two Force Indias were in and around the top ten, but staying there proved difficult as the overtaking aids and the Pirelli tyres gave the faster cars the chance to come through the field.

The strategic thinking started in qualifying, where Lewis Hamilton decided to do only one run in Q3, saving a set of new soft tyres for the race. What exactly did this give him? In comparison to a set that has been used in qualifying, a new set will give a first lap performance boost and will last two to three laps longer than a used set, which has done that much already. On top of that the degradation on a used set means that every lap in the stint will be between 0.1 and 0.2 seconds slower than the new set through the stint. Finally there is another benefit, in that you delay taking the hard tyres – which are around a second a lap slower – for an extra couple of laps. It all adds up to quite a gain.

Why Lewis Hamilton beat Sebastian Vettel

Computer simulations showed that two stops would be faster than three by around 3 seconds over the race, but this was reliant on running in clear air. Vettel went with a two-stop plan, but found himself behind the McLarens after a poor start. His KERS wasn't working properly at the start. It only gave him 30 bhp instead of 80 bhp, which is why the McLarens got the jump on him.

At this point Red Bull had the chance to do three stops. But as Vettel pitted on lap 14, the same time as Button and a lap before Hamilton and came out ahead of both, they decided to stick with two stops. They no doubt thought that their car was fast enough to make the strategy work. Had they followed a three-stop plan from lap 14 onwards Vettel would have won the race.

What none of the simulations prior to the start predicted was how little the tyre life would improve during the race. Experience with the Pirellis in the first two races had shown that the tyre wear was 25 per cent better in the final stages of the race, compared to Friday Free Practice when most teams do their long runs of 18-20 laps. But crucially, this time the circuit did not rubber-in, which meant the surface didn't come to the hard tyres for the final stint, as is normally the case. This is why Vettel and the other two-stoppers, like Ferrari, couldn't keep the pace up and Hamilton, whose tyres were seven laps fresher, caught Vettel in the final laps. It is also the reason why Webber's strategy worked out so spectacularly well, as we will see below.

Lewis Hamilton won the race by getting the strategy exactly right. Saving a set of new tyres played its part in making the three-stop plan work, as did crucial overtakes such as the ones on Button, Massa and Rosberg.

How did Mark Webber go from 18th to 3rd?

"What this race has proved," said Mark Webber afterwards, "is that qualifying isn't as important as it used to be. You don't want to be qualifying 18th every weekend, but you're better off saving tyres for the race than wasting a new set in Q3 for a one-place gain on the grid. Monaco would be the only exception to that rule, of course."

This is true and we may see some of the faster cars doing what Hamilton did and limiting themselves to using just two sets of soft tyres in qualifying, because the benefit in the race is so significant.

Webber ran the three-stop race strategy, but in reverse, starting on the hard tyres and then using three new sets of soft tyres, which he had saved by not doing Q2 and Q3. Webber was the only driver on the grid not to start on softs. This plan gave him plenty of free air to run in and at the end he was running on new soft tyres when all the other drivers were discovering that the track wasn't improving and that the degradation on the hards was therefore worse than expected. New soft tyres gave him a huge pace advantage as proved by his fastest lap, which was 1.4 seconds faster than anyone else.

Webber did exactly the right thing by running the prime tyres early on while stuck in traffic and unable to exploit the pace of his car. Had he started on options, he would have had to use the hard tyres at the end of the race and it would have been much harder for him to make progress.

Nico Rosberg: The one that got away

Nico Rosberg was very upset after the race as he felt that he could have had a podium, and at one stage looked like he might even get his first win. The reason he didn't was a miscalculation of fuel consumption.

Rosberg was fourth on the opening lap, and then thanks to a great piece of strategic thinking by Mercedes early in the race, they brought him in on lap 12 just as he was about to hit traffic. This brought him out in clear air. He was able to run unimpeded at this stage of the race and was in the lead by lap 17, doing impressive lap times on his second set of soft tyres. After his second stop he came out in front of both McLarens and must have thought he was on for a podium. But then it became clear that he didn't have enough fuel to complete the race at competitive speeds, so he had to save fuel and the race got away from him.

In fairness to Mercedes this is an incredibly hard thing to predict. All sorts of things can lead to increased fuel consumption: atmospheric pressure, track conditions, tyre conditions. Rosberg's car was much faster in race trim in China than it had been in Malaysia, and this used more fuel. In Malaysia they had to open the bodywork up to keep it cool, whereas in China they could run the car in its optimal aerodynamic configuration.

All teams run at a fuel deficit at some points in the race, aiming to save fuel in the final stint. Mercedes clearly fuelled the car expecting a lonely race in fourth place, keeping the Ferraris at bay, but the chance arose to do something much better and they couldn't take it for want of a few more kilos of fuel in the car.

Ferrari: Sticking with the wrong strategy

After the race, Fernando Alonso said, "You need to keep focused on your own strategy. And in the end when you have a quick car, any strategy is good, as Webber showed today. When you have a slow car, everything is more difficult."

Ferrari made the same mistake as Vettel in running a two-stop plan, which was a shame because Felipe Massa looked the most competitive he has for a long time, and on a three-stopper could have been on the podium.

Both Ferraris were held up by Rosberg in the first stint. The drivers probably thought they could run quicker in clear air, so they stayed out when Rosberg pitted on lap 12. Massa briefly gained a place on Hamilton, but he and Alonso got split up.

Alonso had been behind his teammate after losing the start to him. He stayed out one lap longer than Massa at the first pit stop and that allowed Massa to stay ahead. Alonso then came out behind Schumacher and he lost a lot of time. It was somewhat surprising that Ferrari stuck so doggedly to two-stops with both cars, you would normally split strategies in that situation.

It's worth remembering that the difference in lap time between old and new rubber, when combined with the fuel load always getting lighter, means it's no longer an advantage to run longer than someone prior to pitting. If the first person to stop does a strong out-lap from the pits, he'll always make time on the person who's stayed out on old tyres.

Turkish Grand Prix
Istanbul, 8 May 2011, 58 laps

The Turkish Grand Prix featured 82 pit stops, a new record for Formula 1, and some spectacular overtaking moves. It was quite a confusing race that requires some decoding, and there are some clear trends emerging, which will have a big effect on the way the races happen from now on. It was also another race all about strategy and not just in terms of pit stops on race day; it was also about planning a strategy for the whole weekend, and particularly for qualifying.

After four races with new rules and new tyres, we are seeing the emergence of some clear patterns in the teams' strategic thinking. There are a number of factors involved. For a start, the DRS wing aiding overtakes mean that it is possible to go for what the computer model tells you is the optimum strategy for your car's pace because you know that you can overtake. It is now unlikely that you will have your race completely ruined, as Alonso's was by Petrov in Abu Dhabi last year, for example.

However, we are also seeing that being stuck in traffic can still lose you vital time, as it did for Jenson Button on Sunday, and this is harmful to anyone trying to get away with making one less stop than the opposition. We have also learned that having even one set of new soft tyres for the race makes a vital difference, as much as 5 to 6 seconds over the course of a typical stint.

Another lesson is that it is preferable now to slant thinking very much towards the race and not qualifying. It's not just about saving a set of tyres, it's also about setting the car up for the race and prioritising that above all else. With the Pirelli tyres the ideal balance for qualifying and race are far apart. In the past it was generally a case of add a bit more front wing for qualifying and take it out at the first stop in the race. Where you qualified was often where you finished. Now it is about setting the car up to preserve the tyres, and this simply isn't compatible with single lap performance. So you are looking to preserve the tyres by dealing with the limitations. In China the tyres were front limited, in Turkey they were rear limited.

Although both Ferraris prioritised a race balance, they failed to save a set of soft tyres from qualifying, which was very odd, especially since Hamilton won the race in China using that tactic. So, the Alonso strategy was right, but not perfect. Massa even used up a set of new soft tyres in Q1 when there was no risk of dropping out because Kobayashi had stopped. No one in the pit lane can understand how that mistake was made.

Teams are also still finding surprises on race day, despite gathering tyre data on Fridays. In China the surprise was that the wear on the hard tyres in the final stint was bad because the track hadn't rubbered-in. In Turkey the track did rubber-in and the surprise was that the lap time difference between the soft and hard tyres was only 0.3 seconds, much less than at any race so far and less than the 1 second per lap it looked like on Friday.

Another point to make is that, even if they have a margin, some drivers are making a final stop for new tyres to cover themselves should a safety car be deployed in the closing laps. Vettel did it with his fourth stop, which wasn't really needed, but if there had been a safety car he would have been a sitting duck at the restart.

Why were there so many pit stops in Turkey?

There are a number of reasons for this. It's mainly because the tyre degradation was severe. The track temperatures were higher on Sunday than during practice and tyres didn't last as long as expected. But it's also because the pit lane in Turkey is relatively short and so you lose less time (just 16 seconds) making a stop there in comparison with other tracks, and because the high peak loading on the tyres through Turn 8 – as much as 1,000 kilos, – takes its toll on tyres.

Why planning to stop four times was the winning strategy

Many teams set out to stop three times, but told their drivers in the early laps of the race that they were moving to "Plan B", which meant four stops. The tyre degradation was huge and that was clear from five laps into the race. It was at this point that many teams switched to four and those who didn't (Button and the Williams drivers) lost out.

Pre-race simulations said that a three-stop strategy would lead a four-stop by 8 seconds after the fourth stop. But then the four-stopper overtakes the three-stopper as his tyres are a second a lap faster. So teams who set out on Friday to run the race as a four-stop strategy did well on Sunday. Ferrari was a case in point with Alonso, who set the car up to be optimised for four stops. He also benefited from a good start, which put him clear of the squabbles over position. We've learned that intense battles speed up tyre degradation.

Why didn't Jenson Button make three stops work?

The limitation for trying to do three stops in Turkey was the front right tyre, which is the one that is punished most by Turn 8. Button found that by running longer stints he developed understeer in all the left-hand corners and that meant he couldn't defend.

Button was racing against Rosberg and Hamilton, both of whom stopped four times. His goal was to do one less stop than them and have enough of a margin when they came out from their fourth stops (around lap 46) for them not to be able to catch him in the 12 remaining laps, despite their newer tyres. This strategy began to unravel on his third stint, when he was on his new soft tyres. This was the moment to build a cushion, particularly as Rosberg was on hard tyres at this time, but on lap 30 he was held up by Massa. Button's laps 30 to 39 should have been in the 1m 31s and 32s, instead they were in the 1m 33s.

This meant that when Hamilton and Rosberg came out from their fourth stops Rosberg was only 8 seconds behind and Hamilton only 2. On tyres that were older and therefore a second a lap slower, Button was a sitting duck.

Similarly, Buemi did well to make his tyres last on a three-stopper so that he was in seventh place with four laps to go. But, on fresher tyres, the two Renaults went past him at the end and he wound up ninth, which is still a good result from 16th on the grid. So again we see that midfield cars that are gentle on their tyres – such as Toro Rosso and Sauber – can run one less stop than their rivals and still get into the points.

Kobayashi copies Webber's China strategy

Kamui Kobayashi was his usual ebullient self on Sunday, making some spectacular overtakes and working his way up from the back of the grid to finish tenth and claim a point. He did this by running on new tyres all race and by getting the hard tyres out of the way at the start when his progress was limited anyway by traffic. He was helped by the hard tyres being faster than expected.

Kobayashi's race again goes to show how much progress you can make if you run as much as possible on new tyres, a situation that is likely to encourage midfield teams to consider throwing qualifying in order to have new tyres for the race.

Spanish Grand Prix
Barcelona, 22 May 2011, 66 laps

This year's Spanish Grand Prix at Barcelona was widely heralded as one of the most exciting largely due to the way strategies played out, meaning that an intense battle for the lead developed in the final third of the race.

The action also saw pole sitter Mark Webber dropping to fourth place, Fernando Alonso, the leader on lap one, finishing in fifth place a lap down on the winner, and the recovery of Jenson Button, from tenth place on lap one to finish on the podium thanks to a bold strategy variation.

Pre-race strategies

On paper going into the race if a driver had new tyres to use, a three-stop strategy was 4 seconds quicker than a four-stop. But few drivers had the luxury of new tyres, most had one new set of softs at best. On old rubber, a four-stop was showing to most strategists as being 10 seconds quicker. So there wasn't much in it, which is why you saw drivers doing different things and ending up in pretty much the same place, with the exception of Button.

The overriding consideration for engineers and drivers was that the new hard tyres were a lot slower than the softs. The gap between compounds was around 2 seconds per lap in practice and that came down to just over a second as the track rubbered-in. So the stints on hard tyres were quite compromised. Drivers wanted to spend as much time on softs as possible.

However, the degradation was such that by half distance some cars, like Webber and Alonso, had already made three stops and so were destined to spend the second half of the race on the hard tyres.

The importance of new tyres

Once again we had several graphic illustrations of how new tyres make a massive difference. We saw some key positions change due to the undercut, where a following driver pits a lap before the car in front and gets ahead of him.

Sebastian Vettel used the undercut to pass Fernando Alonso for the lead. Vettel pitted early, on lap 18, and his out-lap on new tyres was so much faster that when Alonso pitted a lap later Vettel got through to lead the race. It was crucial for Vettel to get past Alonso in this way as Lewis Hamilton was running longer stints and looming as a challenger for the win on tyres four laps younger than Vettel's.

By pitting early and getting clear of Alonso, Vettel was able to stay ahead of Hamilton at the third pit stops on laps 34 and 35, when the drivers switched to hard tyres. We have observed that Red Bull tend to pit on the early side before the tyres start to really lose performance. This is built into their tactical thinking. In contrast, McLaren are willing to run a little longer on the tyres and it brings them very close to Red Bull. In Spain, by running a few extra laps they managed to keep their drivers in clear air, while Red Bull compromised Webber's race early on by bringing him out in traffic after his first stop on lap 10 (see below).

Another clear illustration of how much new tyres count was Nick Heidfeld, who started at the back of the grid after a problem in qualifying and managed to use new tyres all race, almost passing the two Mercedes in sixth and seventh places at the end. This is what Mark Webber did in China and Kamui Kobayashi did in Turkey. Such strategy, however, won't work so well in Monaco where traffic will slow down such progress.

Could Hamilton have used strategy to beat Vettel?

Some people have questioned whether Hamilton might have passed Vettel at the third stop had he stayed out on soft tyres a lap or two longer when Vettel switched to hards.

The analysis shows that in the laps from 34 to 36 Vettel's in- and out-laps were 2 seconds faster than Hamilton's. Their pit stop times were almost identical, but Vettel's flying first lap on new hard tyres was fast enough to make the difference at 1m 28.563. Hamilton had been doing 1m 30.0s on his worn softs, so he would not have passed Vettel by staying out at that pace.

However, in a comparison between McLaren and Ferrari, McLaren knew that Hamilton's pace was better than Alonso's, even on worn tyres, so they nursed tyres and literally shifted everything toward the end of the second stint.

The worn soft tyres on Hamilton's car were faster than the fresh soft tyres on Alonso's car between laps 19 and 21.

Hamilton's soft tyres showed a degradation rate of 0.1625 seconds per lap in the first stint. But McLaren were 0.5 seconds quicker than Ferrari on soft tyres in the race trim so going longer than Alonso was marginal, but he made it work.

How Webber's strategy was compromised early on

Mark Webber started from pole position, looking for the win which would kickstart his season. But he ended the race in fourth place. How did that happen?

Webber's strategy was compromised at the start when both Alonso and Vettel passed him into Turn 1. Webber's starts this year have been a problem: in five Grands Prix he has dropped a total of ten places, so an average of two per race.

To compound the problem by losing position to Vettel, it meant that Vettel had first call on pit strategy so he came in first on lap 9, with Webber forced to wait until lap 10. When he rejoined he was in traffic behind Petrov and Button and this allowed Hamilton, who pitted on lap 11, to undercut him, dropping him to fourth.

After that his problem was being unable to pass Alonso, who stayed in front of him after the second stops on lap 19. From being 4 seconds behind Vettel at that point, he went to 11 seconds behind in ten laps.

He was pitted very early next time around – on lap 29 – and had the tactical advantage of being behind Alonso, so he could surprise him by diving for the pits when it was too late for Ferrari to react. But the element of surprise was lost: Ferrari read it and pitted Alonso at the same time. Red Bull's Dr Helmut Marko has since claimed that Ferrari were listening to Red Bull's radio, which he claims is the only way they could have known the plan, but this has not been confirmed.

Webber was right to try to undercut Alonso. But it was a sacrifice because he was on his only new set of soft tyres and they had only done ten laps. They could easily have gone on for another five or six laps (as Vettel's did on that stint). It had a knock-on effect on the rest of his race and cost him the podium to Button.

From Ferrari's point of view they burned through their soft tyres very quickly in covering other people's strategies. The result was that Alonso had no soft tyres left with 37 laps still to go. In contrast, McLaren managed to get Hamilton six laps further and Button only went to hards with 18 laps to go.

How Button went from tenth to the podium on three stops

Jenson Button had a disastrous start from fifth place on the grid to tenth at the end of lap 1. McLaren reacted by planning a three-stop race. He managed to get to lap 14 on his used softs – the ideal point for a first stop on that plan. – though he dropped around 8 seconds to the leaders by doing the extra four laps. But it was the platform for his successful strategy as he managed to carry the advantage of being on newer tyres than his rivals through the remainder of the race. He came in seven laps later than his rivals at his second stop and 13 laps later for his third.

The delayed first-stop tactic brought him out in sixth place, having jumped Massa, Rosberg and Schumacher, who had lost time behind Petrov.

He got 16 laps out of his new soft tyres (compared to Webber's ten laps)

By stretching it out like this without losing too much time, he was able to go to hard tyres at the same time as Webber, so was not in danger of attack. Also the McLaren turned out to be faster than Red Bull on hard tyres so he was home and dry on the podium.

Monaco Grand Prix
Monte Carlo, 29 May 2011, 78 laps

By looking in-depth at the strategies for each race we can analyse the decisions taken in the heat of battle. Sometimes we see teams and drivers taking big risks; and we also see the part that luck can play in the outcome.

Risk and luck both play a big part when you are trying to get a good result in Monaco. All the strategists know that there is a 71 per cent chance of a safety car here and if it falls at the right time it can make your race – as it did this year for Sutil and Kobayashi. But if it falls at the wrong time, your victory plans fall apart –as they did for Jenson Button.

The 2011 Monaco Grand Prix was shaping up to be a classic until the race was suspended by a red flag for an accident six laps from the end. At that point the three leading drivers were converging. They had all started the race on the same tyres (supersofts) and were all ending it on the same tyres (softs), but in between had done three completely different strategies.

Once again we saw a race in which pre-race expectations on strategy were proved wide of the mark as the tyres performed far better than expected. So, once again, the strategists and drivers really had to think on their feet.

Vettel – forced into a one-stop

Sebastian Vettel is on top of the world at the moment and sometimes when things are going for you, you get a bit of luck. Vettel was forced into gambling on a one-stop strategy on Sunday. If the race had not been red-flagged, it's likely that Alonso would have launched an attack at the end, as Vettel's tyres were 60 laps old, 20 laps older than Alonso's. But the red flag gave Vettel breathing space and he was able to change tyres before the race restarted and take the victory.

Red Bull were caught out by Jenson Button making an early pit stop on lap 15 and taking the lead when Vettel stopped a lap later and lost 3 seconds with a slow tyre change. But they were clever in taking the soft tyres at this point. This gave them flexibility to go either way – take the tyres to the finish in a one-stop, or to come in again later. From lap 16 onwards they were playing it by ear.

On lap 34 when the safety car came out, they saw Ferrari pit Alonso and knew that he would go to the finish on those tyres. From that point on Vettel was committed to staying out.

It seems that the Pirellis fall apart quickly on tracks with medium to high-speed corners, like Istanbul and Barcelona. But on low speed tracks like Monaco they are better than Bridgestones because the surface of the tyre does not grain.

By race-day many strategists felt that it was possible to do 40 to 45 laps on a set of soft tyres, but to do 53, as Vettel did, and still maintain competitive lap times was universally regarded as very impressive.

McLaren gamble with Button; Ferrari play it safe with Alonso

From second on the grid, Jenson Button and McLaren took a big gamble in adopting a three-stop strategy as it relies on being able to exploit new tyres on a clear track – a tactic that will be ruined by a safety car. They were aggressively going for the win by doing something different from Vettel, believing it was the only way to beat him.

But McLaren also made another tactical mistake when Button made his second stop on lap 33, just before the safety car. He pitted just as a Virgin car was stopped on the track. Perhaps McLaren anticipated a safety car, perhaps not, but the mistake was to put on a set of supersoft tyres at that point. This forced them into having to stop again as Button hadn't used the softs yet.

They had taken all the flexibility out of their strategy, something they didn't need to do and which cost Button second place and maybe even the win.

A few laps later the safety car did come out (for the Massa crash) and Alonso pitted immediately, switching to soft tyres. He took these through to the finish. Stopping during a safety car meant it was almost a free pit stop for Alonso. He was 3 seconds behind Vettel before he stopped and, at the restart after the safety car, was only 7 seconds behind on new rubber.

Going into the race Ferrari were confident that the tyres were capable of long stints. Their Friday practice long runs had shown that. They even managed to get 26 laps out of a set of supersofts on Friday, showing that their tyre wear was very light.

So, tactically they gave themselves plenty of options and unlike Red Bull and McLaren they didn't take any risks with Alonso. Pitting under the safety car was the smart thing to do and, when Button had to stop a third time, Alonso passed him and went up into second place.

On tyres that were 20 laps younger than Vettel's, Alonso was waiting for the moment when Vettel's tyre performance started to "fall of the cliff", which may or may not have come in the last six laps. But the red flag prevented him – and us – from finding out whether he would have won.

For the record, Ferrari had split the strategies, with Massa planning to do only one stop. He was in the category of cars that were not quick enough to pull away from the midfield cars and create a gap that you can get into after your pit stop.

Safety car is the game changer

After the controversy at Valencia last year the safety car rules were changed. This had a big effect on Sunday's race.

The rules are complicated, but in a nutshell, the safety car now has to pick up the leader. Anyone ahead of him is therefore able to go around faster than the safety car, make a stop and carry on to the tail of the queue, thus gaining hugely. This happened to Kobayashi and Sutil, who were able to do their only stops of the race under the safety car. With a big window to the next car, they got out of the pits in fourth and fifth places, having started 13th and 15th.

Canadian Grand Prix
Montreal, 12 June 2011, 70 laps

By common consent, the Canadian Grand Prix this year was an absolute classic. It had everything: great racing, safety cars, rain, collisions and some very tight strategy calls, often with little data with which to work. The strategists were really tested on Sunday and it made for a fascinating race. Jenson Button won despite a drive-through penalty, five pits stops, two collisions and a whole lap with a puncture.

Even more incredible is look at it like this: in the 70-lap race there were only 38 total racing laps. The other 32 were safety car laps. On lap 40 Button was in last place. So how did he do it?

The answer is that he won thanks to a mixture of strategy, great lap times and overtakes. He and his strategists basically made it happen for themselves.

Button's race under the microscope

To understand Jenson Button's race we need to go back to McLaren's decision to run his car with a lot more downforce than the opposition, particularly the big rear wing. Although he wasn't demonstrably faster than the others in really wet conditions, the downforce and balance of the car came into its own in the period of the race when he was on intermediate tyres. He made most of his progress in that condition. So, for example, having been last on lap 40 he was ninth on lap 51.

We could examine the pre-red flag period, but it would be academic to the outcome. Button's problems, like his collisions with Hamilton and Alonso, his multiple stops, puncture and drive-through penalty were all in the past by the time the safety car came out in lap 40.

This was the reset moment of his race. From here, with a well-balanced car on intermediates, one more stop to make it onto slicks, DRS enabled for overtakes, he made the race his, passing car after car on the way to the flag.

He was one of the earliest to switch onto slick tyres, on lap 51, and gained the benefit of that. Webber had gone for them a lap earlier and his sector times on lap 50 showed it was the tyre to be on, so from tenth place McLaren pitted Button for slicks and he found tremendous pace on them straight away. At that point he was 27 seconds behind Vettel.

Red Bull had been playing it cautiously at every step with Vettel, waiting a few extra laps in each case to be sure they were making the right call. Webber gambled on slicks first, partly to give himself a chance and partly so Red Bull could look at the data and pick the right moment to pit Vettel. But they remained cautious, leaving it two laps longer than Button. By the time Vettel emerged from his final stop on slick tyres Button was just 15 seconds behind and lapping 2 seconds faster than the champion.

Many fans have asked whether Button could have won without the final safety car on laps 59-60. Vettel certainly saw his lead cut back on several occasions by the safety car, losing a combined total of 20 seconds of lead.

But with regard to the last one in particular, it would have been close: Button was in fourth place and closing fast on Vettel anyway, 17 seconds behind with 12 laps to go he might well have caught him without the safety car. And bear in mind that he caught and passed Vettel using tyres that were two laps older than the German's.

Second guessing the conservatism of the FIA race director

One interesting trend we are seeing is the FIA race director, Charlie Whiting, being quite conservative in terms of the deployment of the safety car and the length of time it stays out, as well as in his instructions to competitors, such as that they must be on wet tyres for the restart after the red flag. He seems more risk averse, and this has become a crucial factor that fundamentally affects race strategy.

Yesterday we saw some teams second-guessing that conservatism, such as Renault and Sauber, who gambled that Whiting would stop the race when the safety car came out for heavy rain on lap 20. Most teams took the opportunity of the safety car to make a stop for new wet tyres, however, Renault left Heidfeld and Petrov out, Sauber did the same with Kobayashi and De La Rosa, Force India did it with Di Resta, while Sutil even stayed out on intermediate tyres. All were gambling on a red flag… and they got one.

Although a pit stop under the safety car had only taken 14 seconds for their rivals, the gamblers all up went the order, and when the red flag came they got the double win because Whiting said that all cars must have wet tyres fitted for the restart, so they got a free tyre change. Heidfeld went from sixth to fourth, Di Resta went from ninth to sixth, Sutil from 17th to 13th.

Kobayashi could only laugh as the likes of Alonso, Rosberg and Schumacher all pitted in front of him for intermediates and then realised their mistake as more rain fell, promoting the Japanese driver to second place. And then he got a free tyre change under the red flag. One has to observe that Kobayashi and the Sauber strategy team have made some bold calls in the last couple of years and made them work. He's not just an exciting overtaker; he gambles on strategy too.

European Grand Prix
Valencia, 26 June 2011, 57 laps

The European Grand Prix at Valencia was the least exciting race of the season so far from the point of view of spectacle. But from a race strategy point of view it was quite interesting. It was less frantic than some of the races we have experienced so far this year and, surprisingly, there was no safety car. As a result the teams had some time to consider their options during the race.

Many had planned to do the race on a two-stop strategy, which on paper was 8 seconds faster than a three-stop, assuming you had a trouble-free run in traffic. But then the conditions changed and race day turned out to be much hotter than the practice days. The track temperature on Sunday was about 20°C hotter than it was on Friday, which is why so many people opted to go conservative and followed a three-stop strategy.

In passing it's worth noting that in previous years with Bridgestone tyres, the Valencia track rubbered-in and lap times improved by about 4 seconds per lap between Friday morning practice and the start of qualifying on Saturday, but the feeling this year was that it was less with the Pirellis, probably closer to 3 seconds.

It's also worth remembering that Pirelli had brought the medium compound tyres to race for the first time and although they were tested in practice, no one had any knowledge of how they would perform with the 47°C track temperatures.

There are some interesting observations to make about the strategy battle between Red Bull and Ferrari, but there's also the opportunity to look at drivers in the midfield who coped with change, did something different, and got great results.

Alguersuari: A fabulous drive under extreme pressure

When he qualified in 18th place, down among the backmarkers for the third race in a row, Jaime Alguersuari knew that the vultures were circling on his career. With pressure on his seat from Toro Rosso test driver Daniel Ricciardo, Alguersuari was fighting for his future on Sunday afternoon. What he did was remarkable. No wonder he jumped into the harbour in celebration after the race!

Starting on a new set of soft tyres, he got a decent start, moving up to 17th place, then quickly dispatched Perez and Petrov, who had both started on the medium tyres. He was now behind teammate Buemi, who had started one place ahead of him on the grid, so both were making similar progress.

They gained places as Heidfeld, Barrichello and Sutil all pitted around laps 11 and 12. When Buemi pitted on lap 14 and Alguersuari continued, it was clear that Toro Rosso were splitting the strategies with the Span-iard going for two stops. He made his first stop on lap 19.

What made his race remarkable, and gave him his ultimate result of eighth place, was his 23-lap second stint on the soft tyres. Not only was the stint long – most teams couldn't have got 23 laps out of the soft tyres – Alguersuari was able to lap at a similar speed to the Mercedes and Renault cars throughout the stint.

Alguersuari's performance caught out most of the midfield teams, who didn't expect him to be able to run so long and stay competitive. The Toro Rosso was not considered to be particularly kind on its tyres, like the Sauber, for example.

When his rivals made their third stops Alguersuari went up the order again. He also did a great job to hold off Sutil in the closing laps. They were both on the medium tyres, having made their final pit stops within a lap of each other (42 and 43), but Sutil couldn't find a way past, even with DRS and a straight line speed advantage of 2.5 mph.

Strategy battle at the front: Red Bull and Ferrari

While Sebastian Vettel had the whole thing covered and was able to maintain a slender lead, not overstressing the tyres at any stage, Mark Webber was locked in a battle with Fernando Alonso's Ferrari.

Red Bull's tactic was to pit earlier and try the undercut. There were three significant factors in the race which helped Alonso take second place from Webber. The first was that he overtook teammate Felipe Massa at Turn 2, and that allowed him to run with Webber. If he'd been behind Massa, he would have found it difficult to pass because the double DRS activation wasn't very effective in Valencia, particularly in the first stint.

The second factor was that Ferrari were very cautions at the beginning of each of the soft tyre stints. After overtaking Webber on lap 21, Alonso allowed himself to be undercut at the second pit stop by Red Bull making the first stop. He must have been worried about tyre wear, otherwise he would have come in earlier. Alonso did not even accelerate at full speed out of the pit lane so that he would not overheat the surface of the tread on his out-lap. He was very cautious about warming up the whole tyre, not just the tread surface.

The final factor was that staying out on the option tyres for three laps after Webber had pitted for new medium tyres on lap 42, again trying the undercut, worked out for Alonso. It was pretty obvious that used options were going to be quicker than new medium tyres – strategists could see that from looking at Kobayashi's lap times on them. Alonso did enough in three laps to take second place when he made his final stop. The Ferrari was surprisingly fast on the medium tyres, having struggled on them in practice.

British Grand Prix
Silverstone, 10 July 2011, 52 laps

This was another very interesting race from a point of view of strategy. There were a lot more unknowns than normal, particularly with the tyres, as there was so little dry running before the race. And then there was the partially wet track at the start, which forced everyone to start on intermediate tyres.

Prior to the start most strategists were thinking of a three-stop race, with some further back on the grid planning to do one less stop to try to make up places.

The wet start meant two things, both of which made life easier. Firstly, drivers would not have to use the much slower hard tyres, and secondly, it essentially shortened the race by 11 laps, making strategies easier to achieve.

The first key decision was how early to come in for dry tyres. This decision was helped by Michael Schumacher who was forced to pit for a new nose on lap 9 and went to dry tyres as he had nothing to lose. By lap 11, when his tyres were up to temperature, he was a second a lap faster than the leader making it clear that slicks were faster; drivers like Jenson Button dived into the pits.

Red Bull: coping with two competitive drivers
Mark Webber took the pole at Silverstone and was competitive in the race, although he surrendered the lead at the start to his teammate. So Red Bull had to manage the race carefully.

At the point of wet to dry changeover, Sebastian Vettel had an 8-second lead over Mark Webber, who was under pressure from Fernando Alonso. Using this to their advantage, Red Bull pitted Webber first so he would not lose time or a place to Alonso. It worked, helped by Alonso losing 2.6 seconds on his stop. But keeping Vettel out for the extra lap cost him 5 seconds. So the team was definitely thinking of Webber's needs when it made the call on the order at the first stop.

However, at the second stop they inadvertently cost Webber a place to Alonso. They did their usual thing of pulling the driver in just before the tyre performance drops off a cliff and Webber pitted on lap 26. Alonso still had life in his tyres, however, and did a 1m 35.5, which was the fastest lap of the race to that point. That and Webber losing 1.5 seconds in his own pit stop meant that Alonso had done enough to undercut him. But then when Vettel's stop went wrong and he lost the lead to Alonso, the German came out in Webber's path, preventing him from attacking Alonso on tyres that were up to temperature.

This was a very rare example in 2011 of a driver undercutting a rival by stopping a lap later; normally new tyre performance means the undercut can only be achieved by stopping first.

Later in the race Webber was catching Vettel on tyres that were two laps fresher, but the team would not allow him to try a pass.

McLaren – race compromised on several fronts

Leaving aside the extraordinary situation where Jenson Button's wheel wasn't attached at his third pit stop, McLaren's race was compromised because Lewis Hamilton did not have enough fuel to finish competitively.

Normally you need around 150 kilos of fuel to do 52 racing laps of Silverstone. But with engine mapping changed for the wet start – less fuel was needed because they were not using it to blow the diffuser – and no real dry running in practice, the team strategists had to estimate the amount of fuel needed.

The opening 11 laps should have played into their hands because you use less fuel in the wet. Indeed many strategists took fuel out when they saw that the race start would be wet. But McLaren's estimate was wrong and Hamilton was forced to save fuel in the last 20 laps, which cost him a podium place to Webber and almost cost him another to Massa.

This is one of the big challenges for race strategists; they want the car to finish with the minimum amount of fuel, because any extra weight you carry for 52 laps slows you down. If you are too aggressive it loses you a lot of positions because you are forced to slow down at the end. If you put too much into the car, it will make you slower in the opening part of the race, but at least you won't lose positions from it.

We've seen very little of this in the last 12 months because teams don't feel underloading on fuel is a worthwhile risk. Starting tenth, McLaren were clearly over aggressive on Hamilton's strategy.

From back to front again for Alguersuari

This year we are seeing a phenomenon which we haven't seen before in F1 strategy: in six of the nine races so far, a driver who is eliminated in Q1 has been able to come through and score points. Alguersuari has now done it three races in a row from 18th place on the grid.

Toro Rosso's official word was that they were caught out by the rain at the end of Q1 and didn't get a lap in on soft tyres, but I've been told that they went for a hard tyre run only in order to save three sets of soft tyres for race day, a tactic that has worked for them in the past.

At any rate, Algersuari drove his customary long stints, taking advantage of the extra life and performance of new soft tyres to stop only twice and finish tenth.

Nico Rosberg and Sergio Perez were the highest placed two-stoppers in sixth and seventh places. The Sauber again showed itself as very gentle on the tyres and consistent.

The importance of the start in race strategy

We are seeing some trends in starts this year, which are making a difference to drivers' results. At Silverstone Nico Rosberg lost three places at the start and did well to finish in P6. Pastor Maldonado qualified a brilliant seventh and then lost three places on the start line. It's a worrying trend for the Venezuelan, who has lost 19 places in nine starts this season. Mark Webber, who lost the lead at the start to Vettel at Silverstone, also has a poor record, losing 12 places in nine starts this year.

German Grand Prix
Nürburgring, 24 July 2011, 60 laps

The German Grand Prix featured three drivers in different cars closely matched on performance. As the winner Lewis Hamilton observed, it was all about being perfect and not making mistakes and this was as true of the strategists and the pit crews as it was of the drivers.

In the end it came down to some inspired driving and finely balanced strategy calls. But further down the field we saw some varying strategies making a difference to the race result, particularly in the case of Adrian Sutil who finished sixth, ahead of the faster Mercedes cars.

The key consideration in deciding the strategy in Germany was the performance on the slower medium tyres. If you were getting a performance difference between the soft and medium tyres of around 1.5 seconds then two stops was the way to go. If the gap was larger then three stops would be the answer with a short final stint on the medium tyres.

Tyre life turned out to be better than expected in Friday practice, so for many teams two stops looked a good option. But heavy rain on Saturday night cleaned the track and that pushed some people towards three stops, believing that the track was very green.

In the Bridgestone days this condition would have led to tyre graining, but that didn't happen with the Pirellis in Germany. Instead, what happened was that the track had less grip so lap times were slower. This took less life out of the tyres as the green surface didn't damage them.

The three-way battle at the front
Bearing all this in mind, even the three-stoppers at the front ran almost a two-stop race in terms of stint lengths. Webber, for example, did 26 laps on his third set of soft tyres. They didn't want to put on the prime tyres, so they stopped as late as possible. Two cars pushed it to the extreme – Vettel and Massa – who pitted for medium tyres on the penultimate lap.

Among the leading trio Webber, who lost the lead to Hamilton at the start, was able to undercut Hamilton at the first stop by pitting first on lap 14. Webber was 0.5 seconds behind Hamilton when he made the stop. A very fast turnaround by the Red Bull crew, plus two very aggressive out-laps by Webber got him into the lead. He pushed hard to open a gap but Hamilton was faster in sectors one and three and Webber knew then that it wasn't going to be his day.

Having pushed his tyres too hard early on, Webber's pace wasn't good at the end of the second stint. He tried the undercut again, but it didn't work out.

Hamilton and Alonso, on option tyres that were two laps younger, were able to increase their pace when Webber pitted. Webber's second stop was 0.8 seconds slower than his first stop, and the end result was that he was down to third.

As for Hamilton and Alonso, they came in together for the first stop but Hamilton pitted a lap earlier second time around. Alonso's in-lap was 0.7 seconds faster than Hamilton's and the pit stop was 0.4 seconds faster. What was interesting was that Hamilton's out-lap on fresher tyres hadn't been significantly faster than Alonso's on worn tyres, which again defied the principle of the early stopper having the advantage.

Alonso came out of the pits in front but the Ferrari's weakness in not warming the tyres up straight away meant Hamilton was able to pass him in Turn 2. So the strategy had worked for Ferrari on paper, but not in reality.

Webber had managed the undercut at the first stop but stopping first didn't work for either Webber or Hamilton at the second stop. This can partly be explained by the damage the extra fuel weight does to the tyres in the first stint, which diminishes by the time of the second stop, and by the durability of the Pirelli soft tyres.

As for the timing of the final stop to the slower medium tyres, that was all about looking for evidence. Maldonado had gone to the mediums early on lap 35 but his lap times were inconsistent. However, when Petrov went to mediums on lap 46 and started setting personal best sector times on his second lap on the tyres, and Kobayashi went faster than his teammate who was still on old soft tyres, it was clear to McLaren that the time had come to take the medium tyres.

Webber was out of the picture by now, 8 seconds behind second place Alonso. McLaren pitted Hamilton on lap 51, but Ferrari did not react, leaving Alonso out for two more laps. Ferrari was more concerned about its pace on the harder tyres. Hamilton's pace was good straight away on the mediums and the race was in the bag. Webber tried to stay out longer and jump them but he was coming from too far back and he couldn't get close.

Sutil vs Rosberg
One of the highlights of the race was the performance of Adrian Sutil in the Force India. He put together a perfect weekend, finishing in sixth place,

ahead of both Mercedes and Renaults. He qualified eighth, two places and 0.8 seconds behind Nico Rosberg's Mercedes. To beat him from there is quite an achievement.

Sutil vs Rosberg was a good example of two stops working out better than three. Force India were one of the teams for whom the simulator said that two stops was as fast as three. With one less stop to make there was less risk of losing time in traffic or with a poor stop.

Sutil stopped on laps 22 and 48; Rosberg on laps 14, 36 and 53. Their lap times were pretty similar in the first stint, but thereafter Sutil had the measure of him. The Mercedes is heavier on its tyres and Sutil closed the gap to Rosberg from 4 seconds down to nothing by the time Rosberg made the first of his three stops. The Mercedes is a faster car, as was proven in qualifying, but their hands were tied by the heavy tyre use and Force India were able to beat them with 10 seconds to spare at the end.

Sutil was very impressive all weekend and he managed to find good consistency from the medium tyres. He was straight onto the pace after he went to mediums and set his fastest lap of the race when they were nine laps old. Many teams found it hard to get temperature into the medium tyres in the cool conditions.

Getting the fuel load right

The possibility of rain on race day had quite an influence on fuel strategy in this race. A lot of people under-fuelled their cars in the belief that it would rain and that forced a lot of people to save fuel late in the race. That's why Alonso eventually finished 4 seconds behind Hamilton, before running out of fuel on the slow-down lap.

After making that mistake and under-fuelling Hamilton at Silverstone, McLaren didn't make the same mistake again.

Hungarian Grand Prix
Hungaroring, 31 July 2011, 70 laps

The Hungarian Grand Prix was a fantastic race, again very close between the top four cars, any one of which could have won it. The closeness of competition and changeable conditions made it another race where strategy was the decisive element.

The winner put together the right combination of decisions, based on the data assembled in practice, and a judgement when a sudden shower fell late in the race not to pit for intermediate tyres but to wait it out. Meanwhile, several drivers saw their races compromised by poor strategy calls and we had three midfield runners in the points, all as a result of good strategy.

Rain had been forecast for Sunday morning but not for the race. There was a lot of doubt among teams about the forecasts.

Overtaking wasn't easy – it never is in Budapest – but the conditions helped in this race. There was much less of a headwind on the pit straight during the race than there had been during qualifying, which is why the DRS zone wasn't particularly successful: a lot of people were hitting the rev limiter without the wind to slow them as it had on Saturday. Another reason why the DRS didn't produce lots of overtaking was down to the relatively short length of the straight and consequent amount of wing run on the cars. They never reached terminal velocity before the braking point.

Let's take a close look at how the decisions were made.

Button makes the right calls

Of Jenson Button's 11 Grand Prix victories, six have come in mixed conditions such as we had on Sunday. A combination of experience, smoothness at the wheel and judgement of grip level are central to this. Button started the race on intermediates, as did everyone else, then switched to supersoft tyres on lap 11.

Webber, Massa and Barrichello had come in on lap 10 and Webber set fastest sector times straight away; all the right signals were there. However, Massa was incredibly tentative on dry tyres on a wet track, struggling to get them up to temperature. Button, in third place, reacted and pitted on lap 11, Alonso didn't. And neither did the leader Hamilton, nor P3 Vettel and P5 Rosberg. They waited until lap 12 to change over. All of them except Hamilton, who had had a 5-second lead, lost time and positions as a result: Button got ahead of Vettel for P2, while Webber got ahead of Alonso and Rosberg into P4.

The supersoft tyres didn't last long. Pre-race predictions were that they would be good for 20 laps, but the reality was more like 15 or 16 – less in

Hamilton's case. He had a new set he had saved in qualifying and pushed very hard on them to open up a 9-second lead on Button. But after 14 laps he had to pit again, Button stopped a lap later, and they remained about 6 seconds apart. The decisive moment came when Hamilton went for another set of supersofts on lap 40. There was no way he'd be able to reach the finish on them. Button went for soft tyres on lap 42, knowing that they would make the finish.

Here's how their decisions were reached: the used supersofts were 0.8 seconds faster per lap than the new soft tyres, so Hamilton's tactic was to open a lead of over 18 seconds in order to pit again and retain the lead. He should have easily done this with a 15-lap stint, but in fact Button was as fast, if not faster on the softs. On lap 47, as light rain began to fall, Hamilton spun, losing the lead to Button. Now behind his teammate and on the wrong tyres, he was caught between a rock and a hard place. Vettel, who was also on soft tyres to the finish, was going to jump him at his pit stop and so was Webber.

Although Hamilton attacked Button and got ahead, he needed a game changing move, which is what the intermediate tyres might have been when he took them on lap 52 as the rain persisted. But it turned out to be the wrong call. Although the lap times went off by 11 seconds, keeping a calm head was vital as the shower died away and within three laps the times were back to normal. The drivers on intermediates had to stop again for dry tyres. Button, Vettel and Alonso did not take the intermediates and stayed ahead of Hamilton, Webber did take them and stayed behind.

Though the decision on intermediate tyres was important to the outcome, it wasn't decisive. The soft tyre decision earlier was the decisive one.

Alonso did many of the same things as Hamilton. Judging by the lengths of his stints, he planned to make four stops, especially after losing time behind Rosberg early on. He was jumped by Webber on the switch from intermediates to slicks because he stayed out too long. His first dry stint on supersofts was 13 laps, second stint 11 laps, third stint 11 laps and fourth stint on softs was 23 laps. He jumped ahead of Webber at the third stop by pitting three laps earlier and he didn't make the mistake of going for the intermediates on lap 50 and so got ahead of Hamilton. It was a good recovery from a messy first half of the race.

The two Toro Rosso drivers had strong results: Sebastien Buemi went from 23rd to 8th, while Jamie Alguersuari got points for the fourth time in five races, by again running a long middle stint on the harder tyres and doing one less stop than the others. This tactic has been so successful for them and Sauber this year it's surprising more midfield teams haven't tried it. But being kind on the tyres is a pre-requisite.

Breakthrough result for Paul di Resta

Paul di Resta got his best F1 finish to date with seventh place, a breakthrough result in many ways. His engineers were amazed at his composure and authority in the tensest moments of the race, such as when it rained on lap 50. It was his call not to pit for intermediates at that point. Di Resta has struggled for results since the early races, but this one will have made other teams sit up and take notice. It was not the drive of a rookie.

It's interesting to look at his race strategy because it exactly matches Button's. Di Resta started on the supersoft tyres, albeit his were new because he didn't get into Q3 and so he had a spare set. Button stopped on lap 27 for another used set of supersofts and Di Resta did the same. On lap 42 Button went for a new set of softs and Di Resta followed suit. There is no suggestion here that he was copying Button, it's just a coincidence. But it's interesting because the two slick tyre choices were based on their data from Friday practice where they got good life and good pace from the soft tyres. It was clear that they would do up to 30 laps on a lighter car close to the end of the race.

Di Resta was racing Rosberg, who had gone for the soft tyres in the second stint. But the Mercedes driver's decision to pit for intermediates decided it in Di Resta's favour. It was the second race in a row that Force India has finished ahead of Mercedes. While it was the seventh time in 11 races that Rosberg has finished lower than his start position.

As a side note, given that Button has now won six of his 11 races in these conditions in recent years, it's probably not a bad idea to copy him – he doesn't often get it wrong!

Belgian Grand Prix
Spa Francorchamps, 28 August 2011, 44 laps

The Belgian Grand Prix saw the top four finishers using four different strategies. Most of the practice was run in wet conditions, so no one had any tyre data. This meant that race day was a voyage into the unknown for both drivers and strategists as they struggled with a number of questions: such as how long the soft tyres would last and how much slower per lap would the medium tyres be than the softs?

What was known after qualifying, as a result of most drivers doing up to six laps in Q3, was that the soft front tyres were blistering, even on low fuel. This meant that several drivers, including both Red Bull drivers, were faced with having to make a pit stop very soon after the start of the race to get rid of their damaged qualifying tyres. How they managed that and the decisions they made about how to run the race from there dictated the outcome, and it's fascinating to look in depth at what happened.

Vettel: Risk, opportunity and reward

Sebastian Vettel started from pole, briefly lost the lead to Rosberg, then regained it. It was a good decision to stop early, on lap 5. It's never easy to make such an early stop when you are pulling away, but the tyres didn't have much more in them (having already done six laps in qualifying and now five in the race). By coming in on lap 5 and rejoining in seventh place, just ten seconds behind the leader, Vettel was now on fresh tyres while all his rivals were still on their old qualifying rubber. His pace during this seven-lap stint is what set up the victory for him.

It effectively gave him a free pit stop when the safety car came out on lap 13, because he had built a sufficient margin that he could pit and only lose track position to Alonso. From there he could manage the race, dividing the remaining 20 laps into roughly equal stints on the softs and then finally on the mediums. By the time he took the medium tyres on lap 30, the team already had a lot of data about them from Mark Webber's car, the Australian having done most of the race on them.

So, Vettel's strategy was all about coping with risk initially, being bold and stopping early, then taking the opportunity of the safety car – from there on he had track position and it was just about managing the tyres.

Did Ferrari make a mistake not pitting Alonso under the safety car?

Fernando Alonso was with Vettel for most of the race, but ended up off the podium in fourth place. Many fans have suggested that Ferrari's strategy was flawed, but it wasn't. They made the right decision to leave him out under the safety car as it maintained track position ahead of the Red Bull and this gave Ferrari and Alonso a shot at the win. Even though Alonso had tyres that were five laps older than Vettel's, he was better off staying out because:

a) Ferrari's tyre wear was good and

b) a stop under the safety car would have dropped him behind Webber.

With Webber on medium tyres, and slower than Alonso after the restart, this would have resulted in Alonso being even further behind Vettel prior to making his last pit stop.

The only thing that Ferrari might have done differently is to spend fewer laps on the medium tyres which may have given Button less of an opportunity to close the gap. But they were trying to do one less stop than Vettel, and Alonso probably needed fresh rubber when he pitted for mediums after 21 laps on his soft tyres. This season with the Pirellis you are constrained into windows in which you have to change tyres simply because of the tyres going off.

Alonso's lap times on the medium tyres remained consistent so it is debatable whether the extra laps on the mediums cost him the position to Button. Most likely he would have lost it either way.

Whatever decision Ferrari made at the safety car moment, Alonso would ultimately have lost out to Webber, either by failing behind under the safety car and then not having the pace advantage to re-pass, or by staying out as they did.

Making good tactical use of the slower medium tyres

Going into the race the talking point was the blistering on the soft tyres, which risked failure if the tyres were pushed for too long on a car heavy with fuel. Mark Webber clearly felt that he couldn't be competitive using the soft tyres and opted to run mainly on the medium tyres, which hurt his ultimate pace but got him a second place.

Many teams seem confident that once they had got rid of the first set of soft tyres, they would be able to manage the blistering issue on the second set. They didn't have much information about how the tyres would behave at Spa, although they do generally have a very good knowledge of the tyres, having raced them at every event this year. There was also a reluctance on most people's account to use the medium tyres because they believed them to be 1.5 seconds or more slower than the softs.

The teams who didn't qualify in the top ten didn't get to run slick tyres in qualifying and so had no idea what would happen with blistering on their cars. It's important to recognise that blistering doesn't harm lap time particularly, it is not the same as degradation. The problem is vibration and ultimately if pushed too hard, there is the risk of a failure.

Michael Schumacher and Jenson Button did the same three-stop strategy: a short early stint to get the slower medium tyres out of the way, pit early and then divide the rest of the race into three flat-out stints on soft tyres. Both drivers were starting out of position: Schumacher 24th after a crash in qualifying and Button 13th after a bad strategy call saw him sitting in the pits in Q2 when the track was at its fastest.

Both came through the field brilliantly, using strategy as well as car and driver pace. Button finished third and Schumacher fifth, ahead of his teammate Rosberg, who qualified fifth. When both made their final stops around laps 30 and 31 Schumacher was just 5 seconds behind Rosberg. But crucially he was now on new soft tyres and Rosberg on the slower medium tyres.

It would not have been possible without the safety car on lap 13, as Schumacher was 20 seconds off the lead at that stage and Button 21 behind. The safety car took away that time gap and made a comeback possible. Also the track allows it; not only is Spa a good track for overtaking, but with the adjustable DRS rear wing, a fast car and new soft tyres, passing was very easy on the Kemmel Straight. This was all factored into Button's and Schumacher's strategies.

The way Button, in particular, came through the field from 13th place after the safety car restart was very impressive. He went through Perez, Petrov,

Sutil, Massa and Rosberg and then bridged the gap to the leading trio. However, it was a consolation prize; Button believed that he had the car to challenge for pole position and the race win in Spa, but that strategy mistake in qualifying cost him that chance and gave Vettel one less rival to deal with. Button saw this race as an opportunity for him to beat Vettel because there was so much variation on strategy, but he knew it was crucial to start alongside him on the front row.

Italian Grand Prix
Monza, 11 September 2011, 53 laps

Sunday's Italian Grand Prix was one of the best races of the season from the point of view of wheel-to-wheel combat and, because of the unique nature of the Monza circuit, it also featured some fascinating decision-making by teams on race strategy, not just in terms of tyre strategy and pit stops, but also in terms of how to set up the cars, particularly wing level and gearing.

With top speeds reaching 220 mph, one of the key decisions was how to balance the use of the DRS wing (which gives a 3.5–4 mph speed boost) while not hitting the rev limiter, which is set at 18,000 rpm. How teams like Red Bull, McLaren and Mercedes, in particular, chose to tackle this had a huge bearing on the outcome of the race.

The battles at the front
It was widely known after qualifying that Sebastian Vettel had chosen to use a shorter top gear than his rivals. This gave him the advantage of a smoother acceleration out of corners like Lesmo and Parabolica, even if he was sacrificing top speed. It also allowed him to use the DRS exactly how he wanted. Vettel was clocked at just 203 mph, the slowest of any driver and 13.5 mph off the fastest, but as he was on pole by half a second the tactic worked.

It would have made him vulnerable if he had lost track position in the race, as he would not have the top speed to overtake on the straights. When he fell behind Alonso at the start, he had to make a very bold move in the Curva Grande to pass him for the lead. But he was then able to use his pace advantage to break the tow and pull away.

Meanwhile, McLaren thought that they'd got the balance right, but hadn't counted on finding themselves behind Michael Schumacher, who had his car set for high top speed and proved very hard to pass after another fantastic start put him at the front.

Schumacher qualified eighth, but was running third after the first corner only dropping back behind Hamilton by the end of the lap. The safety car was deployed for the accident in Turn 1 and, at the restart, Hamilton wasn't sharp and Schumacher re-passed him, staying ahead for the whole of the first stint. Mercedes pitted him on lap 16, putting him on the new set of softs that the team had saved in qualifying by doing only one run in Q3. Hamilton stayed out for two more laps to try to build a gap. His stop was 0.7 seconds faster than Mercedes, but Mercedes tyre planning for the race paid off and on new tyres Schumacher was fast enough to stay ahead of Hamilton. Mercedes top speed without the DRS was equal to the McLaren's top speed with it, so Hamilton couldn't get ahead.

After a warning from Race Control about blocking, in the end Schumacher lost the place by making a late upshift when the engine was on the limiter, this lost momentum and allowed Hamilton to pass.

In the battle for second place between Button and Alonso, the Spanish driver had good pace on the soft tyres, but once again the Ferrari's weakness on the first laps on the medium tyres cost him a position. Button came in on lap 33 and his out-lap was 1.5 seconds faster than Alonso's when he pitted a lap later. Button passed him on that lap. Button's second lap on the tyre was a 1m 28.0, while Alonso's was a 1m 29.3. This has now cost Alonso important positions in three races, including Germany, where he lost the lead to Hamilton in similar fashion to the way Button took him at Monza. Ferrari acknowledges it is a weakness they must address for 2012, as it holds them back strategically.

Mercedes thinking differently

Another important reason why Schumacher was able to compete at Monza was that the soft Pirelli tyres turned out to be more durable than expected. The blistering was not as bad as at Spa, due to strict camber levels imposed by Pirelli and enforced by the FIA. And the degradation was not as bad as in Friday practice because the track improved. Mercedes have struggled this season with wearing out the soft tyres more quickly than their rivals, but Schumacher was able to do 21 laps on his second set of softs.

Knowing that they didn't have the speed to do better than seventh and eighth in qualifying, Mercedes strategists had been focusing on the plan for the race. To this end Rosberg had qualified on medium tyres, which meant that he fell behind Petrov and Schumacher, whom he would normally outqualify. The thinking behind Rosberg's strategy was to avoid starting the race on blistered soft tyres, to run a long opening stint and then two fast stints on new soft tyres. Part of this was due to the fact that Mercedes had high degradation on the softs on Friday and also because the difference in lap time between the softs and the mediums wasn't as great as at Spa. Here it was more like 0.7 seconds to 1.2 seconds, with Mercedes and Red Bull on the lower end of that.

Sadly, we never got to see what Rosberg might have achieved as he was eliminated in the first corner accident. But it is worth noting that as the durability of the soft tyres was better than expected on race day, Rosberg's rivals were easily able to do the race in only two stops, so it's unlikely that he would have finished higher than Schumacher did in fifth place.

Strategy brings midfielders strong results

Rosberg's decision to start on mediums was not unique as it caused a ripple effect. Senna did not set a time in Q3 so he could have the choice of which tyres to start on and, because he was behind Rosberg on the grid he went for mediums, reasoning that there was no point being on the faster tyres if Rosberg, also on mediums, was going to be slower ahead of him in the opening stint. He lost five places in the opening lap chaos and pitted under the safety car on lap 2 for soft tyres and did a three-stop strategy from there. Arguably, he would have been better to stick with the original plan to run mediums and stop twice. It might have left him closer to Alguersuari in the middle stint.

But the Spaniard had great pace in that second stint, which set him up for his career best seventh place. His start was good, coming from 18th to 11th and, because he had been eliminated in Q1, he had new tyres for the whole race. The Toro Rosso is very kind to its tyres, like the Sauber, and the general pattern seems to be that they qualify poorly but race well. In previous years with durable Bridgestone tyres this would have led to no points, but they've played the Pirelli card very well.

Alguersuari's result makes it seven consecutive races – and nine in total out of 13 – in which a driver eliminated in Q1 scores points. It's all down to strategy and this has been one of the most refreshing aspects of the 2011 season.

Behind Rosberg and Senna, several drivers outside the top ten (and therefore able to choose their starting tyre), went for medium tyres too. These included both Saubers and Sutil, their target being to do the race in one stop only. Again, regretfully, all three retired so we never got to see what they might have done.

Perez was looking very good though. He made up seven places at the start to tenth and was running eighth in the opening stint, with Alguersuari. He was in a very good position with good pace on the medium tyres. When the Spaniard pitted on lap 20, Perez could have switched to a two-stopper and come home just ahead of him in P7. But sadly the gearbox failed and he retired. This proved significant in the championship as it allowed Di Resta to score four points and move Force India into sixth place in the constructors' championship, ahead of Sauber.

Singapore Grand Prix
Marina Bay, 26 September 2011, 61 laps

Strategy wise, this race didn't turn out as expected. The key consideration for the strategists on Sunday was thermal degradation of the tyres, especially the rears. This was due to the surface temperature of the tyres being very high, due to braking, traction and very heavy fuel loads at the start. With Singapore being a high fuel consumption track, cars were over 10 kilos heavier at the start than for the average F1 race.

Before the race, the talk was of three-stop strategies at the front and so it proved for the leading four cars. But the way they did it was unforseen and had the safety car stayed out a little longer than four laps, we might have seen some strategists switching to a two-stop. There was, however, one driver who made a two-stop work and he set an example early on, which led all the leading teams to react and copy him.

Di Resta and Force India get it spot on

As the tyre covers came off the cars on the grid, tenth placed Paul di Resta's car caught the eye immediately. He and his team had opted for the soft tyres, while all the other top ten cars were starting on supersofts, including his teammate Adrian Sutil (ninth) and Mercedes' Michael Schumacher (eighth), both of whom had the choice of what compound to start on because they didn't set a lap in the Q3 session. This race strategy was planned on Saturday before qualifying even started.

Force India had realised in practice that they had good race pace and hints that they might even be faster than Mercedes over the race distance, even if they were half a second slower in Q2. They had noticed that Mercedes were struggling with tyre degradation, as they have for most of the season, and reasoned that by starting on the harder tyres they would be able to do one less stop than the Mercedes. They also had an inkling that the difference between the softs and the supersofts might turn out to be less than others imagined. This thought turned out to be the key to their race.

With this strategy in mind they opted not to run in Q3 and then run a longer first stint on a new set of soft tyres in the race. Meanwhile the cars he was racing against: Sutil, Schumacher and Rosberg, all started on used super-softs. Sutil had to do so because he had used two sets of supersofts in Q2. This proved to be a problem for him in the race, as he couldn't quite go long enough on the used set in the opening stint. The Mercedes, meanwhile, was also slightly limited by having a smaller fuel tank, so would not be able to use the blown diffuser to best effect as that consumes a lot more fuel.

Rosberg had to pit early on lap 9 and Sutil on lap 11, while Di Resta went to lap 19. But what had been apparent to Force India was now apparent to everyone else; that they could keep a good pace on the soft tyres relative to the supersofts. So Vettel, Button, Webber and Alonso all put new soft tyres on at their first stop, not what Pirelli had predicted at all. Instead they were all reacting to what Di Resta was showing them.

In the opening laps Sutil was faster, but by lap six Di Resta was matching and beating his lap times. As the supersofts suffered thermal degradation with the heavy fuel loads, especially the rears, it was clear that Di Resta was on the best tyres.

The Force India cars got ahead of Rosberg when the Mercedes driver had to make his second stop on lap 22. Then, on supersoft tyres that were eight laps younger than Sutil's softs, Di Resta passed Sutil on lap 26, crucially before the safety car came out for Schumacher's accident. Both Force India cars pitted under the safety car, as did Rosberg, but the team had to hold Sutil as Perez was coming in and this lost him 4 seconds and a place to Rosberg. With all three now on new soft tyres, Di Resta drove away from the other two in the long final stint to record a career-best sixth place. Looking back, it's surprising that more drivers didn't start on the softs. Only the Virgin drivers, Kobayashi and Petrov did it. Force India certainly thought Perez would do it, given his strategy choices this season.

The question arises, why did Schumacher not do the same strategy as Di Resta given that he had the choice? Unlike Di Resta, Schumacher had saved a new set of supersofts and he was clearly on a "fastest possible race" strategy of three consecutive stints on supersofts and then a final stint on softs. This "sprint" strategy called for him to push very hard and, as we saw, he pushed a little too hard, hitting Perez on lap 29 and triggering the safety car.

Who was helped by the safety car?

Wherever there is a safety car there are always winners and losers. Lewis Hamilton was helped by it as it allowed him to close up after losing so much time with an extra pit stop for a nose change and then a drive-through penalty. By lap 15 he had been in the pits three times.

It also helped the leaders because the slower traffic was a real problem and the safety car bunched everyone up at mid-distance, meaning the leaders had to make half the lapped traffic passes they would otherwise have had to make. Although it helped Button by cutting Vettel's lead of 18 seconds, the revised rules on lapped traffic meant that the German driver had Trulli, Liuzzi and Kobayashi between him and Button at the restart. By the time Button had cleared them all, Vettel was 10 seconds clear of him.

And to round out a day of "reactive strategy" in the final stages of the race, we saw the leading teams covering each other as they stopped for a set of supersoft tyres; so when third place Webber stopped on lap 47, second place Button covered him on lap 48 and then the leader Vettel covered him on lap 49.

Although he gave himself a shot at a podium with another fine start, Alonso was unable to do much on strategy, as the Ferrari was slow on both types of tyre, unlike Monaco and Hungary where it had been relatively competitive on the same tyres. Here the tyre degradation was worse for Ferrari than expected which pushed them into running only the opening stint on super-softs and then the other three stints on softs.

Japanese Grand Prix
Suzuka, 9 October 2011, 53 laps

The Japanese Grand Prix was all about race strategy. With tyre wear much more tricky to manage than expected, throughout the field the drivers who succeeded were the ones whose teams got the strategy right, not just on race day but in qualifying too.

There were some pretty contrasting races at the front. Of the top three, Sebastian Vettel's Red Bull had the worst tyre performance and Fernando Alonso's Ferrari had the best. Alonso was nowhere near as quick as Vettel at the start of each of the stints, but he was always the quickest of the leading cars at the end of the stints, with much less tyre drop off. This gave him the opportunity to take second place, despite only having the car pace to qualify fifth.

Meanwhile, the race winner Jenson Button had the pace to stay with Vettel early on and was able to manage his tyres better in the opening stint so that he could pit a lap later than the world champion and emerge in front of him. But it wasn't easy for him: as the McLaren has got quicker this year, its tyre performance has edged closer to that of Red Bull, as you would expect given that it's putting more load through the tyres.

Getting that little bit extra: Vettel vs Button and Alonso
The top three finishers all did exactly the same strategy with three stints on used soft tyres and a final stint on new mediums. The difference was in the tyre degradation each of them suffered and the laps on which they chose to pit.

I thought as the race unfolded that Red Bull were being conservative with Vettel – knowing he only needed a point to clinch the title – and that offered a chance to Button and Alonso, which both of them took. But closer analysis shows that this wasn't necessarily the case, given that in each stint he only pitted when the tyres started to drop off in performance. Often this season we have seen Red Bull pit first when arguably there has been some life left in the tyres, but they always had enough pace in hand to make early stops and retain track position. In Japan, Vettel couldn't get away with that.

There are two ways of looking at Vettel's strategy on Sunday: on the one hand he stopped early to try and maintain position, which could be considered conservative, but on the other hand being the first to stop was also quite aggressive because he risked running out of tyres late in the race. He went onto the mediums with 20 laps to go, while Button went three laps later and Alonso four laps later, thanks to superior tyre wear at the end of the stints on the softs. This is where he took second place from Vettel.

Vettel had a big gap at the end of his first stint (5.2 seconds) and he only pitted because his tyres were finished (lap 5: 1:39.7s; lap 6: 1:40.0s; lap 7: 1:41.2s; lap 8: 1:41.7s). At the end of the second stint, you can see that his tyres were finished again and he was actually very aggressive at the final pit stop because came out in traffic on the prime tyres. The newer tyres helped him, but Button had him covered all day.

How the safety car changed the midfield battle for points

As we have seen many times this season there was a tremendous scrap among the midfield runners for points positions behind the top three teams. It was always going to be this way at Suzuka with the high tyre wear, and the strategists started planning their race on Saturday before qualifying.

We saw Kobayashi, Schumacher, Senna and Petrov all make it into the top ten in qualifying, but they did not set a flying lap time in Q3. So they had, in the Renaults' case, two sets of new medium tyres and one set of new softs for the race and, in Schumacher and Kobayashi's case, one new set of each compound.

The key calculation here was the crossover point in lap time between the two tyres, and on the day the difference between the mediums and the softs was about 1.2 seconds per lap. Schumacher and Kobayashi started on used soft tyres, while the Renaults went with new mediums.

The two Force India cars, meanwhile, qualified outside the top ten and both started on used softs, while Sergio Perez was down in 17th on the grid and started on new mediums.

The safety car likelihood for this race was 60 per cent and we duly got one on lap 24. The drivers who benefited were Petrov and Perez because they'd started on the medium tyres and the safety car won them back the time they'd lost. They were 43 seconds off the lead and over 20 seconds behind Sutil when the Force India driver pitted, just two laps before the safety car was deployed.

The Force India drivers were on classic three-stop strategies and by lap 20 it was going well; they had three-quarters of a pit stop advantage over their rivals. But the gap went down to zero under the safety car and Perez and Petrov had gained track positions with the Force India stops. Even with DRS it's difficult to overtake at Suzuka. Petrov and Perez were on new sets of options at the end of the race too, while Sutil was on the prime tyres so there was no chance to recover.

As for the two Mercedes cars, Rosberg started 23rd after a hydraulic problem in qualifying. He started on new medium tyres and ended up in 12th place, right behind Sutil's Force India after the safety car. He was essentially on the same pit stop sequence as Force India, but the safety car closed the gap and, with the advantage of using the option tyres at the end of the race, he was able to get ahead and claim a point in tenth place.

Schumacher, meanwhile, ran a pretty standard three-stop race with stops on laps 9, 24 and 41. Interestingly he did a 15-lap second stint on used soft tyres, which revealed that he had better tyre life than the Red Bulls and Hamilton, which hasn't always been the case with Mercedes this year. He was 25 seconds behind the leaders when the safety car came out, so that handed him the chance to close up. A nice long, consistent 17-lap stint on new soft tyres after the safety car brought him out ahead of Massa and underlined once again that the veteran is back on top form in terms of race pace as we get towards the end of his second comeback season. His races have also noticeably improved since Jock Clear, his old rival from Villeneuve/Williams days, became his race engineer.

What happened to Lewis Hamilton?

This was an odd race for Hamilton as he squandered a chance to start on pole because of a collective team and driver timing mistake in qualifying. Then, in the race, he was well off his teammate Button's pace.

A slow puncture at the end of the first stint undoubtedly lost him time (lap 5: 1:40.1s; lap 6: 1:40.8s; lap 7: 1:41.9s) and positions to Alonso and Button. And McLaren have said that it also affected the rest of his race because they made a set up change to the car before realising that it had been handling strangely due to a puncture. They say the changes gave him an imbalance.

Hamilton's second stint was really poor – much worse than the others. He was right with Alonso and Button on lap 12, but by the time he made his stop on lap 20 he had dropped 8 seconds, a second a lap in other words.

Hamilton got a place back, from Massa, by making an earlier pit stop and then exploiting the Ferrari's problems with initial warm up on the mediums to pass the Brazilian on his out-lap. Hamilton's pace was better on the medium tyres, but he lost too much time in the opening two stints to get a decent result.

Wear rates were pretty marginal on the soft tyres, but as always, it was the same for everyone. The puncture didn't help, but it seems that Hamilton also suffered a bit more than the other front-runners. When the tyres are going away it's frustrating for a driver. It's a vicious circle: he's trying to push, but he ends up going slower.

Korean Grand Prix
Yeongam Circuit, 16 October 2011, 55 laps

The Korean Grand Prix threw up many talking points on the matter of strategy, with lots of questions from fans about whether Mark Webber could have won the race if he hadn't pitted at the same time as Lewis Hamilton, and whether Fernando Alonso could have got on the podium if he had got passed Felipe Massa as he had in Suzuka. Hopefully, the answers are all here.

This was one of those races where strategy was always going to be decisive, but where it was vital to be flexible and adaptable. As soon as Pirelli announced its very aggressive tyre choice for the weekend, bringing the two softest compounds to a track with quite a few high-energy corners, all the strategy engineers realised that they were up against it. Throw in rain all day Friday, meaning that there was almost no data on tyre wear on long runs, and there really was a lot of thinking to be done.

Pirelli brought the soft/supersoft compound pairing (usually used on slow street circuits) because they were worried about the graining evident on the Bridgestones last year. The soft tyres this weekend were between 0.8 and 1 second per lap slower than the supersofts.

There were several tactics at play in qualifying with Red Bull saving sets of soft tyres for the race, while Ferrari and McLaren prioritised saving super-softs.

In the race the supersofts turned out to be far more durable than expected and pre-race predictions of three or four stops were revised after the start as strategists and drivers were thinking on their feet. A safety car one third of the way through the race – one of several occurring this year at a critical juncture of the race, after the first pit stops – again changed the game for several drivers. The four-lap safety car period (laps 16-20) helped to conserve tyres and 18 of the 21 finishers ended up doing two stops.

Vettel changes plans and still wins the race

After losing out to Lewis Hamilton in qualifying, Vettel knew he needed to pass the McLaren early in the first stint. He muscled his way past on the opening lap and was never really tested after that. He was able to use his car pace advantage to open a 1-second gap over Lewis Hamilton on the opening lap and that gap was out to 4.7 seconds by the time Hamilton pitted on lap 15.

Vettel had saved sets of soft tyres, thinking they would be the tyres of choice for the race. But having managed 16 laps on the used supersofts, the team switched plans and put him on the same tyres again for the second stint, this time lasting 18 laps. This took him to the window for putting on a set of softs and going to the finish on a two-stop plan, one less than pre-race predictions.

After the safety car appeared on lap 16, giving Vettel a "free" pit stop and fresher tyres, Hamilton had to turn his attention to Mark Webber behind, who was particularly quick on the prime tyres. Vettel cruised to victory; the winning margin over Hamilton was 12 seconds.

Could Webber have won the race if Red Bull hadn't pitted him with Hamilton?

One of the real talking points of this race was the decision by Red Bull to pit third place Mark Webber on the same lap as Lewis Hamilton (lap 33) when Webber, running on soft tyres, was faster than the Englishman on supersofts.

Why did Webber make his final pit stop on the same lap as Hamilton, when he'd radioed the team to say his primes were holding out OK? He was very frustrated after the race. "I think at the second stop we did the worst thing," he said. "We didn't stop before or stop after [Hamilton], we stopped on the same lap. That was disappointing as clearly we had some good pace to pull away from Lewis."

Webber had caught Hamilton who was due a stop. By lap 32, Hamilton's lap times had dropped off by a second a lap. Webber had been sitting behind him since lap 27 and, as the car behind, had the tactical advantage of being able to stop first without Hamilton being able to react and cover him. With Red Bull having the fastest pit work, it is likely that had Webber dived into the pits on lap 32 he would have undercut Hamilton as he had a car pace advantage of 0.5 seconds over the McLaren, and his out-lap, on new soft tyres, was substantially faster than Hamilton's in-lap (lap 33) on used supersofts.

In contrast, staying out a lap longer would not have done the job, as Hamilton's new tyres would more than offset Webber's pace advantage.

As for passing Vettel in the undercut, Webber was quick to point out after the race that Vettel's lap times (lap 31: 1:42.433s; lap 32: 1:42.281s; lap 33: 1:42.044s) were still getting quicker at this stage of the race, so he would not have jumped his teammate. Red Bull cannot therefore be accused of trying to stop him from winning. However, they probably did lose him a second place by not stopping him before Hamilton.

Red Bull were cagey after the race (and keener to talk about the bigger picture of their constructors' championship success) but it's likely that the team thought that Webber had taken more out his tyres than Vettel, due to his scrapping with Hamilton. So they didn't think he'd lap significantly faster in clear air. It's also possible that, given their track record this season, Red Bull fancied their chances of winning a "pit stop race" with McLaren under pressure. Sadly for them that's one race they lost this time.

Could Alonso have finished second?

The Ferrari, with its experimental front wing, was slow in qualifying but Fernando Alonso was very fast on the soft tyres in the race. He spent the opening 34 laps stuck behind his teammate Felipe Massa, costing him about 0.5 seconds per lap if you compare their lap times from lap 38 when Fernando was in clear air having jumped Massa in the pit stops.

After making his second stop on lap 37, Alonso was 7 seconds behind Button, yet that gap was down to one second within ten laps. All the leading cars ran the same new soft tyres in the final stint and they all set similar lap times, though Alonso had exceptional pace.

It is very clear therefore that had Alonso been closer to Button at the second pit stops, he could have got the undercut and challenged Webber and Hamilton. His radio message, "I give up" at the end of the race, was a clear message to Ferrari's management.

Rosberg's heroic efforts fail to stave off Alguersuari

Nico Rosberg did a phenomenal job to do 28 laps – four more than anyone else – on the soft tyres for his final stint. It was a surprise to see any car – and particularly a Mercedes – last that long.

His opening stint was 13 laps on used supersofts. What wrecked his race was that he only did 14 laps – four of which were behind the safety car – on a new set of soft tyres for his second stint because he was forced to pit early after flat-spotting this new set while scrapping with Massa.

Although he kept soldiering on near the end, the tyres were finished and he was passed on the final lap by Jaime Alguersuari for seventh place.

One third distance safety cars becoming a trend

This year we have seen quite a few safety cars deployed at one-third race distance. These favour the drivers running the longer opening stints. The ones that started on the soft tyres and "going long" were Adrian Sutil, Pastor Maldonado and Sergio Perez, and they all benefited from the safety car. Jaime Alguersuari was running the supersoft tyres but hadn't stopped either, so his tyre performance and pace were very impressive and he also benefitted from the safety car.

Toro Rosso's low tyre wear and very high straight line speeds were the two biggest reasons why Alguersuari and Buemi finished in the points. They were first and second fastest through the speed trap (Buemi 199.2 mph; Alguersuari 199.1 mph), whereas Vettel was just 14th fastest (194.4 mph). They were also first and second fastest in sector 1 (Alguersuari 35.0s; Buemi 35.1s; Vettel 35.6s).

Buemi did the longest stint of anyone on the option tyres in the final stint. He pitted for options on lap 36 and his final lap of the race was 1.5 seconds slower than teammate Alguersuari on the primes.

Why did some drivers run out of fuel?
Rosberg and Alonso ran out of fuel on the slowdown lap in Korea, and Button had a similar problem at Suzuka. It begs the question why? Four laps behind the safety car at Yeongam should have given the teams ample opportunity to save fuel.

It appears that it's down to the teams being a lot more aggressive with their fuel tank sizes this year and the attraction of using aggressive engine modes at the start and re-starts.

Indian Grand Prix
Buddh International Circuit, 30 October 2011, 60 laps

Although this was not a thrilling race, it was an intriguing one, mainly because of the difference between the two types of tyres each driver had to use. Like many races this year, it didn't turn out the way pre-race expectations had predicted. In fact, it was quite a surprise.

At the front, Vettel always had something in hand over Button. Although the McLaren was closer at the start of each stint, the Red Bull had the raw pace to ease away each time into a 5-second cushion. This was a margin that Vettel seemed comfortable with, allowing him to lose a second to Button by stopping a lap later and giving him a couple of seconds to play with in case of a poor pit stop. Generally this season he's wanted to have a bigger cushion – more like 7 or 8 seconds – so the short cushion indicates that Button was pressing him. Immediately we can see that it wasn't as easy as it might have looked from the outside.

The thinking behind Vettel's gap management tactic is that he doesn't want to push too hard for fear of damaging the tyres. As the leader he needs to be the last to stop and so cover the cars behind. He does not want to put himself in a position where he has nothing left in the tyres.

With a performance gap between hard and soft tyres, the key as always was recognising the point at which a new set of hard tyres was quicker than a used set of softs.

Webber's hand forced on strategy calls

Mark Webber's race summed up his season in many ways. He lost a place at the start, then had worse tyre wear than his rivals, so was forced on to the back foot strategy wise.

Webber was battling for third place with Fernando Alonso, who got ahead of him at the second round of pit stops. Alonso said after the race that he was surprised that Webber stopped so early. Webber had a gap of around 2 seconds over the Ferrari on lap 35 when his tyres started to go off. On lap 36 he lost a second to Alonso.

Webber's middle stint was just 21 laps before his tyres started to go off, which is seven laps less than Vettel's in the same car. This has been his Achilles heel this season. Alonso pushed hard for two laps and then was able to pit and rejoin ahead of the Australian.

Webber's plight seems all the more strange given that the Pirelli tyres were far more durable this weekend than expected. Michael Schumacher did 32 laps on a set of softs in his middle stint (albeit they were a new set, with no qualifying laps on them).

With the benefit of hindsight, Pirelli could have brought the soft and supersoft tyres this weekend, but they didn't have any knowledge of the circuit. Also the temperatures could have been a lot higher, so it was probably best to play it safe.

Although he has had good pace at times, the story of Webber's season is that he's had poor starts, which have put him in traffic and this has hurt his tyres more. Without strong top speed he also finds it more difficult to pass. He has also lost the strategic freedom by having higher tyre wear, so he has to stop earlier each time.

How Schumacher beat Rosberg

This was another strong race for Michael Schumacher, who beat teammate Nico Rosberg for the third time in recent races where both have finished.

Schumacher started 11th on the grid, four places behind Rosberg, but again got an excellent start to run right behind him in eighth place. He pitted one lap later at the end of the first stint and put on a set of new soft tyres, while Rosberg's had done qualifying laps.

Schumacher's middle stint was what won it for him: he did 32 laps on that set, four laps more than Rosberg. When Rosberg switched to hard tyres on lap 45, he should have been faster than Schumacher on used softs for the five laps before he stopped. But Schumacher kept the pace up, lapping in the 1m 29s, while Rosberg didn't get the speed on the new tyres, so when Schumacher pitted on lap 50 he jumped his younger teammate.

The pair were told they could race, but Schumacher got the hard tyres up to speed more quickly than Rosberg and held him at bay. Mercedes were in a lonely race of their own, too slow to race the leaders, but faster than the midfield.

And it was again more evidence that Schumacher is back on form and ready to shine if Mercedes can build him a good car next year.

Di Resta – counter strategy doesn't work out this time

Although pre-race predictions suggested that the gap between the soft and hard tyres would mean that drivers would want to run the hard tyres as little as possible, it didn't turn out that way at all.

But that only became apparent after Paul di Resta, Vitaly Petrov and Sergio Perez, who started on the hard tyres, had pitted early to remove them. Di Resta pitted on lap 2 and was clearly hoping that the time he had lost by doing it this way would be made up by a safety car period at some stage of the race. We've had five recently. Also teams felt that with inexperienced marshals, who had taken a long time to clear debris during practice, race director Charlie Whiting wouldn't want to take any chances in the race if an incident needed clearing up. It didn't happen.

Di Resta was now committed to the soft tyres for the rest of the race. But instead of stopping just once more, as Perez and Petrov did, dividing the race in half, he was forced to stop twice more because he couldn't make the tyres last long enough.

Early evidence that the hard tyres were, in fact, pretty quick came from Rubens Barrichello in the Williams. After a collision at the start, he was forced onto the hard tyres on lap 1 and once in clean air his lap times were competitive. So Di Resta, Petrov and Perez could have run a more normal length first stint on them.

On the first lap Di Resta was 13th behind the Toro Rossos and, with a normal strategy would have finished behind them, along with Sutil. It's a big call to put yourself out of the game by pitting that early in the race in the hope of a safety car, especially when you are in a competitive position. Force India have a quick car which has scored points consistently and even beaten Mercedes a couple of times. But they were aware that in their championship battle with Toro Rosso, they couldn't afford to give away a lot of points, which they would if a safety car changed the game.

So they went for a gamble here, based on the premise that we've seen a spate of safety cars lately and this was a case of strategists trying to second-guess the race director. It was a gamble over a point, so not much was lost. Arguably, it was a risk worth taking.

Toro Rosso's massive strides

Alguersuari had another very strong run to eighth. The Toro Rosso again had low tyre wear, but the surprising thing in India was that he was able to drive away from Sutil's Force India car in the middle stint. Given that a few races ago Force India was beating Mercedes, it shows how far Toro Rosso has come.

Since Singapore their progress has been amazing. The combination of new front and rear wings, new floor and maximising the exhausts and engine maps has transformed the car.

Abu Dhabi Grand Prix
Yas Marina Circuit, 13 November 2011, 55 laps

This weekend's Abu Dhabi Grand Prix featured six different strategies in the top ten finishers. Pre-race predictions of two stops were the norm, but there was a wide variety of alternatives tried, with Mark Webber doing three stops en route to fourth place and Paul di Resta scoring points for ninth using a one-stop plan.

We also saw McLaren pull off something audacious at the first stop; they pitted Jenson Button on the same lap as the leader Lewis Hamilton, with only a 12-second window between them. Button's total time in the pits was a second slower than Hamilton's but it was a very brave thing to do and showed the team's confidence on the day.

All three podium finishers did the predictable strategy of running two stops with a longish middle stint of around 24 laps on soft tyres before a short final stint on the mediums. Ferrari tried to use the easier tyre use of the car with Alonso to stay out three laps longer than Hamilton and have a go at jumping him at the second stop, because they saw that the McLaren driver was losing time in traffic after his second stop.

It nearly worked. He was only 3 seconds behind when Hamilton pitted on lap 40 and did two very strong laps on worn tyres before pitting. He was about to catch the HRT of Ricciardo and didn't want to lose time, so pitting then when he had pretty much the right gap (21 seconds) over Hamilton made sense. Unfortunately for him, HRT called their stop at the same time and he was held up behind Ricciardo on the way into the pits and a slightly tardy change cost him the chance come out ahead.

But even if he had managed it, Hamilton would have probably passed him as the McLaren was superior to the Ferrari on medium tyres. This scenario is precisely what happened in Germany earlier this year. Though Ferrari must have felt that they had enough margin at that point to call Alonso in, as he still had good pace from his tyres.

Why did Webber change to three stops?

Mark Webber has done some racy strategies this season, mostly to get himself out of traffic, something his teammate Sebastian Vettel hasn't had to do much as he's usually been out at the front.

Webber started out planning to make two stops, like the podium finishers. He lost a position at the start to Alonso. However, with Vettel retiring he was racing Button for a podium until he had a very slow pit stop on lap 17, which cost him 6 seconds. It was an unusually messy stop for the Red Bull team, which tops the league table for quick stops this year along with Mercedes.

Although Button had KERS problems, the gap back to Webber was still significant after this. Webber was then racing Massa for fourth place. The Brazilian wasn't on great form in Abu Dhabi and it was well known that Ferrari were very wary of the medium tyres as they had struggled to get performance out of them in practice, as they have all year.

When Webber pitted again for soft tyres on lap 35, it was clear he had changed strategy. But it wasn't realistic to think that it would help him get at Button, as to do that would require him to have gained 31 seconds in 20 laps over the McLaren.

There have been suggestions from some in the team that he needed to stop to get off his second set of tyres, which wasn't working for him, but after passing and being re-passed by Massa he was sitting behind the Ferrari, and the switch allowed him to try something different to get ahead of the Ferrari. There was a big gap in the traffic for him to slot into and use the pace of a fresh set of tyres.

It worked, but even if he had stayed behind Massa and done a conventional two-stop, he would have easily passed him anyway once they both went onto the medium tyres, because the Ferrari was so slow on them. Massa made life easier for Webber with a spin and by being slow generally.

Massa was lucky that the gap between the Ferrari and the Mercedes was as big as it was, because it meant that despite being 0.6 seconds slower than Alonso he would still finish in fifth or sixth place.

How to win the midfield battle

Many fans have wondered why Force India, having qualified both cars strongly in the top ten, put Paul Di Resta on a one-stop strategy. Di Resta ended up at least where he would have been – ninth behind Adrian Sutil – but the strategy didn't give him a chance to challenge his teammate. The mediums were slower than they needed to be on race day to make a one-stop work.

If you analyse the decision making here, you can see why they did it. Force India's plan was to put one driver on the one-stop plan and the other on a two-stop. Locked in a battle with Sauber and Toro Rosso over sixth place in the championship, which is worth many millions of dollars to them, they were more or less forced to cover off the possibility of their rivals putting one driver on a one-stop strategy and hitting the jackpot if there was a safety car, as we saw last year in Abu Dhabi.

The data showed a 50 per cent chance of a safety car and if one of their rivals had managed to get a free pit stop and been able to run most of the race on the faster tyres, they could have cut into Force India's points lead. This had to be covered off.

The midfield teams race in a different way from the top teams: firstly because the leaders are constrained by starting the race on their qualifying tyres, and secondly they don't take risks because they have the car perform-ance to help them.

There is a significant gap between the top three and Mercedes and then between Mercedes and the midfield, and this gives them a margin for error. They would never gamble on a one-stop in case the medium tyres don't perform; for the midfield it's all about gaining track position and gambles often pay off as we've seen this year.

So it was a smart move by Force India's Dom Harlow and his team. Having qualified strongly, Di Resta's plan cut the midfield pack off from Sutil – by the time the German stopped on lap 15 he had a 15-second lead over the nearest midfield challenger. And if there had been a safety car Di Resta would have been the first car on the road to benefit from it. This is a great example of the depth of strategic thinking that goes into planning a race.

Brazilian Grand Prix
Interlagos, 27 November 2011, 71 laps

The Brazilian Grand Prix brought to an end a season that has seen Formula 1 run to a quite different pattern in terms of race strategy. This is largely due to the Pirelli tyres, but also because the DRS wing has made it easier for cars to overtake.

Although it has felt like a year of change, if you analyse the top six or eight starting positions compared to the finish positions, the amount of variation compared to last year isn't that much: Vettel and Webber normally finish more or less where they start as do the McLarens, Alonso usually makes up a place or two, Schumacher qualifies a bit behind but races though to finish where he should have qualified.

However, though the outcomes haven't changed much they way the races have played out has been fascinating. With more overtaking and better use of strategy, races have become more engaging for spectators.

Last year everyone ran on the same strategy, in pace order for most of the race. This year that has all changed: cars have risen and fallen in position, and this shuffling in the order has created battles within the races, such as the Massa/Hamilton or the Alonso/Webber scraps we've enjoyed this year.

If the leading four teams were closer to each other on pace, as the midfield runners are, it would make for some really interesting races. The midfield battle has been really exciting this year with race strategy used to make significant gains. We've seen Toro Rosso and Sauber in particular finish well ahead of where they have qualified. Force India have also scored a lot of points from qualifying positions on the fringes of the top ten.

There has been a difference this year in the way the teams have used their tyres. However, Pirelli has failed to find a crossover point between the softer and the harder tyres which offers a range of options as to how to run the race, either taking the longer run on the harder tyres or the shorter run on the faster tyres. "What you need is the softer tyres, the supersoft and the soft, to be fast but degrade," says Paul Hembery. "The medium and harder tyres need to be slower but more stable, and basically you have to work out how many laps you go before you are better off being on the other ones."

It's very important that Pirelli achieves this next year otherwise strategies could become a bit generic.

Two stops versus three in Brazil
Today the teams at the front generally decided to run a three-stop strategy, dividing the race into three stints of roughly 20 laps on soft tyres and then a short stint on the slower medium tyres.

Jenson Button did three stops but approached it differently, as we shall examine later. Several of the midfield teams thought that two stops would be possible and a couple of them pulled it off, with Di Resta and Kobayashi scoring points with that plan.

The medium tyres had shown themselves to be around 0.8 seconds a lap slower than the softs in practice and qualifying, but in a race stint it was down to more like 0.5 seconds for most teams, apart from Ferrari who really struggled for pace on them again.

Button was pushed into running two stints on the medium tyres because his third set of softs had proved to be not very good on Saturday. When Button went onto the medium tyres on lap 31, he was at the same pace as Alonso on softs. Button did a 1m 16.9 on lap 3 which looked good and he then ran in the 1m 17s.

The one variation among the top teams was Felipe Massa, who did a two-stop strategy. It was surprising that he hasn't done this more often this season, because running in sixth place as he usually is – the slowest of the top six drivers – he generally has no pressure from behind and if he does the same plan as the McLarens and Alonso in front of him, he'll stay sixth.

Here, the Ferrari strategists decided to try it and it did allow him to take track position over the McLarens for a while, so on that level it worked for them and was worth a try. There is a 71 per cent chance of a safety car at Interlagos and if one had come today it would have played into his hands, as would the rain that was forecast, but which never came.

Rosberg vs Sutil

Force India's Adrian Sutil did a fantastic job to beat the Mercedes of Nico Rosberg for sixth place, and they approached the race in quite different ways.

Rosberg did a very long second stint on a new set of soft tyres – 26 laps. He stopped for the first time on lap 16, which is too short for a two-stop strategy. But was behind Sutil who had better pace. On a new set of softs he couldn't keep up with the Force India car. So from that point, if he did a three-stop plan, like Sutil, then he wouldn't beat him.

The only way he could try to beat him was by doing two stops and trying to get track position after his final stop. It required a very long middle stint on soft tyres. After the final stops, they found themselves on the same tyres and Rosberg's were only three laps older, so the plan was great and should have worked, but Rosberg simply couldn't hold on to the place and in the end he was beaten by a faster car.

Sutil crammed three stops into what would normally be a two-stop window and managed to keep a good pace. His short stints were an aggressive strategy, but with Massa doing only two stops and not being as quick as he would normally would be, he came back towards Sutil and almost impacted on his race.

The Force India was very quick this weekend. Paul di Resta hadn't done as well in qualifying and so the team put him on a two-stop plan. He was racing Petrov and Kobayashi and easily won that battle. Di Resta's two-stop was a defensive strategy, like Rosberg's, because it will give you track position after your second stop and then it's a question of whether you can keep your opponent behind you.

And that was the 2011 F1 season, not a classic in terms of the championship, but fascinating from the point of view of the races themselves, with more overtaking, more battles for position and more strategy. I enjoyed it overall, but the last four races really lacked tension with nothing much to play for except the lower championship positions.

If you take Sebastian Vettel out then there was a good fight among the drivers behind him, which ended up being pretty close. But Vettel was literally in a different league this year and next year he will be very difficult to stop once again.

Despite the rule changes for 2012, which include banning the Red Bull innovated blown diffuser and a subsequent loss of aerodynamic downforce at the rear of the cars, there is no reason why Christian Horner's team should lose their pre-eminence.

The car most likely to win next year will be the one that claws back as much as of that lost downforce as possible. And history shows that when rule changes cut downforce, the man who always comes up with the best solutions is... Red Bull's technical director Adrian Newey.

McLaren made a fantastic job of the second half of the season, with Jenson Button scoring 161 points to Vettel's 176 from Hungary onwards. This shows that had McLaren started the season as they finished it, they would have pressed Red Bull for the title. I think they'll be close at the start of 2012 and we will have a tighter battle, but I still see Red Bull keeping their noses in front.

The pressure will really be on Ferrari, who had a poor year in 2011. Technical director Pat Fry will feel that pressure intensely and Ferrari president Luca di Montezemolo will keep the heat on team boss Stefano Domenicali if the team doesn't deliver wins early in the season.

Another team that needs to progress is Mercedes. They failed to score a podium in 2011, which is very disappointing, not least for the drivers Rosberg and Schumacher. At times they were beaten for pace by Force India and not just towards the end of the season when they were focused on next year's car.

I'm looking forward to 2012, it will be a busy year of sport with football's European Championships and the London Olympics, but I think F1 will deliver some quality entertainment with closer racing and hopefully more of a title fight.

Two days after Brazil, the new season was kick-started with the news that Kimi Raikkonen, Formula 1's most enigmatic driver, will make it a record six world champions on the F1 grid next year when he lines up to race with Lotus-Renault. Fans have been on tenterhooks for months to see whether the 2007 world champion, who is still only 32 years old, would make a comeback, following in the footsteps of Michael Schumacher who spent three years on the sidelines before coming back with Mercedes in 2010.

Like Schumacher, Raikkonen was eased into early retirement by Ferrari. The Finn has been in rallying since he was dropped by the Scuderia after a disappointing 2009 campaign, but started talking to Williams in September about making an F1 comeback. They got a long way down the line, even to the point of discussing promotional days, but it didn't work out.

Instead, he has done a deal with Lotus-Renault, with whom he had a bit of a spat in September 2010 over the subject of a potential comeback. At that time it was a rumour which the team was openly discussing and the Finn didn't like them using his name "for their marketing purposes." At the time Boullier questioned Raikkonen's motivation: "I would have to speak personally with him first, look him in the eyes to see if I see enough motivation there for him to return to F1," he said. "It doesn't make sense to hire somebody, even a former world champion, if you cannot be sure that his motivation is still 100 per cent. Why should you invest in somebody who leaves you guessing?"

The question of motivation is one that has troubled teams about a possible return, but the signs are clearly there that the Finn still feels he has unfinished business in F1 and also an appetite to earn some more money.

It looks like Boullier and Raikkonen have put all that behind them now with this exciting deal, which is great news for F1 fans as it brings back one of the best supported drivers, with a huge worldwide fan base.

"My time in the world rally championship has been a useful stage in my career as a driver," said Raikkonen, "but I can't deny the fact that my hunger for F1 has recently become overwhelming. It was an easy choice to return with Lotus-Renault GP as I have been impressed by the scope of the team's ambition."

Raikkonen has 18 wins, 62 podiums and 16 pole positions to his credit. He is also a close friend of reigning champion Sebastian Vettel, who is a neighbour in Switzerland.

Team owner Gerard Lopez said, "Kimi's decision to come back to Formula 1 with us is the first step of several announcements which should turn us into an even more serious contender in the future. Of course, we are all looking forward to working with a world champion. On behalf of our staff, I'd like to welcome Kimi to Enstone, a setting that has always been known for its human approach to Formula 1."

Index